REMEDIES TO INFORMATIONAL ASYMMETRIES IN STOCK MARKETS

REMEDIES TO INFORMATIONAL ASYMMETRIES IN STOCK MARKETS

PETER-JAN ENGELEN

intersentia

Antwerpen – Oxford

Distribution for the UK:
Hart Publishing
Salter's Boat Yard
Folly Bridge
Abingdon Road
Oxford OX1 4LB
UK
Tel: + 44 1865 24 55 33
Fax: + 44 1865 79 48 82

Distribution for North America:
Gaunt Inc.
Gaunt Building
3011 Gulf Drive
Holmes Beach
Florida 34217-2199
USA
Tel: + 1 941 778 5211
Fax: + 1 941 778 5252

Distribution for Switzerland and Germany:
Schulthess Verlag
Zwingliplatz 2
CH-8022 Zürich
Switzerland
Tel: + 41 1 251 93 36
Fax: + 41 1 261 63 94

Distribution for other countries:
Intersentia Publishers
Groenstraat 31
BE-2640 Mortsel
Belgium
Tel: + 32 3 680 15 50
Fax: + 32 3 658 71 21

Remedies to Informational Asymmetries in Stock Markets
Peter-Jan Engelen

© 2005 Intersentia
Antwerpen – Oxford
http://www.intersentia.be

ISBN 90-5095-484-7
D/2005/7849/70
NUR 784, 793 and 827

TABLE OF CONTENTS

CHAPTER 1
ECONOMIC ANALYSIS OF
REGULATION

0. INTRODUCTION

The behaviour of participants on financial markets, the development of these markets and economic growth strongly depend on the institutional and legal environment in which companies and investors operate. While the empirical studies discussed in section two examine investor protection rules in company laws, bankruptcy and reorganization laws and (intellectual) property rights, the remainder of this book focuses on some investor protection rules in securities regulation. In particular, this book analyses how to solve problems of informational asymmetry and how to organize the dissemination of information by stock exchange listed companies by means of regulation.

While most of such regulations are assumed to be in the public interest to produce better economic outcomes, only a relatively small portion of literature uses explicit economic analysis (Kitch, 2000). However, this is necessary since financial theory and the legal framework can no longer be viewed as inseparable (section two). This book therefore inquires into some aspects of financial theory from an interdisciplinary perspective and attempts to analyse the interaction between financial theory and the law (securities regulation, criminal law). In order to analyse these interactions it adopts a law and economics approach. Section three gives a brief overview of the law and economics methodology, which focuses on the economic effects of alternative legal rules. The chapter starts with some general theories of regulation in section one.

1. WHAT IS REGULATION?

Because the remainder of this book deals with the interaction between regulation and the functioning of financial markets, this section gives a brief overview of some general theories of regulation. Neither legal nor economic literature (Kabir, 1991 and den

Hartog, 2000) contains a universally accepted definition of the term 'regulation'.[1] In general, regulation seeks to alter the behaviour of those regulated (Veljanovski, 1984). Kabir (1991) considers regulation as the intentional restriction of an individual's or an organization's choice of activity by an entity not directly involved in the performance of the activity.[2] We join the definition of den Hartog (2000) who defines regulation as the employment of legal instruments for the implementation of social-economic policy objectives. Several theories exist to explain the existence of regulation.

1.1. THE PUBLIC INTEREST THEORY

The most classical explanation for the existence of regulation is the so-called *public interest theory* of regulation. According to this theory regulation exists in response to public demand for the correction of inefficient or inequitable market practices (Posner, 1974). Government regulation is thus an instrument for overcoming the disadvantages of the market mechanism.[3] Put differently, regulation is intended to improve economic efficiency by correcting market failures. However, for regulation to be undertaken, three conditions must be satisfied: (a) there is a clear failure in the market place, (b) the proposed regulation can be designed to reduce the undesirable activities and (c) the costs of the regulation to society are in balance with the benefits (Phillips and Zecher, 1981). In this and the next chapters we will analyse which regulation is necessary and to what extent it is necessary with respect to information disclosure.

If the public interest theory were correct, one would expect to find regulation mainly in highly concentrated industries or in industries that generate substantial external costs (Posner, 1974). However, regulation is not positively correlated with external effects or with monopolistic market structures (Kabir, 1991). Moreover, it appears that the market mechanism can often cope with any inefficiencies itself, thereby questioning the generally accepted failures of the market (Cowen, 1988 and den Hartog, 2000). Finally, the assumption of the public interest theory that government regulation is effective and virtually costless (Posner, 1974), is questioned empirically (Joskow and Rose, 1989). Phillips and Zecher (1981) conclude that "nearly all regulatory programs have fallen far short of dealing successfully with a real market failure in a cost effective manner (p.19)."

---

[1]   See Ogus (1994) for references on legal scholars using the term 'regulation' in a bewildering variety of meanings.

[2]   For other definitions, see Needham (1983), Mitnick (1980) or Joskow and Noll (1981).

[3]   For an overview see den Hartog (2000) discussing imperfect competition, unbalanced market operations, missing markets and undesirable market results.

1.2. THE CAPTURE THEORY

Besides the public interest theory, some other theories assume that regulation is a process by which interest groups seek to promote their private interests. Through empirical and theoretical research the public interest theory had few defenders in the 1970s, shifting attention from alleged market failures to a closer consideration of the decision-making process (Kabir, 1991). A first type of theories is what Posner (1974) calls the *capture theory*, which is derived from political science. The merit of this theory consists of the insight that regulation serves the interests of the branch of industry involved. Over time the regulatory agencies come to be dominated by the industries regulated so that in the end regulation serves their private interests instead of the public interest. However, the theory has a couple of flaws. First, it does not explain why a regulated party can subject a regulatory agency to its interests, but cannot prevent the mere establishment of the agency itself. Second, the capture theory ignores the regulation that serves the interests of consumer groups rather than of the regulated industries themselves.[4] Especially regulations such as environmental laws, regulation of product safety or labour conditions cannot be explained within the capture theory of regulation.

1.3. THE ECONOMIC THEORY OF REGULATION

Besides the capture theory, this section covers another theory that assumes regulation to be a process by which interest groups seek to promote their private interests. This theory originated from the seminal article 'The Theory of Economic Regulation' by George Stigler in 1971 in which the central thesis was that regulation is acquired by the industry and is designed and operated primarily for its benefit (Stigler, 1971). Although, the *economic theory of regulation* also starts from the premise that regulation serves the private interests of politically effective groups, it differs from the capture theory in several respects. First, it extends the capture theory by including interest groups other than the regulated industries. Second, it replaces the vague 'capture' terminology by explicitly using the economic terminology of supply and demand. Viewing regulation as the outcome of the forces of demand and supply directs attention to factors bearing on the value of regulation to particular individuals or groups (Posner, 1974).

On the demand side of regulation the benefits for interest groups can easily been seen.[5] In short, the benefits a state can provide to an industry are foursome: a direct monetary

---

[4]   Posner (1971) observes that in many cases regulation favours certain consumer groups.
[5]   See Posner (1971) for some examples and evidence.

subsidy, control over entry by new rivals, rules that affect substitutes and complements and price-fixing. However, not all groups will influence regulation to the same extent because the costs of organization will differ among different groups. In general, small interest groups are likely to organize themselves at lower cost than larger interest groups. The smaller the interest groups, the larger the per capita stake in the benefits of the regulation. Smaller interest groups are also more likely to exhibit homogeneous preferences so that it is cheaper to arrive at a common position. Moreover, the free-rider problem is less of a problem in smaller interest groups.

Becker (1983 and 1985) refines the demand side by focusing on the competition between interest groups. Because some interest groups are more efficient in influencing politicians than others, transfers of income occur from less efficient to more efficient groups. Again, politically successful interest groups are small, while the less efficient groups who bear the burden of the transfers will be larger. Regulations are thus dependent on the relative efficiency of interest groups in exerting political pressure and influence (den Hartog, 2000). In this way, regulation reflects the relative power of competing interest groups and the resulting legal framework has little to do with correcting failures in the marketplace (Phillips and Zecher, 1981). According to the economic theory of regulation the public interest may not be an important consideration in the regulatory process. To put it bluntly, "only by accident would this process lead to regulatory programs in the public interest" (Phillips and Zecher, 1981, p.22).

Furthermore, the view of regulation being governed by the laws of supply and demand also directs attention to the factors bearing on the cost of obtaining regulation. This is related to the supply side of regulation, which is formed by the political parties. A politician's only objective is re-election. Therefore, an interest group who seeks regulation must be prepared to pay with votes or resources (Stigler, 1971).[6]

The base model of Stigler's economic theory of regulation can be extended to incorporate cross-subsidisation (Peltzman, 1976) or to incorporate public interest considerations (Keeler, 1984).[7]

---

[6] These include campaign contributions, contributed services, indirect methods such as the employment of party workers, educational programmes to influence voting behaviour.

[7] An example of cross-subsidisation is the supply of electricity to hospitals at a price less than the marginal costs.

1.4. DISTRIBUTION OF COSTS AND BENEFITS

Opposed to the view that the origin of regulation stems from 'public interest' or from 'private or self-interest', Wilson (1974) points out that regulation can have a variety of political causes depending on the distribution of the perceived costs and benefits of the proposed regulation. The costs may be widely distributed (e.g. a general tax levy) or narrowly concentrated (e.g. a tax charged to a particular industry), as well as the benefits that can be widely distributed (e.g. lower prices, lower taxes, better products or services) or narrowly concentrated (e.g. a subsidy paid to a particular industry).

Table 1.1. The sources of regulation based on the distribution of costs and benefits

| | | Benefits | |
		Concentrated	Distributed
Costs	Concentrated	Interest group politics e.g. labour regulation, railway regulation	Entrepreneurial politics e.g. environmental regulations, unsafe products
	Distributed	Client politics e.g. protection of professional groups by licensing	Majority politics e.g. antimonopoly

Source: Wilson (1974 and 1980)

Based on the distribution of costs and benefits Wilson (1974 and 1980) classifies regulation into four categories (see table 1.1). Client politics arise out of a situation where the benefits of regulation are concentrated on a single group, but the costs are diffused. In this case a small, relatively homogeneous group has a powerful incentive to organize and lobby. It will propose a particular regulation in order to obtain the benefits, while imposing the costs on a large number of others, who will not seriously challenge the proposed rules because the costs are distributed at a low per capita rate. A classic example is the protection of professional groups by licensing, e.g. the regulation of the number of taxicab licenses in Austria (Lewisch, 1991), or the self-regulation of professions in Belgium (Van den Bergh and Faure, 1991).[8]

Interest group politics is expected with concentrated benefits and costs. This kind of regulation is the outcome of a political situation in which two or more clearly organized opponents compete for a particular set of rules. A regulation will benefit a relatively small group at the expense of another small group, while the public does not believe it will be much affected one way or another. Typical examples of these two

---

[8]   See also Plott (1965), Svorny (2000), Stephen and Love (2000) and Olsen (2000).

opponents are unions versus management[9], truckers versus railroads[10] or wholesalers versus retailers[11].

When benefits are diffused and costs are concentrated, the form of policy is denoted as entrepreneurial. In this case a small group, which faces the possibility of an increased burden, is unable to defeat a proposed regulation that benefits a large group, for whom the benefits to each individual are unclear and diffuse. Typical examples are environmental rules[12] and consumer regulation[13]. This kind of regulation is difficult to explain with the economic theory of regulation (den Hartog, 2000). As Wilson (1980) puts it: "Since the incentive to organize is strong for opponents of the policy but weak for the beneficiaries, and since the political system provides many points at which opposition can be registered, it may seem astonishing that regulatory legislation of this sort is ever passed."[14]

Finally, majoritarian politics is the result of diffused costs and benefits. In this case, most of society expects to gain as well as to pay. Because no small, relatively homogeneous group is expected to capture a disproportionate share of the benefits, there is little incentive to lobby.

1.5. CONCLUSIONS WITH REGARD TO THE THEORIES OF REGULATION

None of the above theories has universal explanatory power to explain the existence of every piece of regulation. Because the regulatory process is very complex, a particular set of rules can have public interest aspects as well as private interest aspects. But as a whole, the combination of the above theories can give a better insight to describe the origin of a particular regulation. Moreover, it is a very useful exercise to analyse who gains and who loses from a particular set of rules. Even if a certain regulation may seem to be in the public interest, the question who benefits most from this rule can yield some important additional insights. In the next chapters, we will come back to this question when discussing disclosure regulation and insider trading.

---

[9] For a law and economics analysis on labour regulation, see e.g. Dau-Schmidt (1992), Posner (1984), Rubin and Kau (1981), Schwab (1987) and X (2000a and 2000b).
[10] See Wilson (1974, 1980).
[11] For a law and economics analysis on retail, see e.g. Van den Bergh (1986).
[12] See e.g. Eide and Van den Bergh (1996) and Faure (2000).
[13] See e.g. Arcuri (2000).
[14] Although private interests can also explain regulation in the areas of safety, environment and health. Setting rules and standards is in the interest of existing firms already complying with the standard. In this way, entry barriers for new producers are created, thereby limiting competition to existing firms. See e.g. Bartel and Thomas (1987) and Pashigian (1984).

2. LAW AND FINANCE LITERATURE

The importance of the institutional and legal environment for the behaviour of actors on financial markets, the development of these markets and economic growth only recently attracted the attention of research in corporate finance, in particular the so-called law and finance literature. This new research area was initiated by the seminal papers of La Porta, Lopez-de-Silanes, Shleifer and Vishny (1997, 1998, 1999, 2000). These papers investigated the relationship between a country's legal framework and its financial development. Their analysis focuses on company laws and bankruptcy and reorganization laws. The analysis says nothing about securities regulation, disclosure rules or how companies communicate with the financial markets.[15] This is the subject of the remainder of this book.

Since investor protection determines the readiness of investors to finance firms, it is of crucial importance that corporate finance turn on these legal rules and their enforcement. In their first paper La Porta et al. (1998) examine whether laws on investor protection differ across countries and whether these differences matter for corporate finance. Investor protection rules are defined as rules that determine the ease with which investors can exercise their powers against management (and controlling shareholders), or put differently, *how investors can extract the returns on their investment from these managers*. Indeed, Johnson et al. (2000) show how tunnelling or the transfer of assets and profits out of the firm occur for the benefit of those who control them at the expense of minority shareholders. This may happen in the form of transfer pricing, asset stripping or investor dilution. Johnson et al. (2000) show that especially in French civil law countries such as France, Italy, and Belgium, much of the tunnelling is even legal compared to common law countries. This is mainly due to the fact that such transactions are assessed by courts in French civil law countries in light of their conformity with statutes and not on the basis of their fairness to minority shareholders such as in common law countries.

Investors get cash only because they have power. Investors' rights, in La Porta et al. (1998), are both shareholder rights and creditor rights. The different bundles of rights to which an investor is entitled are determined by laws and are not inherent in the securities themselves, implying that legal rules matter. Other rights include disclosure rules, accounting rules and securities regulation. La Porta et al. (2000) point out that such rules are established to provide investors with information they need to exercise the other rights.

---

[15] Other aspects of regulations which are not dealt with are banking and financial institution regulations and merger and takeover rules. See e.g. Heremans (2000) and Bittlingmayer (2000).

In line with comparative legal scholars, La Porta et al. (1998) classify the national legal systems of 49 countries into four families of law. Historically speaking, common law is case law developed by precedents from judicial decisions. Common law countries include the U.K., the United States, Canada and British colonies. Civil law countries, on the contrary, are characterized by the codification of abstract rules and rely heavily on legal scholars. Civil law countries can be divided into three families: French[16], German[17] and Scandinavian[18]. Their results show that investor protection is determined by the legal family to which a country belongs. This is an important observation. La Porta et al. (1999, p.9) conclude that "because financial legal families originated long before financial markets have developed, it is unlikely that laws were written primarily in response to market pressures. Rather, the legal families appear to shape the legal rules, which in turn influence financial markets."

With regard to shareholders they examine voting powers (one-share-one-vote rules), the ease of participation in corporate voting (vote by mail, the necessity to deposit one's shares with a financial intermediary several days prior to a shareholder meeting, cumulative voting for directors) and legal protections against expropriation by management (minority shareholders legal mechanisms, percentage of share capital needed to call an extraordinary shareholders' meeting). Finally, the right to a mandatory dividend is examined. The analysis very clearly shows that common law countries offer the best legal protections to shareholders (see table 1.2). Shares are never blocked before a shareholder meeting (0%), voting by mail is frequently allowed (39%), laws protecting oppressed minorities have a high incidence (92%), relatively few shares (9%) are required to call an extraordinary shareholder meeting. These countries therefore have an overall score of 3.39 with regard to anti-director rights.

---

[16]   This legal family includes France, Belgium, Spain, Portugal and several Latin American countries.
[17]   This legal family includes Germany, Austria, Czechoslovakia, Hungary and Switzerland.
[18]   This legal family includes Denmark, Finland, Norway and Sweden.

Table 1.2. Shareholder right according to legal family

Legal family (averages)	One share – one vote	Proxy by mail allowed	Shares blocked before meeting	Cumulative voting for directors	Oppressed minority	% of share capital to call an ESM	Antidirector rights index°	Mandatory dividend°°
Common law	22% – PS	39% – PS	0% – PS	17% – PS	92% – PS	9% – PS	3.39	0%
French civil law	24% – PS	9% – PM	43% – PM	19% – PS	33% – PM	14% – PM	1.76	14%
German civil law	33% – PS	17% – PM	67% – PM	17% – PS	33% – PM	5% – PS	2.00	0%
Scandinavian civil law	0% – PM	25% – PS	0% – PS	0% – PM	25% – PM	10% – PS	2.50	0%
Total	22%	22%	27%	16%	53%	11%	2.44	6%

Legend: Percentages are expressed as a fraction of one legal family
PS – pro-shareholder laws; PM – pro-management laws
° ranging from one to five; °° as percentage of net income
For a precise definition of all variables, see La Porta et al. (1998)
Source: La Porta et al. (1998)

In contrast, French civil law countries offer the worst legal protection of shareholders: the lowest incidence of voting by mail (9%), a high incidence of blocking shares before the shareholder meeting (43%), a low incidence of laws protecting oppressed minorities (33%), the highest percentage of share capital (14%) required to call an extraordinary shareholder meeting and a score of 1.76 with regard to anti-director rights. Their results show that the differences between common law and French civil law countries are large and statistically significant. It is not surprising to see that the weak legal protection of shareholders in French civil law countries coincides with the existence of a mandatory dividend, such as in Greece or Portugal, to serve as remedial legal protection. This does not exist in the other legal families.

Furthermore, La Porta et al. (1998) examine five creditor rights variables: automatic stay on assets[19], secured creditors paid first, restrictions on reorganizations, the stay of management pending the resolution of the reorganization and the existence of a legal reserve as a percentage of capital. Again, common law countries offer creditors better legal protection against managers (e.g. they place restrictions on managers seeking court protection from creditors – 71%, and the lowest incidence of allowing managers to stay on the job in reorganization proceedings – 24%), while French civil

---

[19] Procedure to prevent secured creditors from getting possession of loan collateral. This rule protects managers and unsecured creditors against secured creditors and prevents automatic liquidation.

law countries offer creditors the weakest protections against managers (e.g. allow automatic stay on assets – 74%, and lowest guarantee that secured creditors are paid first – 68%). Scandinavian and German civil law countries have some pro-management and some pro-creditor laws (see table 1.3). As was the case with mandatory dividends with respect to shareholders rights, the existence of a legal reserve can serve as a remedial creditor right when other investor powers are insufficient to extract from management the returns on their investments. It is therefore not surprising to see that they do not exist in common law countries, with the exception of Thailand.

Table 1.3. Creditor rights according to legal family

Legal family (averages)	Restrictions for going into reorganization	Automatic stay on assets	Secured creditors first paid	Management stays during reorganization	Legal reserve required as a % of capital
Common law	71% – PC	29% – PC	94% – PC	24% – PC	1%
French civil law	42% – PM	74% – PM	68% – PM	74% – PM	20%
German civil law	33% – PM	33% – PC	100% – PC	67% – PM	28%
Scandinavian civil law	75% – PC	75% – PM	100% – PC	100% – PM	16%
Total	54%	52%	85%	57%	13%

Legend: Percentages are expressed as a fraction of one legal family
PC – pro-creditor laws; PM – pro-management laws
For a precise definition of all variables, see La Porta et al. (1998)
Source: La Porta et al. (1998)

Another important topic La Porta et al. (1998) look into is the enforcement of investor protection rules because a strong system of legal enforcement could even compensate weak rules. Using five measures for the quality of enforcement (efficiency of the judicial system, rule of law, corruption, risk of expropriation, likelihood of contract repudiation by the government), once again, the analysis shows that law enforcement is strongest in Scandinavian countries, whereas it is weakest in French civil law countries. The analysis in La Porta et al. (1998) reveals that the quality of law enforcement does not compensate for the lack of quality of laws.

Moreover, their empirical results show that good shareholder protection and enforcement are highly negatively related with the concentration of ownership. It appears that highly concentrated ownership is a response to poor investor protection.

However, if small investors are not well protected, companies are unable to raise capital from them and entrepreneurs cannot diversify their holdings.

Table 1.4. The rule of law and accounting standards

Legal family (averages)	Efficiency of judicial system°	Rule of law°	Corruption°	Risk of expropriation°	Risk of contract repudiation°	Rating on accounting standards°°
Common law	8.15	6.46	7.06	7.91	7.41	69.62
French civil law	6.56	6.05	5.84	7.46	6.84	51.17
German civil law	8.54	8.68	8.03	9.45	9.47	62.67
Scandinavian civil law	10.00	10.00	10.00	9.66	9.44	74.00
Total	7.67	6.85	6.90	8.05	7.58	60.93

Legend: Percentages are expressed as a fraction of one legal family
° ranging from one to ten (highest is best); °° as a score on 90 items
For a precise definition of all variables, see La Porta et al. (1998)
Source: La Porta et al. (1998)

In a follow-up paper La Porta et al. (1997) show that the legal environment is highly relevant for the size and extent of a country's capital markets. An investor is only willing to surrender funds to a company in exchange for securities, if he is protected against expropriation by management. A good legal environment, as measured by both legal rules and the quality of enforcement, therefore, expands the ability of companies to raise external finance through either debt or equity. Using three equity measures (ratio of stock market capitalization to GNP, the number of listed domestic companies and the number of initial public offerings) their regression results show that low shareholder protection causes smaller equity markets as well as lower access of firms to external equity. Similar results are found with regard to the debt market. Using two variables (the total bank debt of the private sector and the total face value of corporate bonds, relative to GNP), their results show that debt finance is more accessible in common law than in French civil law countries. Examining the impact of the quality of enforcement, they also find that it has a significant impact on the ability of companies to raise external debt or equity finance. In conclusion, La Porta et al. (1997) offer strong evidence that the legal framework has a large effect on the size and the breath of capital markets across countries. And, importantly, it has an effect on both equity and debt markets.

Several other papers confirm similar relations between the legal framework and financial development. Using a sustainable growth model, Demirgüç-Kunt and Maksimovic (1998) identify externally financed companies and link the availability of external finance to the legal framework. The access to long-term external finance depending on the origin and efficiency of a legal system is also demonstrated by Demirgüç-Kunt and Maksimovic (1999). Similar results are also reported by Rajan and Zingales (1998). Beck, Demirgüç-Kunt and Maksimovic (2002) show that firm growth is more affected by reported constraints in countries with underdeveloped financial and legal systems and higher corruption. This is especially true for small and medium sized companies (SMEs). As a policy recommendation they argue that improving financial and legal development and reducing corruption will promote firm growth, especially in the case of SMEs. Cassimon and Engelen (2005) also report the negative impact of legal constraints on the amount of long-term debt as well as short-term debt.

La Porta et al. (1999) elaborate their analysis to the corporate governance context. Instead of focusing on the traditional difference between bank-centred and market-centred corporate governance systems, they argue that the law and finance approach appears to be a more fruitful way to understand corporate governance. The legal approach to corporate governance holds that the key mechanism is the protection of outside investors. They observe that "Italy and Belgium have developed neither debt nor equity markets because no outside investors are protected there" (La Porta et al., 1999, p.23). They stress the importance of investor protection as an important factor contributing to the development of financial markets. Again, this is an important finding, because recent research shows a clear link between the development of financial markets and economic growth.

Klapper and Love (2002) examine the relationship between the legal framework, corporate governance and operating performance and company valuation. Examining 374 firms in 14 emerging markets they examine the impact of good (bad) corporate governance on Tobin's-Q as a measure of the market valuation of assets and ROA (return on assets) as a measure of operating performance. They confirm that firms in countries with a good legal environment have better market and operating performances. But, more importantly, their empirical results reveal that firm-level corporate governance matters more in countries with poor overall minority share-holder protection. It appears that even the smallest improvement of a company's corporate governance compared to country-average is very important to investors in countries with poor legal environment or with weaker investor protection from the courts. A relative improvement through company charters of corporate governance compared to the country-average in countries with poor investor protection improves the valuation and operating performance of such companies and acts as a rough and partial replacement for the poor country-level legal environment. Therefore, Klapper and Love (2002) conclude, in line with the conceptual model of Shleifer and Wolfensohn (2002), that companies "cannot completely compensate for the absence of strong laws and good enforcement."

Several recent empirical studies furthermore found a link between financial development and economic growth. Controlling for causality, King and Levine (1993) found a relationship between indicators of financial development and indicators of economic growth. The empirical results in Levine and Zervos (1998) and Rousseau and Wachtel (1998) show a statistically significant relationship between initial stock market development and subsequent economic growth. Financial development can enhance subsequent economic growth in several ways (Levine, 1997 and Beck, Levine and Loayza, 2000): enhanced savings, capital accumulation, efficiency improvements and technological innovation. The link between legal framework and economic growth is clear: investor protection enhances financial development, which in turn accelerates economic growth. So, from a social point of view, the legal framework is an important element for creating economic growth.

This section stressed the importance of the institutional and legal environment for the development of financial markets and economic growth. Investigating the relationship between a country's legal framework and its financial development, the law and finance literature shows that differences in the legal framework and in law enforcement affect ownership structure, the availability of external finance (capital structure), and corporate governance of companies.

3. LAW AND ECONOMICS

Since the previous section showed that the functioning of financial markets and the legal framework can no longer be viewed as inseparable, we will analyse financial markets from an interdisciplinary perspective by adopting a law and economics approach. After giving a brief overview of the specific nature, the development and the state of the art of the law and economics movement, the law and economics methodology is explained in more detail.

3.1. THE LAW AND ECONOMICS MOVEMENT

The application of economic principles to legal instruments, questions and procedures, better known as law and economics, or as some authors prefer to call 'the economic analysis of law' (Posner, 1998 and Dnes, 1996), was up until the 1960s limited to areas such as antitrust and the regulation of natural monopolies (Posner, 1998). This period is generally referred to as 'old' law and economics (Van den Bergh, 1996). In this period economic science focused on empirical research that required hard data instead of the verbal analysis of lawyers. Things have changed drastically since the emergence of the so-called 'new' law and economics that began with the articles of Guido Calabresi (1961) on torts and especially the seminal article of Ronald Coase (1960) on social cost.[20] 'The Problem of Social Cost' was the breakthrough of the transaction cost approach, which allowed an in-depth analysis of alternative legal rules and institutions with regard to their capability to save on transaction costs (Van den Bergh, 1996). But a real milestone is obviously the publication of Richard Posner's '*Economic Analysis of Law*' in 1973 and the work of Gary Becker (1968, 1976, 1981).

This gave rise to the economic analysis of law in areas that do not regulate avowedly economic relationships, such as tort, property, contracts and criminal law. The table of contents of Posner's (1998) 'Economic Analysis of Law' reveals a wide array of law and economic applications in new areas such as intellectual property, pollution, the regulation of sexual behaviour, the war on drugs, the transmission of wealth at death, civil and criminal procedure, the economics of federalism, racial discrimination or freedom of speech, besides more traditional areas such as the theory of monopoly, antitrust laws, taxation, the regulation of the employment relation or the law of business organisations and financial markets. Posner (2000) concludes that few areas of legal scholarship remain untouched by economics, so that "law and economics has had interesting things to say about virtually every area of law, and this makes it of potential relevance to anyone working in one of those areas, who might be a practising lawyer, an economic consultant, a sociologist, psychologist, historian, or philosopher (p.xiii)."

It is quite clear that law and economics is an established discipline in the United States, that provides a major input to legal scholarship (Ogus, 1998 and Herzel and Braendel, 1998). The law and economics literature has exploded in recent years and several journals are devoted exclusively to the field, such as the *Journal of Law and Economics* published at the University of Chicago since 1958, the *Journal of Law, Economics, and Organization* published at Yale University since 1985, the *Journal of Legal Studies*, and

---

[20]   However, Rowley (1998) points out that the political philosophers and economists of the Scottish Enlightenment, such as David Hume (1739), Adam Ferguson (1767) and Adam Smith (1776), already made the link between law and economics, as did Jeremy Bentham (1776, 1789). Also Posner (1998) refers to the work of Beccaria (1764) and Bentham's 'Principles of Penal Law' who use economics in analysing criminal law and Pigou (1920) as early examples of the use of economics in analysing law.

the *International Review of Law and Economics*.[21] The classification of the *Journal of Economic Literature* assigned a separate index to 'Law and Economics' (letter K). The latest edition of the *Encyclopedia of Law and Economics* lists over 20,000 law and economics publications (Bouckaert and De Geest, 2000b). The Nobel Committee also recognized the importance of this discipline by awarding the Nobel Memorial Prize in Economic Science to Ronald Coase, Gary Becker and George Stigler. Moreover, several prominent law and economics scholars have become U.S. federal judges, such as Richard Posner and Frank Easterbrook (U.S. Court of Appeals for the Seventh Circuit), Guido Calabresi (U.S. Court of Appeals for the Second Circuit) and Stephen Breyer (U.S. Supreme Court). Cooter and Ulen (1997) list several other indicators of the impact of economics on law, including the presence of at least one economist on the faculty of each of the top law schools in the States or joint degree programmes (a Ph.D. in economics and a J.D. in law). Furthermore, there are several professional organizations in law and economics (Posner, 2000).

The situation in Europe is quite different where the law and economics movement only started in the 1980s (Van den Bergh, 1992). However, it has grown rapidly during recent years (Van den Bergh, 1996), leading Posner (2000) to conclude that the movement is now clearly international. However, the situation differs heavily from country to country. While the law and economics movement is barely non-existing in France (Montagé, 2000), it is an important discipline in Germany (Kirstein, 2000), while in other countries the research into law and economics almost coincides with a few legal scholars, such as Erling Eide (2000) in Norway, Göran Skogh (2000) in Sweden, Pardolesi and Parisi in Italy (Pardolesi and Bellantuono, 2000), or the pioneering work of Bouckaert, Heremans and Van den Bergh in Belgium (De Geest, 2000 and Engelen, 2000).[22]

Van den Bergh (1996) argues that a strict disciplinary divide between law and economics is harmful. Economics provide behavioural theory to predict how people respond to changes in law. In fact, regulation acts in the same way as prices or taxes, which provide incentives influencing human behaviour. Economic science has (mathematically) precise theories and empirically sound methods to analyse such behaviour (Cooter and Ulen, 1997). If policy makers were more aware of the consequences of their decisions on welfare, adverse effects could be avoided (Van den

---

[21]   Besides law and economics journals many articles on law and economics were published in the 1970s in economic journals such as *American Economic Review* or *Bell Journal of Economics* and in the 1980s in American law reviews such as *Harvard Law Review*, *University of Chicago Law Review* and *Virginia Law Review*.

[22]   For an overview of the state of the art of the law and economics movement in other countries, see Weigel (2000), Lando (2000), Nuolimaa and Timonen (2000), Hatzis (2000), Holzhauer and Teijl (2000) and Pastor and Pintos (2000).

Bergh, 2000). Economists, on the other hand, will benefit from this interdisciplinary approach by drawing their models closer to reality. Section two clearly demonstrated that financial theory should not operate in an institutional vacuum.

The Coasean approach especially offers a powerful framework to predict the effects of policies on efficiency.[23] Economic science is very relevant to studying law because it "is the science which studies human behaviour as a relationship between ends and scare means which have alternative uses" (Robbins, 1932). Van den Bergh (1996) points out that to make efficient outcomes possible, the policy goals should be to reduce transaction costs.[24] In this way, a comparative analysis of alternative rules to reduce transaction costs becomes relevant. Transaction costs include search and information costs, costs of negotiating and monitoring and enforcement costs (Van den Bergh and Heremans, 1987). Obviously, besides transaction costs, other aspects have to be incorporated in a law and economics analysis as well, such as incentive costs and risk allocation (Van den Bergh, 1996). The incentive analysis examines whether legal rules create incentives for the relevant individuals or firms to behave efficiently, meaning in such a way that global welfare is maximized (Polinsky, 1983 and De Geest, 1994). Risk allocation refers to the question whether legal rules efficiently allocate risk among the relevant individuals or firms (Polinsky, 1983). It involves the transfer of risks to superior risk bearers, i.e. persons who are better suited to bear such risks (De Geest, 1994). It is desirable to reduce the risk borne by a risk-averse party. Therefore, if the risk cannot be eliminated, it can be shared among the parties (risk sharing), it can be shifted entirely to one of the parties or it can be shifted to an insurance company (risk pooling).

3.2. THE LAW AND ECONOMICS METHODOLOGY

The economic analysis of law can have normative as well as positive aspects. The positive approach explains legal rules as they are rather than change them to make them better (Posner, 1998). The normative approach studies the effects of a set of rules on social welfare. It analyses how the law ought to be and applies efficiency as a prominent criterion in designing legal rules (Van den Bergh, 1996).

---

[23]   Besides efficiency economic science can also predict the effects of regulation on the distribution of income and wealth (Cooter and Ulen, 1997).

[24]   If transactions costs are equal to zero, the Coase theorem holds that efficiency can be reached through negotiations regardless of the choice of the legal rule. So the efficient outcome will occur regardless of the choice of legal rule. If there are positive transaction costs, the efficient outcome may not occur under every legal rule. In this case, the preferred legal rule is the rule that minimizes the effects of transaction costs (Polinsky, 1983).

Van den Bergh (1991, 1996) classifies the different forms of the law and economics methodology into three categories: predictive, explanatory and normative analysis. The former two can also be grouped as positive analysis. An explanatory law and economic approach tries to explain the existing legal rules as a consequence of evolving towards efficiency. The economic analysis provides a framework to reconstruct the legal arguments (Mercuro and Medema, 1997).[25] Such an analysis reveals that complex legal reasoning can be replaced by economic concepts. Sometimes positive analysis shows that existing law cannot be explained on efficiency grounds thereby falsifying the efficiency enhancing character of that legal rule. Economic theory therefore explains which legal rules can be expected on efficiency grounds and then confronts it with the existing legal rules (Van den Bergh, 1991). However, in a positive analysis no attempt is made to say how legal rules should be adapted because this is the subject of a normative analysis. If legal rules create inefficiencies, two causes can be found. First, other values besides efficiency such as redistribution of income can cause an inefficient outcome of a legal rule. Second, alternative theories such as the public choice theory can explain the existence of inefficient legal rules because rent-seeking private interest groups try to influence regulation in such a way that it benefits them (see supra). In this case, private interest groups thus lobby for regulation to be inefficient decreasing social welfare.

A predictive law and economics approach uses economic models to explore the behavioural effects of the law (Van den Bergh, 1996). Contrary to a normative analysis, these legal impact studies contain no value judgements and they only try to predict ex-ante the effects of legal rules. Such an analysis can reveal desired as well as undesired effects or side-effects of legal rule making. For instance, predicting whether the number of accidents will increase or decrease in response to a change in traffic regulations such as the introduction of a driver's license with penalty points.

Finally, a normative law and economics approach evaluates legal rules by reference to the efficient allocation of scare resources. This type of analysis is not value free because it sees efficiency as a goal to be reached because it increases wealth (Mercuro and Medema, 1997). Legal rules are assessed as good or bad with respect to its impact on economic efficiency. The law is seen as an instrument to alter economic performance. Changing legal rules is evaluated by its impact on efficiency:

$$\Delta \text{ Law} \rightarrow \Delta \text{ Economic performance} \qquad [1.1]$$

---

[25]   This also refers to the classic view of the Chicago School of Law and Economics that sees 'common law' as a whole of legal rules developed by case law that enhance allocative efficiency. The development of common law can be explained as if its goal was to maximize allocative efficiency: "common law is best understood […] as a pricing mechanism designed to bring about an efficient allocation of resources (Posner, 1987, 5)."

The evaluation of the economic performance is typically undertaken by the tools of microeconomics and welfare economics, such as the concepts of Pareto-efficiency and Kaldor-Hicks efficiency (Mercuro and Medema, 1997 and Zerbe, 2001).[26] Changes in regulation are Pareto-improvements if at least one person is made better off as a result of the new rule while no person is made worse off. However, this criterion is a difficult guide for public policy because few policies have no losers. Therefore the Pareto criterion requires that gainers explicitly compensate losers. If not, the Pareto principle implies that any loss of welfare to even one person is sufficient to veto any possible gains to others, regardless of their size (Zerbe, 2001). A solution to this problem is offered by the Kaldor-Hicks efficiency or the potential Pareto improvement. A change in regulation is said to be Kaldor-Hicks efficient when the gainers are able to compensate the losers (Van den Bergh, 1996). Stated differently, the gainers must gain more than the losers lose. In that case the gainers can compensate the losers. Although this criterion does not require actual compensation, it must merely be possible in principle (Cooter and Ulen, 1997).[27]

This book analyses the functioning of financial markets, particularly the dissemination of price-sensitive information on these markets. In order to evaluate the legal rules governing the dissemination of information within a law and economics perspective, we need a framework to assess the current disclosure regulation with respect to allocative efficiency.

Capital markets are a major financing source for companies because these markets allocate scarce financial resources to various securities. A normative goal for securities regulation is to encourage the establishment of allocative efficient markets, in which the companies with the most promising investment opportunities have access to the needed funds (Sharpe, Alexander and Bailey, 1999). Given a specified degree of risk, investors will select (portfolios of) securities with the highest possible return (Elton and Gruber, 1995). In order to be allocative efficient, prices need to be accurate. In this way, resources are channelled to the place where they will do the most good. The return of a security is determined by the future cash flows that investors expect, based on all currently available information. A security market operates allocative efficient if information is quickly and widely disseminated, thereby allowing security prices to adjust instantaneously and fully all relevant new information so that its price reflects its fundamental value. This property of securities markets is generally referred to as market efficiency or the efficient markets hypothesis and is explained in detail in chapter two.

---

[26] For an extensive discussion of the Pareto efficiency in exchange, the Pareto efficiency in production and Kaldor-Hicks efficiency, see the appendix to chapter one in Mercuro and Medema (1997).
[27] Mercuro and Medema (1997) point out that the different schools of thought within the law and economics movement do not give equal credence to the various criteria of efficiency.

In order to evaluate the allocative efficiency of securities regulation, financial theory uses the efficiency of a financial market. If securities markets function according to the efficient markets hypothesis, security prices are a reliable criterion for the optimal allocation of scarce financial resources at a 'fair' price that reflects the true potential. More accurate pricing of securities thus contributes to more correct economic decisions throughout the economy, which subsequently enhances economic output by society as a whole (Kitch, 2000). Market efficiency will therefore be a benchmark in our law and economics analysis of the disclosure regulation.

Analogously to the research question for law and economics in general as put forward in Van den Bergh (1991), the following relevant questions can be asked with regard to regulating how corporations speak to the market:
(1)   Under which conditions will disclosure regulation be efficient?
(2)   Which existing disclosure regulation rules can be viewed as efficient?
(3)   Which factors other than efficiency considerations can explain the existing disclosure rules?
(4)   What are the economic consequences of the existing disclosure regulation?
(5)   Should the existing disclosure regulation be changed to enhance the degree of efficiency?
(6)   Which other values can prevent the normative question from being solved on efficiency grounds?

Question one is answered in chapter two. We will see that the vague legal goal of securities regulation, being investors' protection, can be replaced by financial economic concepts, being market efficiency and market liquidity. To enhance allocative efficiency, chapter two will show that the two major goals of securities regulation are market efficiency and liquidity because companies as well as investors value efficient and liquid stock markets because it allows a quick and cheap disposal of their securities and gives them low-cost access to information in such a way that they can rely on current market prices. Insofar as market liquidity and market efficiency are crucial characteristics of the quality of a financial market, investors and companies will desire rules that facilitate market efficiency and liquidity. These two policy goals for establishing securities regulation offer a clear and powerful framework in order to analyse the desirability and effectiveness of a certain set of rules from an economic point of view.

Chapter two furthermore shows that in a semi-strong efficient market investors can rely on the fact that all available information is incorporated in security prices and that they can therefore rely on the accuracy of the market prices for making investment decisions, without the need for every investor to collect, analyse and process all information individually. Given these conditions, the answer to question two is analysed with regard to mandatory disclosure. Chapter two will show that current mandatory regulation might be inefficient. Factors other than efficiency can explain the existence of mandatory disclosure rules. It appears that such regulation tends to favour relatively small and well-organised groups that have a high per capita stake in the regulations, at the expense of relatively large, poorly organized groups with a lower per capita stake (question three and four – public choice). To enhance efficiency, we analysed the use of trading halts in disseminating information, the use of selective disclosure and an abolition of the ban on insider trading (question 5).

Finally, besides efficiency, other values may play an important role in establishing regulation. Equity or the distribution of income among individuals especially may be an important policy goal. If transactions costs are equal to zero, the Coase theorem holds that the choice of the legal rule has no impact on efficiency. However, it does affect the distribution of income (Holzhauer and Teijl, 1995). Polinsky (1983) points out that it is no problem when it is possible to redistribute income at no cost; in this case the distributive consequences of an efficient legal rule can be corrected. If income cannot be costlessly redistributed, there may be a conflict between efficiency and equity. In situations where parties are in a contractual or market relationship, Polinsky (1983) points out that it is very difficult, if not impossible, to redistribute income. In situations where parties are strangers, redistribution through the legal system is possible, but is generally cheaper to realize redistribution through the government's tax and transfer system than through legal rules. Also Kaplow and Shavell (1994) demonstrate that redistribution through legal rules offers no advantage over redistribution through the income tax system and generally is less efficient. Consequently, we adopt efficiency as the primary criterion for evaluating legal rules on the dissemination of price-sensitive information about listed companies (question six).

4. OUTLINE OF THE REMAINING CHAPTERS

The law and finance literature clearly and convincingly show that the legal framework matters for corporate finance. To better understand financial theory it therefore seems crucial to analyse the impact of different set of rules on the functioning of financial markets. While the empirical studies referred to above examined investor protection rules in corporate law, bankruptcy and reorganization laws and (intellectual) property rights, the remainder of this book focuses on some aspects of securities regulation, in particular problems of informational asymmetry and the dissemination of information by stock exchange listed companies. In order to analyse the interactions between financial theory and the law (securities regulation, criminal law), we adopt a law and economics approach.

Chapter two presents a general framework for the disclosure of information by listed companies. In order to be able to evaluate the disclosure regulation, chapter two starts by explaining the origin of securities regulation. After examining the functions of an exchange and the goals of securities regulation, the mandatory disclosure rules are examined within the context of market efficiency in chapter three. Besides this system of broad public disclosure, several other mechanisms for a company to communicate to the market are being examined such as selective disclosure through financial analysts and signalling devices such as (legal) insider trading. Two aspects of solving asymmetric information problems, i.e. the use of trading halts and insider trading, are discussed in chapters four and five.

In order to solve the problem of informational asymmetry, chapter two will show that securities regulation can be classified according to the level of intervention by supervisory bodies in the trading process: no, weak, moderate or strong intervention. The next chapters then examine the levels of moderate and strong intervention in the trading process. In this way, chapter four studies trading suspensions as a moderate level of intervention. It examines if such an intervention, i.e. a temporary interruption of trading, can be justified on theoretical and empirical grounds.

Next, a strong level of intervention in the trading process is analysed, i.e. the prohibition of all trading in case of insider information. Chapter five examines the necessity of such a regulation. After considering the pros and cons of such regulation, we shall argue from a law and economics point of view that a (partial) legalization of insider trading can be considered. Chapter six examines several aspects of regulating insider trading by using a clinical study. Finally, chapter seven examines the effectiveness of criminal regulation on insider trading.

CHAPTER 2
ASYMMETRIC INFORMATION AND
SECURITIES REGULATION

0. INTRODUCTION

One rationale for regulation is the improvement of economic efficiency by correcting market imperfections, as was shown by the public interest theory in the previous chapter. One type of market imperfection on markets in general and financial markets in particular results from asymmetric information. In general, a situation of symmetric information occurs when a market participant does not have useful information that the other market participants do not possess. In the opposite case, a situation of asymmetric information arises.

This chapter analyses the problem of asymmetric information on securities markets in section one. Next, the chapter focuses on the scope of securities regulation in section two. After analysing the functions of an exchange, the goal of securities regulation are discussed. The chapter ends with an overview of the different forms of securities regulation.

1. ASYMMETRIC INFORMATION

The section starts by explaining the problem of adverse selection ultimately leading to the non-existence of a market. Several solutions to the 'market for lemons' are considered. Next, the problem of asymmetric information on securities markets is examined.

1.1. THE MARKET FOR 'LEMONS'

The problem of asymmetric information was first explored in industrial economics where buyers and sellers do not have the same information and it refers to every situation in which one party to the transaction is better informed (e.g. the seller) than the other party (e.g. the buyer) about a material fact (e.g. the quality of the product) (Carlton and Perloff, 1994).

This problem of non-observable product characteristics was first examined in the seminal paper of Akerlof (1970) examining the 'market for lemons'. In a market where buyers cannot distinguish between good and bad used cars, an adverse selection effect may occur, leading to the non-existence of a market or only to the sale of the lowest-quality product. In the used-car market the current owner who decides to sell his car, has more knowledge about the quality of the car because, after owning the car for some time, he will have a good idea of its quality. However, the buyer cannot tell the difference between a good car and a bad car. Buyers only know the probability of getting a good car (q) and the probability of getting a lemon (1-q). Therefore all used-cars will sell at the same average price (Akerlof, 1970). In such a market good cars are undervalued and lemons are overvalued.

Consider the stylized example of a used-car market in which buyers believe that half of the cars in the market are good cars (with a value of EUR 4,000) and half of the cars are lemons (with a value of EUR 2,000). Because the buyer cannot distinguish good cars from bad, he is willing to pay EUR 3,000, being ½ × 2,000 + ½ × 4,000, for a random used-car. Put differently, a buyer is willing to pay more than the value of a bad car because there is a probability of q that the car is good, but he is not willing to pay the full value of a good car because there is a probability of 1-q that the car is a lemon (Carlton and Perloff, 1994).

In such a market, bad cars drive out good cars because the owner of a good car is unwilling to sell his car for less than its value and owners of bad cars are more than willing to sell their car for more than its value. No good cars will be placed on the market. Buyers recognize this and are willing to pay even less because the average value of low quality cars is now lower, starting a vicious cycle (Stiglitz, 1997). So it is possible that "the bad driving out the not-so-bad, driving out the medium, driving out the not-so-good, driving out the good in such a sequence of events, that no market exists at all (Akerlof, 1970, p.490)." This is clearly a market failure because no trade takes place even when there are people willing to sell their car at a price which other people are willing to pay if they only knew the true value of the car. So, if buyers and sellers had symmetric information, no market failure would occur.

While the 'market for lemons' caused adverse selection because sellers are better informed than buyers, examples can also be found where buyers have more information than sellers. This occurs, for instance, in the life insurance market. In this case the buyer is better informed about specific risks than the seller. People who are increasingly certain that they need the insurance will have an incentive to buy insurance. If prices of insurance increase, low-risk individuals will not buy insurance. As a result no insurance sales may take place at any price.

1.2. SOLUTIONS TO THE MARKET FOR LEMONS

How can the problem of asymmetric information and adverse selection be solved to avoid market failures? First of all, the market can often solve this problem itself through the pricing mechanism, by information gathering or some signalling devices. Only if the market cannot solve the problem of information asymmetry itself, a mandated provision of information through regulation or even farther-reaching interventions may be necessary.

In some markets *prices* may convey the necessary information to infer the relative quality of products (Stiglitz, 1997). Baron (1996) gives the example of stock markets, where investors have different information, but the market aggregates all the information through its security prices. We will analyse this function of the stock market in detail in section 2.1. Carlton and Perloff (1994) point out that where costs of obtaining information are relatively low, consumers or sellers obtain the information and markets function smoothly. If costs are high, however, the information is not gathered and inefficiency results. For instance, with respect to the used-car problem, a buyer can take the car to a mechanic for inspection and with regard to the life insurance-problem insurance companies can require a physical examination of the customers.

Besides, markets have several other devices for solving information asymmetry. First, the quality of the product can be conveyed by the use of *warranties* or *guarantees*. A company is only expected to provide warranties if it assumes the chances of defects to be low. Companies willing to provide a credible warranty signal that they are selling high-quality products (Grossman, 1991 and Stiglitz, 1997). Second, in markets where consumers and companies repeatedly deal with another, a *reputation* can signal that goods are of high quality (Shapiro, 1982). A common form of establishing a reputation is the use of brand names (Akerlof, 1970). Third, an agent or *expert* can be hired who is more knowledgeable than the consumer. For instance, the publications of consumers union (Carlton and Perloff, 1994), good department stores as intermediaries between producers and consumers (Stiglitz, 1997) or the sale of securities through investment bankers (Fischel, 1984; Leland and Pyle, 1977). Finally, several other devices to reduce uncertainty about quality can be used such as *advertising*[1], the use of *standards*[2] and

---

[1] See e.g. Bagwell (2001) or Chapter 15 'Advertising and disclosure' in Carlton and Perloff (1994).
[2] This is a metric or scale for evaluating the quality of a particular product.

certification[3] (Carlton and Perloff, 1994) or *licensing* of e.g. doctors and lawyers (Akerlof, 1970).

However, Magat (1998) points out that signalling may not be necessary for companies to fully disclose information about the quality of the product. Grossman (1981) develops a model in which full disclosure occurs if product quality is fully observable ex post. Although the quality cannot be observed in advance of the purchase, no company would claim that its product is of higher quality than it really is because it can be prosecuted for fraudulent claims. If the company makes less than full disclosure, consumers with rational expectations will assume that the true quality of the product is of the worst possible quality consistent with his disclosure. Realizing this, companies will fully and voluntarily disclose the true quality of their products. In such cases mandatory disclosure rules are unnecessary. Therefore, Magat (1998) sees regulation of information only as a facilitator to allow natural market forces to provide the incentive for a full disclosure of the quality of the products. Beales, Craswell and Salop (1981) distinguish three sorts of such regulation: (a) removing information constraints, (b) correcting misleading information and (c) increasing the supply of information.

1.3. ASYMMETRIC INFORMATION IN FINANCIAL MARKETS

Analogous to product markets, stock markets are also characterized by asymmetric information, which makes it difficult for investors to distinguish high quality from low quality securities. A similar reasoning can therefore be made. If there are no mechanisms for making such a distinction, investors will value all securities as average in quality resulting in Akerlof's well-known 'lemons' market (Akerlof, 1970). In such a market high-quality securities can only be sold at a lower price than would be the case if their true quality could be revealed. In this way, only low-quality companies have an incentive to offer shares and they will dominate the market as a consequence. Because this decreases allocative efficiency by guiding resources to the least good investment opportunities, social welfare will decrease. Proponents of mandatory disclosure rules in securities markets use this rationale to support governmental regulation.

Clearly, one way for high-quality listed companies to distinguish themselves is to simply disclose information to investors. However, Fischel (1984) points out that there is a serious moral hazard associated with disclosure because low-quality listed companies can mimic this disclosure strategy thereby eroding the information content

---

[3]   This is a report that a particular product has been found to meet or exceed a given level on a standard.

of disclosure. In this way, investors cannot distinguish between high-quality and low-quality securities. As the previous section explained, the regulation of information is only necessary if the market mechanism itself cannot deal with solving the asymmetric information problem. So, jumping to the conclusion of the necessity of mandatory disclosure rules is skipping devices that signal the true quality of the investment opportunities to the stock market.

A first step to convince investors of the quality of the company is to allow accountants to review the books and records and to have them certify the accuracy of the firm's representations (Easterbrook and Fischel, 1984). Next, there are several market-induced incentive-signalling mechanisms that can reveal the true quality of the company's investment projects. A signalling mechanism should have two characteristics to work optimally: it should be inexpensive and it should be convincing (Vermaelen, 1986). Besides administrative costs and the competitive disadvantage costs, the cost to be convincing and credible should be as small as possible. Moreover, a signalling device should be designed in such a way that it is more expensive for a low-quality company to mimic good-quality companies (i.e. to lie) than it is to tell the truth.[4]

These signalling mechanisms include a systematic dividend policy (Easterbrook, 1984), pursuing a certain capital structure policy (Ross, 1977), the sale of securities through investment bankers (Fischel, 1984), allowing insiders to trade (Carlton and Fischel, 1983), the percentage shares owned by insiders (Leland and Pyle, 1977) and share repurchase tender offers (Vermaelen, 1986). Another device is the use of intermediaries such as financial analysts who are more knowledgeable than ordinary investors in distinguishing high-quality and low-quality securities. Finally, similar to warranties in the product market, Easterbrook and Fischel (1984) consider the possibility of managers warranting their statements. Managers could make legally enforceable promises to pay investors if the company does worse than promised, e.g. with respect to a market index. Chapter three will analyse these solutions to asymmetric information in financial markets in more detail.

2. THE SCOPE OF SECURITIES REGULATION

The number of different topics that are addressed in the literature on securities regulation is enormous. Moreover, because securities regulation includes different fields of law (criminal law, company law, banking law, etc.) that regulate almost every aspect of the securities industry the literature is rather diffuse. For instance, the literature on the market for corporate control only focuses on the regulation of

---

[4]   See for this condition section 1 in chapter three.

mergers and acquisitions; an area that developed almost independently from other aspects of securities regulation.[5] Other examples of very specific securities regulations are derivatives regulation, the regulation of automated trading systems or securitisation. In order to get a broader view of securities regulation, section 2.1 focuses on the different functions of the financial system, while section 2.2 analyses the different goals of securities regulation. For this purpose, the efficient market hypothesis is explained in detail.

2.1. THE FUNCTIONS OF AN EXCHANGE

Levine (1997) gives a good overview of the functions of financial markets and intermediaries. Financial markets and intermediaries arise to ameliorate the problems created by market frictions such as information costs and transaction costs. Five basic functions of the financial system can be distinguished: (1) it facilitates the trading, hedging, diversifying, and pooling of risk; (2) it allocates resources; (3) it monitors managers and exerts corporate control; (4) it mobilizes savings and (5) it facilitates the exchange of goods and services.[6]

First, financial intermediaries, of whom a stock exchange is a specific form, facilitate the trading, hedging, diversifying, and pooling of risk. Levine (1997) considers two types of risk: liquidity risk and idiosyncratic risk. Liquidity is the ease and speed with which investors can convert their assets into purchasing power at agreed prices. Put differently, in a liquid stock market, investors can easily and quickly sell their shares if they seek access to their savings. On the other hand, a liquid stock market gives companies a permanent access to the capital invested by the initial shareholders. This is a very important characteristic of a stock market. Companies can only sell their shares to the public when there is a liquid secondary market. When investors fear an illiquid aftermarket, they are willing to pay less for the shares offered, thereby raising the cost of capital to companies (Macey, 1991). Idiosyncratic or company-specific risk arises from investing all one's money in one company; investors would have to buy and sell entire companies. Stock markets allow investors to hold small ownership

---

[5]   See for a recent overview Bittlingmayer (2000).

[6]   Alternatively, Merton and Bodie (1995) distinguish six core functions performed by a financial system: (1) to provide ways of clearing and settling payments to facilitate trade; (2) to pool funds to undertake large-scale indivisible enterprises or for the subdividing of shares in enterprises to facilitate diversification; (3) to transfer economic resources through time, across borders and among industries; (4) to provide ways to manage uncertainty and control risk; (5) to provide price information to help coordinate decentralized decision-making in various sectors of the economy and (6) to deal with incentive problems in case of information asymmetries or when one party is an agent for another. The functions of a financial system are also briefly discussed by Cole and Slade (1991).

fractions in a wide range of companies. In this way, investors can diversify the company-specific risk (Elton and Gruber, 1995). Therefore, it involves the creation of small denomination instruments so that investors can hold diversified portfolios.

Second, financial intermediaries such as stock exchanges facilitate the acquisition of information about investment opportunities and thereby improve the allocation of resources. Information costs create an incentive for financial intermediaries. Instead of each investor collecting and processing all the information on a wide array of companies, the quality of management and economic conditions, it is more efficient for a financial intermediary to do all this work for its members, thus realizing economies of costs. Stock exchanges disseminate prices through published market prices. Investors do not have to collect and process information that is reflected in the market price by the information obtained by others. This is the consequence of the semi-strong form of the efficient market hypothesis (see infra).

While financial intermediaries can reduce the cost of information gathering ex-ante, for the same reasons they can also reduce the cost of information acquisition of ex-post monitoring of managers and of exerting corporate control. This is the financial system's third function. Stock markets make the separation of ownership and management of a firm possible. Or, as Brealey and Myers (1996, p. 24) put it: "Managers do not need to know anything about the personal tastes of their shareholders and should not consult their tastes.[7] Their task is to maximize net present value. If they succeed, they can rest assured that they have acted in the best interest of their shareholders." For, if stock prices reflect managers' investment decisions, investors can monitor their managers through market prices. Poorly performing management is disciplined by the market for corporate control, either through hostile takeovers (Marris, 1963 and Manne, 1965), proxy fights (Ikenberry and Lakonishok, 1993; Dodd and Warner, 1983; DeAngelo and DeAngelo, 1989 and Pound, 1988 and 1991) or through a market for (majority) share stakes (Renneboog, 1996 and Franks, Mayer and Renneboog, 1996). Moreover, the use of equity-linked compensation schemes aligns the interest of shareholders and managers (Brickley, Bhagat and Lease, 1985; Brindisi, 1985; Murphy, 1985; Baker, Jensen and Murphy, 1988; Mehran, 1995; Mishra, McConaughy and Gobeli, 2000; Core, Guay and Larcker, 2003, Murphy, 2003 and Tian, 2004).

Fourth, financial systems mobilize or pool savings from disparate savers for investment. The pooling of savings is costly. However, the use of financial intermediaries can overcome the transaction costs from collecting savings from different individual

---

[7]   Shareholders can transform the wealth created by managers into whatever time pattern of consumption they wish.

investors and they can make savers feel comfortable in relinquishing control of their savings (Sirri and Tufano, 1995).

Finally, financial systems that lower transaction costs can increase specialisation, technological innovation and growth. Myers (1999) points out that venture capital markets will not work without a stock market that accepts initial public offerings (IPOs) by young high-tech companies. The existence of a stock market for growth companies such as NASDAQ offers venture capitalists the possibility of an exit from these firms at the time of the IPO (Black and Gilson, 1998). Moreover, also entrepreneurs, that commit their entire (human) capital in a start-up company, will only do so ex-ante, if they can share in the ex-post profits through an exit on a stock exchange (Myers, 1999).

Kitch (1996, 2000) translates these fundamental functions of a stock exchange into a number of expanded functions. First, it limits access to trading facility on the exchange, thereby eliminating concern about the identity and trustworthiness of any particular counter party. Second, it standardises trading rules. In this way, transacting parties only have to focus on the transaction price. Third, clearing procedures clarify the obligations of the transaction parties to deliver the security and pay the transaction price. Next, an exchange can specify specialized roles for some members, such as dealers or specialists. Fourth, an exchange can provide dispute-settlement procedures. Fifth, the exchange can regulate access to information that is generated through the trading activity (see infra). Finally, listing requirements can be developed to ensure minimum procedural and quality requirements. However, each of these functions can be traced back to one of the five basic functions as explained by Levine (1997).

2.2. THE GOALS OF SECURITIES REGULATION

While the previous section analyses the functions of a stock exchange, this section now looks into the goals of securities regulation.[8] Given the functions a stock exchange can fulfil, it is clear that investors care about the quality of the financial market in which they trade. The better these markets operate, the better the risk diversification, the better the allocation of resources, the more savings mobilized, etc. There appears to be a relationship between the functioning of financial markets and the quality of these markets. As chapter one showed, there is a clear impact of investor protection in company laws and bankruptcy laws on the development of financial markets.

---

[8]   In this section we only develop goals for securities regulation, not for banking laws, company law and bankruptcy and reorganization laws.

Although investor protection is the most cited objective with regard to securities regulation, it is unclear what this 'protection' constitutes (Kitch, 2000). It is a very vague term that can include almost all regulation. As a result, the concept of 'investor protection' is sometimes abused to promulgate regulation that only benefits a particular interest group.[9] Because of its unclear content, it is very difficult to analyse the desirability and efficacy of a certain set of rules from an economic point of view. One of the three conditions for regulation to be undertaken was that its costs to society had to be in balance with its benefits.[10] Using a vague term such as 'investor protection' as a policy goal for securities regulation is therefore problematic. To evaluate a regulation from an efficiency point of view, a more sophisticated and a more operational version of the 'investor protection' goal has to be established.

What kind of protection are investors looking for when they execute transactions on a financial market? Both at the selling-side and at the buying-side investors care about the quality of the financial market in which they trade. When buying securities, investors must be 'protected' from buying mispriced securities. This means that the market price must reflect all available information about the company. This market characteristic is referred to as *market efficiency*. When selling securities, investors must be able to dispose of their securities easily, at short notice and at an appropriate price. This market characteristic is referred to as *market liquidity*.

Besides investors, companies raising external finance value liquid and efficient stock markets because it gives them permanent access to financial resources. Companies can only sell their shares to the public in a liquid and efficient secondary market. When investors fear illiquid or inefficient aftermarkets, they are willing to pay less for the shares offered, thereby raising the cost of capital to companies. Therefore, both companies and investors value efficient and liquid stock markets (Wu, 1968).

2.2.1. Market efficiency

A central goal for securities regulation in general and information disclosure by stock exchange listed companies in particular is the concept of market efficiency (Gilson and Kraakman, 1984 and Kahan, 1992). A financial market operates efficiently if security prices instantaneously and fully reflect all relevant available information. In an efficient financial market, market prices are therefore a reliable criterion for the investment value of securities. A more explicit definition can be found in Malkiel

---

[9]   See in general section 1 of chapter one.
[10] See in detail section 1 of chapter one. The other two conditions are: a clear failure in the market place and the fact that the proposed regulation can be designed in such a way that it can reduce the undesirable activities.

(1992): "A capital market is said to be efficient if it fully and correctly reflects all relevant information in determining security prices. Formally, the market is said to be efficient with respect to some information set if security prices are unaffected by revealing that information to all participants. Moreover, efficiency with respect to an information set implies that it is impossible to make economic profits by trading on the basis of that information set." One method to measure the efficiency of a financial market is to ask what set of information is reflected in securities prices. Traditionally three types of information can be distinguished: information in historical market prices, publicly available information and all information, irrespective of its public or non-public character. Based on these three types of information, three forms of the efficient market hypothesis can be distinguished: the weak form, the semi-strong form and the strong form of market efficiency (Fama, 1970).

a.   The fair game model

Fama (1970) expresses the efficient market hypothesis as a fair game model. In a fair game model there will be no difference between the actual change in security prices across an interval of time and the expected change in security prices based on the information available at the beginning of the interval of time. Price expectations for securities are generated by the following equation:

$$E\left(P_{i,t+1}\middle|\Phi_t\right)=\left[1+E\left(R_{i,t+1}\middle|\Phi_t\right)\right]P_{i,t} \qquad [2.1]$$

where $P_{i,t+1}$ is the price of security i at time t+1, $R_{i,t+1}$ is the return on security i during period t+1, Φ_t is the set of information available to investors at time t and $E(\cdot)$ is the expected value operator. Equation [2.1] expresses that the expected price of security i at the end of the next period, $E\left(P_{i,t+1}\middle|\Phi_t\right)$, is based on the

security's expected normal return over the forthcoming period, $\left[1+E\left(R_{i,t+1}\middle|\Phi_t\right)\right]$,

which itself is conditional on the information set available at the beginning of this period (Φ_t). The fair game model postulates that if a financial market is efficient, investors cannot earn abnormal profits by trading on the available information set Φ_t (other than by chance). The abnormal return of a security can be calculated as:

$$AR_{i,t+1} = R_{i,t+1} - E\left(R_{i,t+1}\middle|\Phi_t\right) \qquad [2.2]$$

In an efficient market, the expected return, given an information set, will equal its actual return. This means that the following equation must hold:

$$E\left(AR_{i,t+1}\middle|\Phi_t\right)=0 \qquad [2.3]$$

The magnitude of each information set Φ_t depends on the particular form of market efficiency being considered. Three information sets are being considered: historical market prices, all publicly available information and all public and private information (see figure 2.1).

Figure 2.1.Three sets of information and three forms of market efficiency of financial markets

$$E\left(AR_{i,t+1}|\Phi_t\right) = E\left[R_{i,t+1} - E\left(R_{i,t+1}|\Phi_t\right)\right] = 0$$

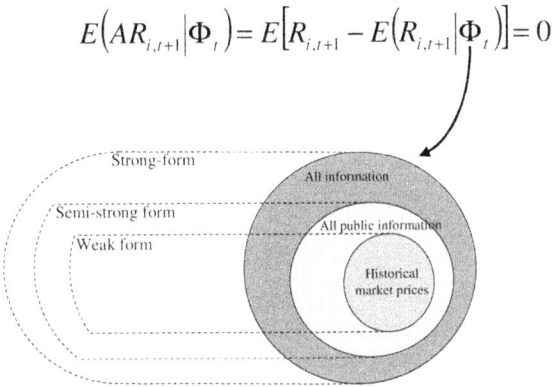

b. Three versions of the efficient market hypothesis

"Weak-form" market efficiency says that all information that may be contained in historical market prices is fully reflected in today's security prices. This means that historical patterns in securities prices are of no use in predicting future stock price movements. An important characteristic of the weak form of market efficiency is that security price changes occur as a random walk (Saari, 1977). If securities prices already incorporate all historical information, prices can only change if new information appears on the market. New information is by definition unpredictable. In this way, security price changes can only reflect this unpredictable or surprise component of information. Therefore, security price changes occur randomly. Supposing there is a predictable pattern in stock prices, technical analysts will recognize this pattern and try to earn abnormal profits by trading on this phenomenon. Increased demand will cause stock prices to rise up to the point where abnormal profits disappear. If a sufficient amount of investors trades in a certain predictable pattern, this pattern will disappear when it is detected. Consequently, if a financial market is weakly efficient, an investor cannot earn abnormal returns (other than by chance) by analysing historical data (for instance, by using technical trading rules). Put differently, "the market has no memory" (Brealey and Myers, 1999).

Figure 2.2. Stock price reaction to the arrival of new information in a semi-strong form efficient stock market

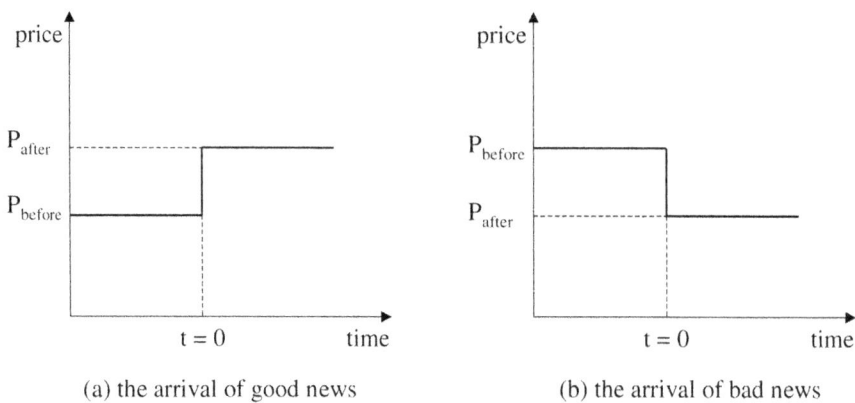

(a) the arrival of good news   (b) the arrival of bad news

The "semi-strong-form" version of market efficiency hypothesizes that security prices fully reflect all publicly available information, such as annual reports, quarterly earnings reports, earnings estimates in analyst reports, articles in newspapers, published investment recommendations, the announcement of a bonus dividend or macro-economic data on interest rates, inflation, etc. A trading strategy based on this publicly available information will not generate an abnormal return (other than by chance). If new information appears on the market, security prices will respond quickly by adjusting the market price to new levels. This is illustrated in figure 2.2. Panel a show how the stock price should react in an efficient market when good news arrives. Up to the moment of the release of new information about the stock the stock price amounts to P_{before}. After the release of the new information, the stock price moves to its new level P_{after}. In a semi-strong form efficient market the adjustment of the stock price occurs on the arrival of the new information (t=0). Panel b illustrates the analogue case of bad news.

Especially the *speed* of adjustment of stock prices to the new information is important (Gordon and Kornhauser, 1985). Speed refers to how fast security prices react to the release of new information. The occurrence of abnormal returns after the announcement of new information is therefore inconsistent with the semi-strong form of the efficient market hypothesis. Figure 2.3 illustrates the speed of adjustment in a semi-strong efficient stock market. If new information arrives at the market at time t=0, then a slow stock price adjustment as in figure 2.3, where the new information is incorporated at time t=1, is inconsistent with semi-strong market efficiency. Therefore, the speed of adjustment is very important in a semi-strong efficient market. Stock prices are supposed to adjust instantaneously in a semi-strong efficient market, as is the case in figure 2.2.

Figure 2.3. Slow stock price reaction to the arrival of new information inconsistent with semi-strong form efficiency

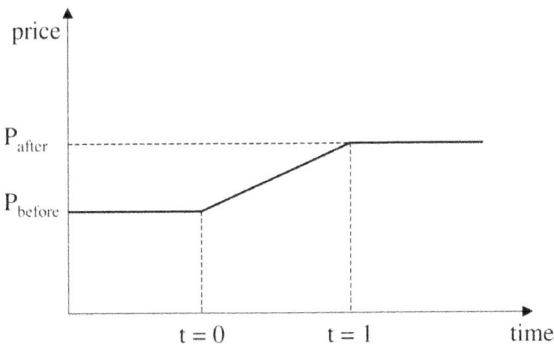

According to "strong-form" market efficiency all information is reflected in security prices, irrespective of the public or non-public character of the information. If a financial market is strongly efficient it implies either that there is no other relevant information besides the public available information (in this case no one has monopoly access to information), or that information that is not publicly available, the so-called private or inside-information, is fully reflected in security prices (Ayres, 1991). If a financial market is strongly efficient, no investor can earn an abnormal return based on non-public information (other than by chance).

Empirical studies generally confirm the weak and semi-strong form of market efficiency, but not the strong form.[11] Tests of the efficient market hypothesis show that financial markets are highly semi-strong form efficient. Security prices seem to impound quickly all relevant information about investment values. Sharpe, Alexander and Bailey (1999, p.103) conclude that "investors cannot easily expect to earn abnormal profits trading on publicly available information, particularly once the costs of research and transactions are considered." However, no empirical evidence is found on strong-form market efficiency (Engelen, 1999). Based on nonpublic information, it is therefore possible to earn a better return than the market. Finnerty (1976), Baesel and Stein (1979), Penman (1982), Heinkel and Kraus (1987) and Seyhun (1986, 2000) show clearly that insiders realise abnormal returns.

It is important to note that the original goal of Fama's classification of different types of information into three versions of the efficient market hypothesis (weak, semi-strong, strong) was only intended to classify empirical tests (Fama, 1970). In his recent article Fama (1991) uses another classification. The weak-efficiency tests are replaced

---

[11]   See for an overview Fama (1991) or Elton and Gruber (1995).

by a more general category of tests of return predictability, while semi-strong form tests are replaced by event studies and studies of announcement. Gilson and Kraakman (1984, p.556) point out that "over time, scholars have pressed the weak, semi-strong, and strong form categories beyond their original service as a classification of empirical tests into a more general duty as a classification of market responses to particular kinds of information." They oppose to the idea of describing an entire market as weak, semi-strong or strong form efficient. A financial market is therefore neither strictly efficient nor strictly inefficient (Haugen, 2001). It may be very useful to use a finer partitioning of different information sets than the three general categories. A further subdivision of each dimension of efficiency is useful because an efficient market response to one set of information does not necessary imply that the market will respond efficiently to a different set of information (Gilson and Kraakman, 1984). It may very well be the case that security prices reflect some types of public information faster than other types of public information (Ayres, 1991). Because it is very likely that security prices will not be uniformly efficient as to all types of information Macey and Miller (1990) argue that a more complete taxonomy of market efficiency is necessary. This is a crucial insight with respect to securities regulation. If security prices are less efficient with regard to a particular piece of information, securities regulation should be concerned to improve the efficiency (production and processing) of particular sets of information instead of focusing on all sources of information in order to obtain semi-strong form efficiency.

c.   The area of tension between lawyers and economists – efficiency versus equal access to information

Traditionally, many regulatory bodies supervising financial markets in the US or Europe pursue equal access to information for all market participants. Many legal scholars also allege the equal treatment of shareholders in equal circumstances as a general goal for the regulation of information dissemination. Although the idea of equal access to information for all investors is a nice principle in theory, in reality it is merely a utopian concept (Kripke, 1973). In reality there is a continuum of informed market participants ranging from very well informed to poorly informed (Engelen, 1999). It is clear that corporate insiders are better informed about their own company than market professionals, which in turn are better informed than small investors and the public in general. Market professionals are specialised in obtaining new information in order to differentiate themselves from other market participants and to obtain a higher profit. Market professionals are therefore always in a position to respond faster to new information than the average market participant. Or, as the US Supreme Court expressed: *"informational disparity is inevitable in the securities markets"*.[12] Thus, small

---

[12]   *U.S. v. O'Hagan, Federal Securities Law Reports*, 1997, nr.99-482, p.97-245, column 2.

investors have a structural informational disadvantage compared to other market participants. Pursuing equal access to information for all market participants is therefore not very useful because this goal cannot be reached in reality (Saari, 1977). Consequently, the policy of equal access to information for all market participants cannot be supported because it does not solve the information asymmetry between insiders and outsiders. The goal of equal access to information is therefore "as unsophisticated as the investors it is supposed to protect" (Easterbrook and Fischel, 1984, p.694), because such a goal ignores the functioning of the financial markets to incorporate information. As seen above, the goal of the disclosure of information should be situated within the scope of the efficient markets hypothesis (Gilson and Kraakman, 1984 and Kahan, 1992).

If financial markets are semi-strong form efficient, market prices are a reliable criterion for the investment value of securities. As long as sufficient market participants process information about companies, market prices will fully reflect all publicly available information, regardless of its distribution among the different market participants. Or as Saari (1977, p.1071) puts it: "In an efficient market, therefore, the greater the sum of information possessed, analysed and used by all market participants, [...] the more assurance each individual investor has that the market price of each security represents its intrinsic value." In a semi-strong form efficient market an investor can rely on the fact that every piece of public information is already reflected in security prices, without the necessity to collect and process the information himself. In this way, semi-strong form efficiency provides individual investors low cost access to the production and dissemination of all relevant information to value securities.

d. Fundamental efficiency

The previous sections discussed whether current market prices immediately reflect different information sets (speed of adjustment). The efficient market hypothesis therefore refers to the so-called "informational" efficiency. This form of efficiency has to be distinguished from another form of efficiency that measures whether security prices, conditioned on the information available, exclusively reflect the underlying or fundamental profits of the company (Ayres, 1991). This form is sometimes referred to as "fundamental" efficiency. It is concerned with the question whether security prices accurately reflect investors' expectations about the present value of future cash flows (Elton and Gruber, 1995). Although some authors do not distinguish between the two forms of market efficiency or use the term "efficiency" to apply to both situations, several authors do appreciate this distinction. While Ayres (1991) refers to "informational efficiency" versus "fundamental efficiency", Elton and Gruber (1995) use the terms "(informational) efficiency" and "market rationality" to make a clear distinction between both ideas. A similar distinction is made by Fischel (1989) who refers to "trading-rule efficiency" and "value efficiency". Trading-rule efficiency "focuses on the speed with which market prices reflect publicly-available information and whether the price reaction to new information is without bias. Under this definition, a market is efficient if it is impossible to devise a trading rule that systematically outperforms the market (net of transaction costs) absent possession of inside information", while value efficiency "focuses on the extent to which security prices reflect the present value of the net cash flows generated by a firm's assets" (Fischel, 1989, p.913).[13]

The two forms of efficiency are however closely related. Fundamental efficiency requires that security prices are equal to the present value of the future cash flows investors expect the company to generate, discounted by the appropriate risk-adjusted rate of return. The expectations about future cash flows are formed based on the information available to the market. This is in turn based on the degree of informational efficiency of the market. While informational efficiency determines what categories of information are available to investors, fundamental efficiency determines how the market reacts to this available information (Ayres, 1991). Fundamental efficiency therefore determines what sort of information the market considers relevant or valuable.

These two dimensions of efficiency are represented in figure 2.4. The vertical axis captures the different versions of the informational efficiency of the efficient market hypothesis. Historical stock prices have no impact on future price changes according to weak form efficiency (areas A and H); the publicly available information has no effect on future price changes according to semi-strong form efficiency (areas A, B, G and H), while public as well as private information has no impact on future price changes (areas A, B, C, F, G and H) according to strong form efficiency. The horizontal axis divides the amount of information into different types of non-fundamental information (areas A, B, C and D) and fundamental information (areas E, F, G and H). Information that is relevant to underlying profitability of the firm is considered to be fundamental, while information that causes changes in stock prices more or less than predicted by fundamentals is considered to contain non-fundamental components.[14] According to fundamental efficiency or market rationality non-fundamental information has no impact on future stock price changes (areas A, B, C and D).

---

[13]   Several authors use some other terms to make this distinction. Gordon and Kornhauser (1985) make a distinction between "speculative" efficiency and "allocative" efficiency, while Wang (1986) uses the terms "information-arbitrage" and "fundamental-valuation".

[14]   Examples of non-fundamental information include the news that the CEO has dyed his hair, news about sunspots or the coffee price in Latin-America with respect to the stock price of a software company.

Figure 2.4. Fundamental versus informational efficiency

Fundamental efficiency

	Non-fundamental information	Fundamental information
Future information	D	E
Present private information	C	F
Present public information	B	G
Present price information	A	H

Informational efficiency

Source: Ayres (1991)

Suppose that a financial market is semi-strong form informationally efficient and fundamentally efficient. Semi-strong form informational efficiency implies that all publicly available information is included in current stock prices, hereby eliminating areas A, B, G and H. Fundamental efficiency would imply that non-fundamental information has no impact on future stock prices, hereby eliminating areas A, B, C and D. Combining both forms of efficiency means that future stock prices are only affected by current private fundamental information and new fundamental informa-tion (areas E and F). If markets are strong form informationally efficient and fundamentally efficient, only new fundamental information can affect security prices (area E).

2.2.2. Liquidity

When investors sell securities on a financial market, they care about market liquidity. Investors are unwilling to trade on a financial market or in financial instruments that exhibit liquidity risk. This risk refers to the potential decline from a security's quoted market price when the security is sold (Weston and Copeland, 1989). Put differently, liquidity refers to the cost of selling a security 'in a hurry'. Levine (1997) points out that liquidity risk arises due to the uncertainties associated with converting assets into a medium of exchange. A house is thus a relatively illiquid asset because it is more difficult to obtain a fair price when sold quickly. Therefore, by facilitating trade in securities, stock markets play an important part in reducing liquidity risk (Wu, 1968). It is reasonable to assume that investors will find more liquid financial markets or more liquid financial instruments to be more attractive, keeping everything else the same (Sharpe, Alexander and Bailey, 1999).

Macey (1991) distinguishes three components of market liquidity. The first component is the ability of an investor to sell a security quickly. This component of liquidity focuses on the speed at which a security can be sold. For instance, 'blue chip' stocks are typically more liquid than some small, unknown shares because they can be sold immediately while small stocks are sometimes lacking a matching buying order.

Besides the speed, the second component requires that the price at which the security is sold is set at the appropriate level at any particular time, or put differently, that the price is unbiased. When an investor sells illiquid securities (e.g. lacking willing buyers), he faces the danger that the transaction price is lowered by these artificial conditions. An unbiased price will therefore be obtained if an investor can convert his securities into cash at a price that is similar to the price of the previous trade, assuming that no new information has arrived since the previous trade. This is the case when at any given time the market price of a security reflects the present value of the expected returns that the security will generate for its investors in the future. The previous section showed that this occurs in an efficient market.

The final component of market liquidity is the low-cost access to information. Unbiased prices require information to be produced and disseminated at low cost. Again, this is linked to market efficiency. For, in an efficient market investors can rely on current market prices because they reflect the information obtained by others.

2.2.3. Towards a clear goal of securities regulation

The two previous sections showed that investors and companies value market liquidity and market efficiency as two important properties of financial markets. While market liquidity allows investors to sell their securities quickly at an appropriate price, market efficiency yields a low-cost access to financial markets (Macey, 1991). In an efficient market investors only have to observe market prices and rely on the market to incorporate information into securities prices without the need to spend private resources to acquire and process information that is almost immediately publicly available through the pricing mechanism (Levine, 1997).

Insofar as market liquidity and market efficiency are crucial characteristics of the quality of a financial market, investors and companies will desire rules that facilitate market efficiency and liquidity. A financial market with an adequate legal framework enhancing liquidity and efficiency will therefore be preferred over a market with a less optimal legal environment. Moreover, the vague and unclear goal of 'investor protection' can therefore be replaced by two clear policy goals, i.e. market liquidity and market efficiency. These two policy goals for establishing securities regulation offer a clear and powerful framework in order to analyse the desirability and efficacy of a certain set of rules from an economic point of view.

Ideally, one would like stock markets to be strong form informationally efficient. Currently, stock markets seem to be semi-strong form informationally efficient. However, as will be explained in the next chapter, there are several signalling devices or selective disclosure mechanisms to incorporate private information in security prices, thereby enhancing strong form efficiency of stock prices. Investors will therefore prefer a legal framework enhancing strong form efficiency. As the next chapters show, this implies the abolition of certain rules (e.g. the ban on selective disclosure through financial analysts or the ban on insider trading) or the establishment of other rules which serve as a facilitator to allow natural market forces to provide the incentive to incorporate private information in security prices (e.g. the notification of holdings and transactions of corporate insiders).

Figure 2.5. The goals of securities regulation and the functions of an exchange

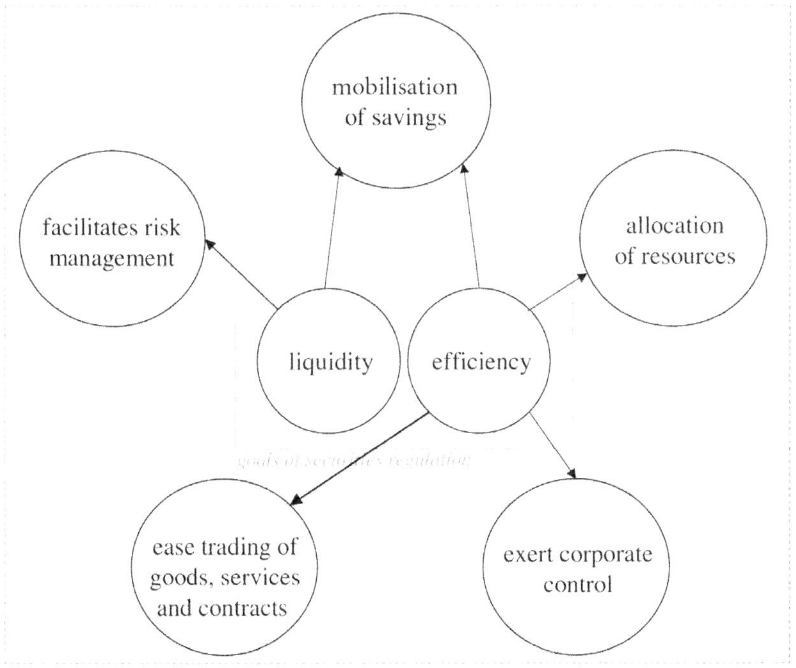

Notice that these goals of securities regulation are in line with the five basic functions of financial systems, as explained in section 2.1. Liquidity facilitates the reduction of liquidity risk and the diversification of idiosyncratic risk (small denominations). Efficiency improves the allocation of resources because of the low-cost acquisition of information about investment opportunities (see figure 2.5). The monitoring of management and the exerting of corporate control requires a fair price in order to be a reliable measure managerial performance; this condition is satisfied in an efficient market. The mobilization of savings can only be successful if investors feel safe to relinquish control of their savings, i.e. a quick and easy conversion into cash (satisfied by market liquidity) and solving problems of asymmetric information (satisfied by market efficiency).

2.3. DIFFERENT FORMS OF SECURITIES REGULATIONS

There are several ways to classify the complete securities regulatory system. A first classification of securities regulation is a *functional division*. Grundfest (1998) distinguishes four broad categories of securities regulation.[15] A first set of rules defines the domain of financial instruments, transactions and market participants that are subject to its jurisdiction. These rules determine the jurisdictional boundaries of securities regulation compared to other regulatory systems such as banking, insurance or derivatives regulation as well as geographical jurisdiction (domestic versus abroad).[16] A second set of rules imposes mandatory disclosure requirements on issuers of publicly traded securities. These requirements include initial disclosure requirements as well as periodic disclosure requirements such as annual and quarterly reports and occasional reporting requirements. However, the theoretical debate as well as the empirical studies on mandatory disclosure remains controversial (see next chapter). The third set of rules compromises antifraud rules that impose civil or criminal penalties on market participants who provide false statements or omit certain important information. Although these antifraud rules generally include prohibitions on insider trading, it remains a controversial issue, especially in the law and economics literature (see chapter five). The final set of rules regulates market structure (e.g.

---

[15]   Compare to Kabir (1991) who uses three categories to classify securities regulation: (a) issuance of securities; (b) trading of securities and (c) financial intermediation. The first set of rules consists of initial disclosure requirements with regard to the sale of new securities. The public offering on the primary market is prevented unless adequate information about the company is provided. The second set of rules regulates the secondary market and includes rules on periodic accounting disclosure, insider trading and trading halts. The final set of rules regulate financial intermediation and include rules on the establishment, the activities and the management of financial intermediaries in order to maintain the stability of the financial system and protect investors against losses.

[16]   In the European Union there is some harmonization between member states of minimum standards for the prudential supervision of financial institutions (e.g. approval of 'regulated' market). Furthermore, there is the mutual recognition by each member state of the competence of the supervisory bodies for the governance of minimum standards in each other member state (e.g. the 'European passport' to provide services freely throughout the European Union). A third concept is the assignment of the supervision of a financial institution to the home-country of that financial institution (Lee, 1998c).

specialist regulation on the NYSE and dealer regulation on NASDAQ) and trading practices (e.g. fixed versus competitive commission rates or the use of circuit breakers).

Table 2.1. Level of intervention in the trading process by the supervisory authorities

Level of intervention	Kind of regulation	Functioning
No intervention	None	Market price sanctions corporations
Weak intervention	Initial disclosure Listing requirements Periodic disclosure Corporate governance recommendations	Minimum compliance before trading can start
Moderate intervention	Trading halts Circuit breakers Disciplinary trading suspensions Order imbalances	Temporary suspension of trading
Strong intervention	Insider trading regulation	Prohibition of all trading
	Delisting	End of all trading

Securities regulation can also be classified according to the *level of intervention* by supervisory authorities in the normal trading process on the stock market (table 2.1). Because the market mechanism is the most basic device to allocate scare resources in capitalist economies[17], as a rule, the first level is one of no intervention. It is ultimately the market price that distinguishes good-quality from bad-quality investments. Regulation is necessary only when the market mechanism fails. However, the need for regulation does not automatically imply that supervisory authorities have to interfere in the normal trading process of securities. Such forms of intervention only occur in very specific circumstances. A first moderate intervention is the temporary interruption in trading of one security that occurs in case of a trading suspension (see chapter four). Even more severe is the use of circuit breakers because it involves a temporary market-wide halt of trading of all stocks. Both regulatory measures are addressed to all market participants. A very strong form of intervention in the normal trading process of stocks is the regulation on insider trading. Although the regulation is only addressed to a particular group of market participants, i.e. insiders, it prohibits all trading in a given security. While the suspension of trading in case of trading halts is rather short in time (several hours to one or two days), the prohibition in case of insider trading can span several weeks. However, most of the securities regulation has

---

[17]   Den Hartog (2000) referring to Arrow (1985) points out that it can be demonstrated that, under certain circumstances, the allocation of resources by means of the market mechanism is optimal.

less impact on the trading process. Initial disclosure and listing requirements can be seen as a priori interventions in the trading process. It imposes minimum compliance before trading can start. As long as listed companies conform to these minimum compliance rules no further intervention in the trading process will be necessary. Intervention will occur only in the case of non-compliance, such as a disciplinary trading suspension. The category of 'weak intervention' differs from the 'no intervention' category because it is not left to the market mechanism to distinguish between high-quality and low-quality securities.

Another classification distinguishes between two forms or models of regulatory law enforcement: *compliance and deterrent systems* (Veljanovski, 1984 and Reiss and Biderman, 1980). The objective of deterrent systems is to secure conformity with law by detecting and prosecuting violations of the law and by using legal penalties to punish lawbreakers to deter violations in the future. In securities regulation antifraud provisions such as the prohibition on stock price manipulation or on insider trading are examples of deterrent systems. Compliance systems secure conformity with the law by ensuring compliance or taking action to prevent potential law violations without the necessity to detect, prosecute and penalize violators (Reiss, 1984). The use of legal sanctions is in this case only an enforcement device of last resort. Examples of compliance systems in securities regulation are initial disclosure requirements, listing requirements and periodic disclosure requirements. Only in the case of non-compliance legal sanctions may occur such as a disciplinary suspension of trading. The design of both models is quite different. Deterrent systems are post-monitory aimed at detecting and processing violations once they have occurred. In this way, the levying of a penalty is a mark of the success of such a regulatory system. In contrast, compliance systems are premonitory and try to prevent the occurrence of a violation. In this system, penalties are only used as threats and the actual carrying out of a penalty is a mark of the failure to secure compliance. As such, violations in compliance systems, e.g. the failure of following the periodic disclosure requirements, are merely seen as 'technical' violations, i.e. behaviour that violates a condition designed to prevent unwanted conditions (Shapiro, 1980). As such 'sanctions' are typically withdrawn on demonstration of a state of compliance. For instance, the suspension of trading will be lifted once the listed company demonstrates compliance with all reporting requirements. While the basic assumption of deterrent systems such as the regulation on insider trading is the causal effect of sanctions to deter future violations, the compliance systems presume knowledge of what causes violations and how to prevent them (Reiss, 1984). This is the general idea behind mandatory disclosure regulation: better information about the listed company protects investors from price manipulations and corporate mismanagement.

Securities regulation can also be classified into *public and private regulation*. Two classic examples of this distinction are the public US regulatory system versus the U.K. private or self-regulatory system (Cheek, 1996)[18]. A public regulatory system is based on statutes and public sector institutions that derive their authority from the legislator[19]. Failure to comply with the regulation can be penalized with fines and imprisonment (Kabir, 1991). On the other hand, the private regulatory system consists of private sector institutions that derive support from the general acceptance of their decisions by the members. Historically, the U.K. had a system of securities regulation with a minimal statutory base and relied more heavily on self-regulation (Cheek, 1996). Failure to comply with private sector regulation can only result in disciplinary actions.

Finally, a distinction can be made between *soft laws and hard laws*. Hard laws are all forms of actual regulation put down in statutes, royal decrees, etc. Issues governed by soft laws are clearly not unregulated, but are not fully legally enforceable. A soft law approach merely depends upon the voluntary observance of these rules by the 'regulated' parties. It is often based on the moral authority of the supervisory body enacting these rules. An example of soft law regulation is the current corporate governance recommendations in many countries. Figure 2.6 summarizes the different classifications of securities regulation.

3. CONCLUSION

After explaining the problem of asymmetric information on securities markets, this chapter analysed the scope of securities regulation. The vague policy goal for securities regulation being 'investor protection' was replaced by a more sophisticated and more operational version with closer connection to the economic reality. Both investors and companies value market liquidity and market efficiency as two important properties of securities markets. While market liquidity allows investors to sell their securities quickly at an appropriate price, market efficiency yields a low-cost access to financial markets. In an efficient market investors only have to observe market prices and rely on the market to incorporate information into securities prices without the need to spend private resources to acquire and process information that is almost immediately publicly available through the pricing mechanism. A security market with an adequate

---

[18]   See furthermore Green, Braverman and Schneck (1996) and Perry (1996). Also Benston (1976) compares the public US and the private UK regulation of corporate financial disclosure.

[19]   For instance, in the US, the public model consists of seven statutes: the Securities Act of 1933, the Securities Exchange Act of 1934, the Public Utility Holding Company Act of 1935, the Trust Indenture Act of 1939, the Investment Company Act of 1940, the Investment Advisers Act of 1940 and the Securities Investor Protection Act of 1970. The Securities and Exchange Commission (SEC) has the principal job of implementing and enforcing this US regulatory scheme. See Cheek (1996).

legal framework enhancing liquidity and efficiency will therefore be preferred over a market with a less optimal legal environment. In this way it offers a clear and powerful framework in order to analyse the desirability and efficacy of securities regulation from an economic point of view. Finally, the chapter concluded with a taxonomy and classification of the complete securities regulatory system.

Figure 2.6. The different classifications of securities regulation

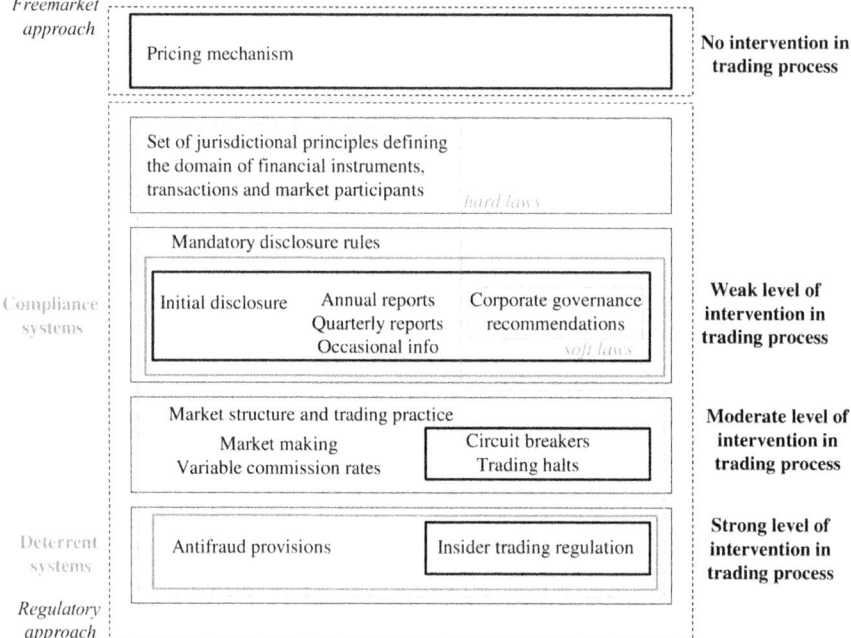

CHAPTER 3
SOLUTIONS TO ASYMMETRIC
INFORMATION IN STOCK MARKETS

0. INTRODUCTION

The previous chapter clearly showed the importance of enhancing market efficiency to solve asymmetric information between market participants by incorporating new information in securities prices. This chapter analyses how companies can be encouraged to disclose information about their activities making stock markets more efficient. There are several devices that can reveal the true quality of the investment projects of listed companies, and solve the problem of asymmetric information.

First, there are several market-induced disclosure incentives that lead to voluntary disclosure of information by corporate insiders (Vermaelen, 1986). These devices signal the true quality of companies to investors. Signaling devices are also referred to as a freemarket approach, in contrast to a regulatory approach for disseminating valuable information about companies to the market. The regulatory approach aims at enhancing market efficiency by mandatory disclosure regulation (see infra). Section one focuses on three signalling devices: maintaining a certain capital structure policy, the percentage shares owned by insiders and share repurchase tender offers.

A second way to solve asymmetric information in financial markets is the use of intermediaries, such as the dissemination of information through financial analysts. Such selective disclosure is discussed in section two.

Finally, if the market mechanism itself cannot deal with solving the asymmetric information problem, mandatory disclosure rules may be necessary. However, as section three will show, the information content of mandatory periodic reports can be questioned. It is doubtful that the limited information value of these financial reports balances against the huge costs related to a system of mandatory disclosure. In this view, mandatory disclosure is totally redundant because companies will disclose the optimal amount of information voluntarily (Grundfest, 1998). Compared to a system of mandatory disclosure, the elimination of such a system "will thus not affect the amount of information available to investors, but will reduce issuer compliance costs" (Dennis, 1987, p.1209).[1]

Companies cannot freely choose whether or not to release information because a shortage of information will increase the risk for investors. If a listed company discloses no information, investors assume the worst and discount the price they are willing to pay for the shares. This in turn will cause the cost of capital of companies to rise (Grundfest, 1998). Because a company can be seen as an open financial system, the financial manager, as an intermediary between the company and the financial markets, has to control permanently the quality and quantity of information flows from the company to the financial markets. A company can only rely on permanent financial resources from capital markets if returns to investors are market based. Adequate investor relations can therefore decrease the cost of capital, which implies cheaper access to capital markets (Diamond, 1985). Information about the decisions of management will reach the financial markets through different communication channels. Financial markets constantly assess those decisions and translate it in the market price of the share.

1. SIGNALLING

As a first solution to revealing the true quality of securities, this section looks at some market-induced incentive-signalling mechanisms that can motivate and implement the release of private information as an alternative to the mandatory disclosure of information. Moreover, disclosure may not always be possible, for instance when the disclosure of the information may cause it to lose its value. If the information is publicly disclosed, the company reveals valuable information to its competitors. In that way, its competitors can take a free ride on the efforts involved in creating new information (Easterbrook and Fischel, 1982). To avoid disclosing the information itself, firms dispose over several mechanisms for overcoming the problem of asymmetric information by communicating the essence of the information indirectly through observable variables without the need to reveal the valuable information. Such signalling mechanisms include, among others, maintaining a certain capital structure (Ross, 1977), the percentage shares owned by insiders (Leland and Pyle, 1977) and share repurchase tender offers (Vermaelen, 1986).

We will illustrate the signalling approach by using the model of Ross (1977). This model describes how signalling can be used to deal with information asymmetry. According to this model the amount of debt managers issue signals the company's

---

[1]   See the empirical evidence in section three.

future performance to investors. The model distinguishes two types of companies, A and B and assumes a one-period world. At time 1, A companies will have a total value of V_{1A} (successful company) and B companies will have a total value of V_{1B} (unsuccessful company), with $V_{1A} > V_{1B}$. Investors cannot distinguish between A companies and B companies. However, investors will perceive a company to be successful (A-type) if it issues an amount of debt above a critical level D^* and unsuccessful (B-type) if it issues debt below this critical level. For this signal to be credible two conditions must be satisfied. First, managers must have the incentive to always signal the truth, even in case of bad news, and secondly, unsuccessful companies cannot mimic the signal of a successful company. This is achieved by managers' compensation in such a way that the payoff from telling to truth is greater than from telling lies. Expressed mathematically, the managers' compensation at the end of the period, M, can be seen as equation [3.1]:

$$M = (1+r)\gamma_0 V_0 + \gamma_1 \begin{cases} V_1 & \text{if } V_1 \geq D \\ V_1 - L & \text{if } V_1 < D \end{cases} \qquad [3.1]$$

where
γ_0, γ_1 = positive fractions of the value of the company which are paid to the managers
r = the one-period interest rate
V_0, V_1 = the current and the future value of the company
D = the face value of debt
L = a penalty imposed on the manager if the firm is bankrupt at time 1 (if $V_1 < D$).

Equation [3.1] shows that the compensation at the end of the period consists of a fraction, γ_0, of the market's current assessment of the value of the company, V_0, and of a fraction, γ_1, of the future market's assessment of the company's value, V_1. If the company goes bankrupt managers receive a penalty, L, which decreases their compensation substantially. Assuming that D^* is the maximum amount of debt an unsuccessful company can issue without going bankrupt, if a company chooses a debt level $D \geq D^*$, investors will assign a current market value of $V_0 = V_{1A}/(1+r)$. If a company chooses a debt level $D < D^*$, investors will assign a current market value of $V_0 = V_{1B}/(1+r)$. We will show that managers have the incentive to send the true signal to investors.

The compensation of managers of a successful company, M_A, can be calculated as equation [3.2]:

$$M_A = \begin{cases} \gamma_0 (1+r)\dfrac{V_{1A}}{1+r} + \gamma_1 V_{1A} & \text{if } D \geq D^* \quad (\textit{tell the truth}) \\[2mm] \gamma_0 (1+r)\dfrac{V_{1B}}{1+r} + \gamma_1 V_{1A} & \text{if } D < D^* \quad (\textit{lie}) \end{cases} \qquad [3.2]$$

Clearly, managers of successful firms have no incentive to choose a debt level below
D˙ ('lie to the market') because their compensation is maximal giving the true signal
(remember $V_{1A} > V_{1B}$.). Similarly, managers of unsuccessful companies will have no
incentive to provide a false signal. This can be seen, when analysing the managers'
compensation payoff in equation [3.3]:

$$M_B = \begin{cases} \gamma_0(1+r)\dfrac{V_{1A}}{1+r} + \gamma_1(V_{1B}-L) & if\ D \geq D˙ \quad (lie) \\[2mm] \gamma_0(1+r)\dfrac{V_{1B}}{1+r} + \gamma_1 V_{1B} & if\ D < D˙ \quad (tell\ the\ truth) \end{cases} \qquad [3.3]$$

Managers of unsuccessful companies will also provide the true signal when the payoff
from telling the truth exceeds the payoff from lying. Or, expressed mathematically:

$$\gamma_0 V_{1A} + \gamma_1(V_{1B}-L) < \gamma_0 V_{1B} + \gamma_1 V_{1B}, \qquad [3.4]$$

or

$$\gamma_0(V_{1A}-V_{1B}) < \gamma_1 L \qquad [3.5]$$

Thus, managers will provide a true signal if the gains from the false signal,
$\gamma_0(V_{1A}-V_{1B})$, are less than the penalty paid by managers if the firm goes bankrupt,
$\gamma_1 L$. Unsuccessful companies cannot mimic successful companies because they do
not have the cash flow to pay off the amount of debt above the critical level and
because managers have the incentive to tell the truth.

Summarizing, a signalling equilibrium is achieved if managers of successful companies
choose debt levels above the critical amount, thereby maximizing their compensation
under the true signal, while managers of unsuccessful companies choose debt levels
below the critical amount. Managers of unsuccessful companies cannot mimic the
signal of successful companies because of the substantial penalty against them if the
company goes bankrupt.

The percentage of shares owned by insiders appears to be another powerful and reliable
signalling mechanism through which management can reveal inside information to
the financial markets without disclosing valuable, confidential information to
competitors. It is more expensive for managers to hold large fractions of the shares
of their company when they believe the market price overstates its fundamental value
(Leland and Pyle, 1977). Especially changes in the fraction of insider ownership are
a powerful signal to investors, which is more reliable than a public disclosure of the
information (Fischel, 1984). It therefore makes very good sense to oblige insiders to
report such transactions. In the U.S. 'officers', 'directors' and beneficial owners of more
than ten percent of any class of stock need to disclose their fraction of share ownership
and their transactions in shares of their company based on section 16 Securities

Exchange Act (Wu, 1968).[2] Within ten days of obtaining their insider status, insiders have to disclose their initial fraction of ownership in the company via a Form 3. Subsequent changes in their fraction of ownership have to be disclosed via a Form 4 by the tenth day of the month following on the month of the transaction. Moreover, insiders have to disclose their fraction of ownership within 45 days after the fiscal year-end via a Form 5. The SEC distributes these notifications to the investment public through the publication "Official Summary of Security Transactions and Holdings". The value relevance of these notifications of transactions by insiders is empirically confirmed (e.g. Jaffe, 1974a; Finnerty, 1976 and Givoly and Palmon, 1985). Because these notifications are strong information signals for investors, there are special investment magazines and websites in the U.S. that focus on reporting and analysing insider trading.[3] See also Seyhun (2000) for specific investment strategies based on insider trading information.

Closely related are the share repurchases that signal inside information to investors. Empirical studies strongly confirm the value relevance of share repurchases; the studies of Masulis (1980), Vermaelen (1981), Dann (1981), Asquith and Mullins (1986), Comment and Jarrell (1991), Bagwell (1992) and Ikenberry, Lakonishok and Vermaelen (1995) clearly show the reliability of this information signal. This signal implies that the premium management is prepared to pay above the current market price reveals the undervaluation as it is perceived by management (Van Horne, 1998). The signal is convincing to investors because management buying back shares at a premium above the fundamental value of the company would bear significant losses. This information signal is more reliable if managers own more shares in their company, buy back more shares and pay larger offer premiums (Vermaelen, 1986).

The credibility of this information signal also depends on the tender method used by the company. Van Horne (1998) points out that the signal is the most credible for a fixed-price tender offer compared to a Dutch-auction tender offer. The least reliable signal is given by open-market purchases. With a fixed-price tender offer, the company makes a formal offer to stockholders to purchase so many shares, typically at a set price. With a Dutch-auction tender offer, each shareholder is given the opportunity to submit to the company the number of shares he is willing to sell at a particular price.

---

[2]   See section 16a-3 (a) Securities Exchange Act of 1934: "Initial statements of beneficial ownership of equity securities required by section 16(a) of the Act shall be filed on Form 3. Statements of changes in beneficial ownership required by that section shall be filed on Form 4. Annual statements shall be filed on Form 5. At the election of the reporting person, any transaction required to be reported on Form 5 may be reported on an earlier filed Form 4. All such statements shall be prepared and filed in accordance with the requirements of the applicable form." This is legal insider trading and has to be distinguished from illegal insider trading prohibited by section 10(b) of the Securities and Exchange Act of 1934 and SEC rule 10b-5.

[3]   See e.g. www.insidertrader.com

In advance, the company typically specifies a minimum and a maximum price and the total number of shares it wishes to repurchase. After receiving all tenders, the company determines the lowest price that will result in the full repurchase of the offered shares. This price is paid to all shareholders who tendered shares at that price or below.

2. SELECTIVE DISCLOSURE

A second method to reduce information asymmetry in financial markets is the use of intermediaries who are more knowledgeable than ordinary investors to distinguish high-quality and low-quality securities. As an alternative to broad disclosure by means of public announcement, a more selective disclosure through financial analysts may be a more efficient way of disseminating valuable information. Financial analysts can therefore play an important part in the dissemination of financial information by listed companies. Or as it was put by the US Supreme Court: "Market efficiency in pricing is significantly enhanced by their initiatives to ferret out and analyse information, and thus the analyst's work redounds to the benefit of all investors."[4] This section shows that the question whether selective disclosure should be allowed is answered affirmatively on economic efficiency grounds (section 2.1), while the question is answered in the negative by a legal analysis referring to 'fairness' considerations (section 2.2). Section 2.3 will show that this legal choice might lead to adverse effects.

2.1. ECONOMIC ANALYSIS OF SELECTIVE DISCLOSURE

Dissemination through financial analysts has some clear advantages compared to a public disclosure of the information. First, a disclosure of valuable information in this manner allows the value of the information to be reflected in the stock prices without the need to reveal the confidential information itself (such as investment opportunities) to the public at large. Because confidential information will also reach competitors in this way, such disclosure can be detrimental to the company. By using financial analysts as an intermediate link, the listed company can screen off the strategic information and, at the same time, communicate the information to the market indirectly through the advices of the financial analysts (Fischel, 1984). In this way, the information is fully reflected in security prices causing security markets to be efficient. Although valuable information is revealed to the market in an indirect way, the same result is obtained as would be the case with a public disclosure, i.e. securities prices

---

[4]   *Dirks v. SEC, Federal Securities Law Reports*, 1983, no. 99-255, p.96-126, column two.

reflect the information set. However, in the case of a selective disclosure the information remains confidential.

Suppose a listed company has two alternative ways to communicate a particular set of information to the financial markets: a public disclosure or a disclosure through financial analysts. The first alternative implies the company to disclose all information publicly by the distribution of a press release. In a semi-strong form efficient market, the new information will be incorporated instantaneously in security prices. However, the disadvantage of such a system is the fact that valuable strategic information will also be revealed to its competitors, which can be harmful to the interests of the company and, consequently, of its shareholders. For instance, it is exactly this case, in which the Belgian Royal Decree Occasional Information explicitly provides the possibility that a listed company is relieved by the Market Authority from its obligation to promptly disclose all facts or decisions, of which it has knowledge, that can influence significantly the market price of its securities.[5] The condition for this exemption is the fact that the release of certain pieces of information is harmful to the legitimate interests of the company.

The second alternative solves this problem automatically. Instead of a public announcement, the company opts to selectively disclose the information to financial analysts. Through the recommendations of these analysts the same set of information will be incorporated in security prices *without* harming the interests of the company. Both alternatives achieve the same goal, i.e. a particular set of information is reflected in the security's market price. However, disclosure through financial analysts is preferable to a public disclosure because the company does not have to reveal its confidential information.

Secondly, information disclosure through financial analysts clearly realizes economies of scale (Fischel, 1984). Financial analysts have a comparative advantage in analysing and verifying information as compared to small investors. Small investors can save a lot of costs for the search and analysis of information they can obtain through the recommendations of analysts. In this way, they obtain the same information by observing security prices without spending private resources to analyse the information. Levine (1997) points out that economizing on information acquisition costs improves resource allocation and may have important growth implications.

---

[5] Royal Decree of 3 July 1996 on the obligations with regard to occasional information of issuers whose securities are listed on the first market or on the new market of a public stock exchange, *Belgian Gazette*, 6 July 1996, modified by the Royal Decree of 13 January 1997, *Belgian Gazette*, 25 January 1997 and the Royal Decree of 9 June 1997, *Belgian Gazette*, 2 July 1997, errata, *Belgian Gazette*, 12 September 1997 [in short: *Royal Decree Occasional Information*].

2.2. LEGAL ANALYSIS OF SELECTIVE DISCLOSURE

The mere fact that listed companies voluntarily use financial analysts to disclose valuable information shows that selective disclosure is an efficient way of communicating information.[6] In the US companies such as Microsoft, Dell Computer's, Tellabs, Apple Computer, Wal-Mart Stores and Exxon used this method to communicate with the financial markets (Levy, 1999 and Serafino, 1999). In its policy note of April 1999 the 'Stichting Toezicht Effectenverkeer', the supervisory body in the Netherlands at that moment put a restraint on the distribution of analysts' reports.[7] In 2000, the SEC also changed its policy with regard to selective disclosure on 'fairness' grounds by promulgating the so-called 'Regulation FD', which requires issuers that intentionally disclose material information, to do so through public disclosure, not through selective disclosure.[8] Both visions cannot be supported because they ignore the part financial analysts play in disseminating information on financial markets.

Likewise, in Belgium the mechanism of selective disclosure is prohibited by the regulation on insider trading because primary insiders are not allowed to disclose privileged information to financial analysts.[9] In turn, it is prohibited for financial analysts to give recommendations based on the privileged information to which they have access by virtue of their profession (Engelen, 1999). The problematic nature of this regulation was brought to light in some insider trading cases. The Belgian Market Authority reported two incidents in 1996. In one case privileged information was distributed among analysts through a press release which was withheld (the Quick-case), while in the other case price-sensitive information was released during an analyst

---

[6] However, this view was not shared by Arthur Levitt, the chairman of the SEC, who put it this way: "… it is very clear to me and to the SEC's Enforcement Division, that issuers should not selectively disclose information to certain influential analysts, in order to curry favour with them and reap a tangible benefit, such as a positive press spin." See Levitt (1998).

[7] Policy note of the 'Stichting Effectenverkeer' with regard to the position of research, research reports, publications and recommendations in the Statute supervision securities trading 1995, Policy note 99-0001/GO, 9 April 1999.

[8] FD stands for 'Fair Disclosure'. Under rule 100 of Regulation FD when an issuer, or a person acting on its behalf, discloses material non-public information, to certain enumerated persons (in general, securities market professionals or holders of issuer's securities who may well trade on the basis of the information), the issuer must make public disclosure of that same information simultaneously (for intentional disclosures) or promptly (for non-intentional disclosures). See Securities and Exchange Commission, *Selective disclosure and insider trading*, Release Nos. 33-7881, 34-43154, IC-24599, File No. S7-31-99, 15 August 2000. The new rules took effect October 23, 2000. The public disclosure requirements are met by filing a Form 8-K, by distributing a press release through a widely disseminated news or wire service. The SEC also allows the use of new technologies such as web casting of conference calls or other conferences that interested members of the public may attend or listen to either in person, by telephonic transmission, or by electronic transmission.

[9] Art. 183 Statute of 4 December 1990 on Financial Transactions and Financial Markets, *Belgian Gazette*, 22 December 1990, erratum, *Belgian Gazette*, 1 February 1991.

meeting.[10] The Market Authority points out that neither may price-sensitive information be released during an analyst meeting in any circumstance, nor be sent by means of telegraph to analysts during market hours.[11]

If a financial analyst receives price-sensitive information in any way, he cannot use this information to trade on the stock market. In its activity report of 1998 the Market Authority reports one case of insider trading in connection with an analyst meeting. During an analyst meeting the management of a listed company revealed that its expected earnings figures had to be revised downwards. A financial analyst distributed this information through a recommendation to two pension funds, which subsequently executed a selling order.[12]

2.3. ADVERSE EFFECTS OF BANNING SELECTIVE DISCLOSURE

Although the legislator or supervisory bodies adopt a policy banning selective disclosure on 'fairness' grounds, it must be stressed that such a choice might lead to adverse effects. Regulation may be 'overshooting' in a sense that the group it is supposed to protect, is worse off than in a situation without the regulation. By cutting off the communication channel through financial analysts based on the regulation on insider trading, a suboptimal level of regulation is therefore achieved (Fischel, 1984). First, companies are forced to use other communication channels that are probably more expensive and less efficient. Second, the investment public at large has to spend unnecessary resources to interpret and verify information about investment opportunities to achieve the same final object, i.e. the incorporation of new information in security prices. Third, financial analysts are compelled to use more expensive methods to acquire information in order to try to replicate the information set companies would have distributed to them voluntarily. Cutting off the communication channel through financial analysts therefore does not decrease information asymmetry; on the contrary, it decreases and slows down the informational efficiency of security prices. This adverse effect is clearly not beneficial to small investors. The suboptimal level of regulation forces investors to pay more to obtain the same information. These are real cash outflows that will decrease the net return on investment (Fischel, 1984).

---

[10] "Beurswereld in de knoei met efficiënt markttoezicht", *De Financieel Economische Tijd*, 13 July 1996.
[11] *Activity report of the Market Authority of the Brussels Stock Exchange 1996*, Brussels Stock Exchange, 1997, p.28.
[12] *Activity report of the Market Authority of the Brussels Stock Exchange 1998*, Brussels Stock Exchange, 1999, p.43.

3. MANDATORY DISCLOSURE

Finally, this section examines whether mandatory disclosure rules are necessary in order to solve problems of asymmetric information in financial markets. It appears that asymmetric information is solved automatically in informationally efficient stock markets (section 3.1 and 3.2). Empirical studies examining the introduction of mandatory disclosure reports question their value-relevancy (section 3.4). It appears that quarterly reports contain some information value. However, as explained in the previous chapters these benefits must be balanced against the costs of a mandatory disclosure system (section 3.5). Finally, the mandatory disclosure system in Belgium is briefly examined (section 3.6).

3.1. THE IMPACT OF THE EFFICIENT MARKET HYPOTHESIS ON REGULATING THE DISSEMINATION OF INFORMATION

This section analyses the implications of the efficient market hypothesis for securities regulation regarding the disclosure of information. If financial markets were strong form efficient, then any regulation of mandatory disclosure of information by listed companies would be totally redundant (Engelen, 1999). In such cases, all public and private information is already incorporated in security prices. Regulating the dissemination of information by mandatory disclosure does not benefit the financial market, but imposes a serious cost on the listed companies. In this way, a socially suboptimal level of regulation is reached.

As the previous chapter showed, empirical research generally supports the semi-strong informationally efficient markets hypothesis. However, even in this case, the implication of a mandatory disclosure of information is not straightforward. In a semi-strong efficient market, the structural inequality of access to information between professional market participants and small investors is an insufficient basis for the mandatory disclosure by listed companies of price sensitive information to all market participants simultaneously (Easterbrook and Fischel, 1984). As long as sufficient professional market participants analyse and process the information, stock prices will reflect all available public information, regardless of its distribution among the different market participants (Engelen, 1999 and Saari, 1977). In a semi-strong efficient market the apparent initial unequal access to information is therefore not a problem. In such a market an investor can rely on the fact that all available information is incorporated in security prices. In this way, equality among the different market participants with regard to information arises *automatically*, without the need for every investor to collect, analyse and process all information himself. If stock markets are semi-strong informationally efficient, investors can rely on the accuracy of market prices. As such market efficiency resolves the initial unequal access to information because prices behave 'as if everyone knows' the relevant information (Gilson and Kraakman, 1984).

It is doubtful that an annual report still contains much information for small investors in a semi-strong form efficient market. By the time that public information concerning listed companies is disclosed to the investment public at large by means of annual reports, it is of no use to small investors because all publicly available information is already incorporated in security prices. This is especially the case because supervisory authorities focus on the disclosure of historical information, which is already reflected in security prices in an efficient market (Engelen, 1999). Investors, in contrast, only value future information. Or as Easterbrook and Fischel (1984, p.708) put it: "Everything in an annual report is old hat by the time it is mailed, and the dissemination of the report itself does not assist in making better decisions about investments." Put differently, a further analysis of this public information will not yield an extra return to small investors.

Although there seems to be little theoretical arguments in favour of a mandatory disclosure of information by listed companies, there may be an important reason why companies would not disclose voluntarily the optimal amount of information, i.e. the existence of so-called third party effects (Easterbrook and Fischel, 1984). In this way, a suboptimal amount of information will be disclosed because there may be incentives for underproduction of information (Grundfest, 1998). Third party effects are external effects that occur when the valuable information that is voluntarily disclosed by a company with respect to its investment projects, also has value for its competitors. In this way, companies are only willing to disclose such information if other companies are also required to do so. When regulatory bodies promulgate standardised rules with respect to disclosing certain information, all companies would reciprocal benefit from these external effects. This collective goods argument can support a mandatory disclosure system (Grundfest, 1998). However, as explained above, a system of selective disclosure could be a good alternative.

3.2. COSTLY INFORMATION

Because market professionals are always in a position to respond faster to new information than small investors, it is sometimes argued that market professionals earn higher profits at the expense of small investors. This view cannot be supported. These profits are normal compensation for acquiring and processing a wide array of information on companies and economic conditions. On financial markets investors do not have costless access to information. Therefore, this compensation is the logic consequence of costs market professionals bear to collect and process information. As pointed out by Grossman and Stiglitz (1980), in a world without a costless access to information, market professionals will be able to identify mispriced securities. Their gross returns will show that they have earned abnormal returns, but their net returns will show that they have earned nothing but a fair return (Sharpe, Alexander and Bailey, 1999). This is because the gains from analysing the information will be exactly offset by the increased costs from acquiring and processing the information. Moreover, their efforts benefit all market participants through security prices. Although information is not immediately available for free to all market participants, market prices will act as if it were (Gilson and Kraakman, 1984). In this way, small investors can even free-ride on the efforts of professional analysts (Fischel, 1982 and Schwartz and Wilde, 1979). Therefore, small investors have few incentives to spend private resources to acquire information that is almost immediately available to all investors. Small investors can simply observe security prices that reflect the information obtained by others because semi-strong form efficient markets aggregate and disseminate information through published prices (Levine, 1997).

Regulatory bodies supervising financial markets should therefore reject their unrealistic model of investor protection through equal access to information disclosure for all investors and replace it with the goal of securities regulation which is in the true interest of investors, i.e. market efficiency. Or as Stigler (1964, p.124) puts it: "efficient markets are even more important than the protection of investors – in fact efficient capital markets *are* the major protection of investors."

3.3. REGULATION OF PRICE INFORMATION

In a semi-strong form efficient market investors can rely on market prices because all available information is incorporated in security prices. In this way, there is no need for every investor to collect, analyse and process all information himself. Through the price mechanism of the market the different market participants will have automatic equal access to information. Consequently, market transparency is of the utmost importance. Investors have to know almost instantaneously (a) who has bought or sold, (b) at what moment in time, (c) at what price, (d) how many stocks. If prices are an important device for disseminating information about securities among the different market participants, some regulation making it available to all investors can be necessary. This requires the answer to several questions such as: Which data should be published? To whom? How quickly? What prices may be charged for this information? What constraints may be placed on their use? Lee (1998b) points out that there are no universally accepted answers to these questions.

In order to make price and quote data available to market participants in the US the SEC requires that the prices, sizes and locations of all trades and all quotes in the largest exchange-listed and NASDAQ-listed securities are being published via the Consolidated Tape Association and the Consolidated Quotation System. The SEC is a strong supporter of market transparency by the full publication of trades and quotes. However, SEC-rules allow an exchange to charge a fixed access charge for the price and quote information which it sells.[13] Moreover, the SEC also relaxed the amount of price and quote information an exchange is required to distribute in some specific circumstances (Lee, 2000).[14]

For each transaction carried out in the order book Euronext disseminates immediately the (a) quantity, (b) price and (c) time of execution of such transaction.[15] Transactions carried out outside trading hours must be published before market opening on the following trading day (rule 4504/2 Rule Book).[16]

3.4. THE VALUE-RELEVANCY OF THE MANDATORY DISCLOSURE SYSTEM

The implicit assumption of a mandatory disclosure system is that the pricing of securities improves as a result of such a disclosure programme to disseminate information and that the improved pricing mechanism justifies the costs of such a regulatory programme. Although several theoretical considerations can be developed, the issue is ultimately an empirical one. The value-relevancy of a mandatory disclosure system has therefore been the subject of several empirical studies. First, the seminal studies of Benston and Stigler are examined. Next, other empirical studies are analysed.

3.4.1. The Stigler and Benston studies

Stigler (1964a) examined the impact of the SEC regulation on newly issued securities. He analyses whether investors are better off after the promulgation of the U.S.

---

[13]   SEC, *In the matter of Bunker Ramo Corporation, GTE Information Systems Incorporated, Options price reporting authority*, 1978, release no. 15372, file no. 4-280.

[14]   SEC, *SROs; Notice of filing of proposed rule change by the NYSE relating to the NYSE's closing-price session of its off-hours trading facility*, 1990, release no. 34-28639, file no. SR-NYSE-90-52 and SEC, *SROs; Notice of filing of proposed rule change by the NYSE relating to the NYSE's aggregate-price session of its off-hours trading facility*, 1990, release no. 34-28640, file no. SR-NYSE-90-53.

[15]   See rule 4504/2 Rule Book. See the Ministerial Decree of 29 May 2001 on the approval of the market regulations of Euronext Brussels [*In short: Rule Book*], *Belgian Gazette*, 8 June 2001, modified by the M.D. of 6 September 2001, *Belgian Gazette*, 21 September 2001. See also section V of Euronext Instruction nr.4-01, Euronext cash market trading manual, Notice nr.2001-3807, 29 October 2001 and 2001-3840, 30 October 2001 (applicable as from 29 October, 2001) [*In short: Notice*].

[16]   Besides the post-trade publication, rule 4504/1 Rule Book also regulates pre-trade transparency.

Securities Act of 1933, because the paramount goal of this regulation was to protect investors. More mandatory information was supposed to lead to better investment decisions and accordingly to improved security prices. To test this hypothesis Stigler (1964a) compares a sample of new issues in the pre-regulation period (1923-1928) and in the post-regulatory period (1949-1955) and measures the performance of both samples during the first five years after the issue.[17] In this way, it is tested if investors are better off after the SEC was given control over the registration of new issues, compared to the period before. His results show that investors in common stocks in the 1950s did not do significantly better than in the 1920s.[18] These empirical results show that the mandatory information requirements with respect to new issues had no important effect on the quality of new securities sold to the public. Investors 'protected' by this regulation were no better off than they were before the Act was passed. These results are also reported by Jarrell (1981).

The Stigler-study was however heavily attacked in critical replies of Friend and Herman (1964a) and Robbins and Werner (1964). They argue that Stigler's sample contains some data errors and omissions, recalculate his empirical results and reach just the opposite conclusion by stating (p.398) that "we find evidence of superior relative price performance of new issues in the post-SEC period."[19] However, using revised data, Stigler (1964b) confirms his earlier conclusion that this regulation did not significantly improve the market performance of new issues: "The data revisions and the new analysis do not call for amendment of this conclusion (p.419)."[20] Although the results of the Stigler-study may be questioned, it shows that it is possible to study the effects of public policies (Posner and Scott, 1980, chapter 11) and "not merely to assume that they exist and are beneficial (Stigler, 1964a, p.124)." Moreover, "grave doubts exist whether if account is taken of costs of regulation, the SEC has saved the purchasers of new issues one dollar (Ibidem, p.124)."

In his seminal article Benston (1973) examines the value relevance of mandatory disclosure regulation by comparing 'disclosure' and 'non-disclosure' listed companies. The first group consists of companies that voluntarily disclosed sales information prior to the enactment of the Securities Exchange Act of 1934, while the second group contains companies that disclosed this information once it was obligatory. The effect of the 1934 Act is thus tested by analysing the differential impact on the securities that were and were not affected by this new regulation. If the mandatory disclosure were crucial to investors, one should observe this effect in the security returns of the companies in the period after the enactment of the 1934 Act, because investors would

---

[17] Adjusting for market movements in both periods.
[18] See table 1 in Stigler (1964).
[19] Notice that one of the authors was formerly an official of the SEC.
[20] Again these results were questioned by Friend and Herman (1965).

alter their previous estimates of the relative value and riskiness of the listed companies. The empirical results show that "the disclosure provisions of the 1934 Act were of no apparent value to investors (Benston, 1973, p.149)." Because the 1934 Act had no measurable effect on the security returns of disclosure and non-disclosure companies, this finding is "consistent with the hypothesis that the market was efficient before the legislation was enacted, at least with respect to financial data. [...] The 1934 Act did not make the stock market a 'fairer game' for investors (Ibidem, p.152)." Benston (1969) already showed that the SEC had no positive effect on the use of stock markets by corporations. Again, the conclusion that the Securities Exchange Act of 1934 had no measurable positive effect on security prices and was therefore not needed nor desirable, was questioned by Friend and Westerfield (1975) and replied by Benston (1975). The empirical question whether mandatory disclosure matters, therefore remains open to heated dispute (Grundfest, 1998).

3.4.2. Other studies on the value relevance of periodic reporting

Other studies examine the value relevance of specific periodic reports. Two aspects are important: (a) do accounting numbers have information content and (b) is this information timely or is it anticipated by the stock market? Ball and Brown (1968) and Beaver (1968) question the value relevance of annual reports. It appears that financial markets anticipate to a large extent the information contained in the annual report before its actual release.[21] From an investors' point of view, an annual report seems merely irrelevant because it contains little or no information and unexpected information is reflected rapidly in security prices.[22] Apparently, the information is reflected in security prices by more timely sources of information. The information content of quarterly earnings reports is more valuable.[23] This is not surprising because such information is timelier than in annual reports. However, the value relevance of accounting information in the U.S. remains unclear (Lev, 1989). Alford, Jones, Leftwich and Zmijewski (1993) show that accounting earnings are more valuable in countries such as Australia, France or the Netherlands (see also Kabir, 1997).

With regard to Belgium, Hawawini and Michel (1987) examined the impact of the introduction of the Royal Decree of 1976 on accounting standards and financial reporting. This empirical study compared the stock returns of listed companies that

---

[21]   About 85% to 90% is already reflected in security prices by the time of the actual release of the annual report.

[22]   See also Korhonen (1975), Forsgardh and Hertzen (1975), Firth (1976, 1981) reporting similar results.

[23]   See Joy, Litzenberger and McEnally (1977), Griffin (1977), Foster (1977), Watts (1978), Beaver, Lambert and Morse (1980), Aharony and Swary (1980), Patell and Wolfson (1984) and Foster (1986). Sometimes a post-announcement drift is found. See Rendleman, Jones and Latane (1982) with regard to the U.S. The post-announcement drift especially questions fundamental efficiency.

disclosed the information required by the Royal Decree of 1976 voluntarily to that of listed companies that only disclosed this information after it was legally mandatory. No statistical significant difference was found between both groups. Hawawini and Michel (1987, p.143) conclude that "the information conveyed by the new financial data had already been impounded in securities' prices by the time the data were required to be publicly disclosed." Apparently financial markets obtain and process this information through more timely communication channels.

3.5. COST-BENEFIT ANALYSIS OF DISCLOSURE REGULATION AND PRIVATE INTERESTS

Although financial markets seem to anticipate to a large extent the information contained in periodic reports, the previous section showed that they still contain some information value. The only relevant question is then whether the limited information value of financial reports balances against the costs related to such a system of mandatory disclosure of information through the publication of financial reports. Companies may have other channels for communicating information to the market, such as disseminating information through financial analysts or by using several signalling devices (see supra). A cost-benefit analysis of the mandatory disclosure system may therefore be useful. Regulation should only be undertaken if the costs of the regulation to society are in balance with the benefits. However, very little evidence exists on this cost-benefit analysis because neither the cost nor the benefit side permits easy measurement (Easterbrook and Fischel, 1984). While evidence that disclosure regulation produces benefits observable in investors' returns is unclear, measuring the costs is not straightforward either. Direct costs include expenses for compiling and distributing disclosure documents, the opportunity costs of the persons involved in this process (e.g. corporate executives, lawyers) and the costs borne by supervisory authorities. Easterbrook and Fischel (1984) point out that some indirect costs have to be included as well, such as disclosing valuable information to competitors.

With regard to the U.S. an interesting, although incomplete, attempt is the study of Philips and Zecher (1981).[24] They examine the cost of disclosure of 54,640 periodic disclosure reports filed by nearly 10,000 listed companies in 1975 and 2,813 new issue disclosure documents.[25] With respect to the fiscal year 1976, they estimate the annual costs of filing periodic reports at $213 million plus $12.5 million for the supervision and administrating by the SEC (see table 3.1 in more detail). Besides these costs of

---

[24] They do not include the opportunity costs of the persons involved in the disclosure process, nor do they measure any indirect costs.
[25] Forms 10-K, 10-Q and 8-K, respectively, Forms S-1, S-7, S-14 and S-16.

periodic reporting, they also estimate the costs of new issue registration documents ($192 million in 1975). The costs of the SEC's disclosure system are estimated to be close to $1 billion per year in 1980. The costs have to be balanced against the social benefits of the disclosure regulation. However, Philips and Zecher (1981) find no pricing efficiency benefits and conclude that the SEC disclosure system fails the cost-benefit test of social desirability. It appears that this regulation does not serve the public interest because only some interest groups benefit from it. Philips and Zecher (1981, p.22) do not hesitate in identifying these interest groups: the disclosure system "tends to favour (subsidise) relatively small and well-organized groups that have a high per capita stake in the regulations, at the expense of relatively large, poorly organized groups with a lower per capita stake in the program." The major supporters of these programmes are the SEC itself, securities lawyers, financial accountants, financial analysts, portfolio managers and other securities market professionals. These interest groups clearly benefit from the disclosure system, while the costs are borne by the listed companies and ultimately by their consumers, suppliers, employees and shareholders.

Table 3.1. Cost estimates of preparing mandatory periodic disclosure documents by listed companies in the U.S., by size of the listed company, in 1975

Assets	Number of firms	Costs of 10-K, 10-Q and 8-K ($1,000)	Total cost ($1,000)	Cost as a percent of assets
Over $1 billion	734	57.1	41.9	0.0022
$100 million to $1 billion	1,859	19.6	36.4	0.0073
Less than $100 million	7,191	18.8	135.2	0.0723
Totals	9,784		213.5	

Source: Philips and Zecher (1981)

With the exception of the limited evidence of Philips and Zecher (1981) no other recent empirical studies measure the costs and benefits of the disclosure system. Easterbrook and Fischel (1984, p.714) conclude that "there is no good evidence that the disclosure rules are beneficial. On the other hand, there is no good evidence that the rules are harmful or very costly." Grundfest (1998, p.414) also concludes that "the empirical research is relatively uninformative about the optimal structure of a mandatory disclosure regime, and it is generally difficult to draw sweeping assertions that individual mandatory disclosure requirements are socially harmful or beneficial."[26] However, if disclosure regulation were in the public interest, one would expect the

---

[26]   Although some authors do not share this conclusion. Posner (1998, p.487) concludes that the fact "that regulation of new issues does not help investors, is now widely accepted by economists."

government and the supervisory bodies to spend substantial regulatory resources to assess the effectiveness of the stated policy goals, measuring both the costs and the benefits of the regulatory programmes (Philips and Zecher, 1981). Again, the lack of such cost-benefit analysis questions the public interest character of the disclosure regulation.

3.6. EVALUATION OF THE DISCLOSURE REGULATION IN BELGIUM

By way of illustration, we shall briefly discuss the mandatory disclosure rules in Belgium. Within the confines of this book a full overview of these rules cannot be given.[27] Evaluating the mandatory disclosure rules, one can question the value-relevancy of annual reports. In a semi-strong informationally efficient stock market, annual reports will not contain value-relevant information for investors. One essential aspect of mandatory reports is timing. For a report to contain value-relevant information, the report has to be disclosed as soon as possible. Although the Belgian Royal Decree on Periodic Information reduced the deadline for publication of semi-annual reports from four till three months[28], even this is probably too long. For instance, it is still twice as long as the requirement on NASDAQ. Only a timely periodic report is of relevance to investors. Moreover, the frequency of the publication of periodic information in Belgium is too low. By the time a semi-annual report is published, its information content has already decreased because the information will have reached the market through other communication channels. If one favours a mandatory disclosure system, it is necessary to increase the frequency and demand for Belgian companies to publish quarterly reports.

Table 3.2. Comparison of periodic disclosure requirements

Stock exchange	First market	NASDAQ
Frequency of periodic informa-tion	Semi-annual	Quarterly
Deadline	Within 3 months after the first half-year	Within 45 days of the end of the quarter
Cash-flow statements	No	Mandatory
Content	Limited	Extensive

Source: Engelen (1999, p.114)

---

[27]   See in detail Engelen (1999).
[28]   Art. 1, 1° R.D. 17 December 1998, *Belgian Gazette*, 16 January 1999.

Moreover, not only the timing or the frequency should be increased, the content of such reports should be improved as well. Currently, the legislator especially stresses the inclusion of historical information in the periodic reports. For instance, the quantitative part of a semi-annual report contains historical data, which must be compared with the results of the same period of the previous year. However, in a semi-strong informationally efficient stock market, historical information is already incorporated in the current stock price. It is difficult to see how the disclosure of such information can improve investor decisions. On the contrary, only future information is relevant to investors because the current stock price is the discounted value of the future cash-flows a company is expected to generate. Therefore, in a semi-annual report, the qualitative part will contain the most value-relevant information. To be of use to investors, it must include information such as the company's strategy, a forecast of turnover, risk management aspects, and a sectorial analysis instead of focus on historical accounting data.[29]

Besides mandatory disclosure, there are several market-induced devices for distinguishing between high-quality and low-quality companies. However, the supervisory authorities largely ignore such mechanisms. Section 2.2 already showed that the use of intermediaries such as financial analysts to selectively disclose information is banned by the supervisory authorities on the basis of insider trading rules. Besides disclosure, signalling devices could be used. Although share repurchases are important signalling devices, the Market Authority does not pay much attention to optimizing the functioning of this signal. Furthermore, while the percentage shares owned by insiders is another powerful and reliable signalling mechanism, no regulation in Belgium obliges managers and members of the board of directors in Belgian companies to disclose their holdings and transactions of shares in their company, similar to section 16 Securities Exchange Act in the U.S. We therefore favour such regulation as a facilitator to allow natural market forces to provide the incentive for a full disclosure of the quality of the companies.

4. CONCLUSIONS

This chapter analysed several solutions to the problem of asymmetric information on securities markets. In a semi-strong form efficient market an investor can rely on market prices because all available information is already incorporated in the price. In this way, equality among market participants arises automatically, without the need

---

[29]   A similar problem occurs with respect to the prospectus requirements. The focus is on the inclusion of historical accounting data. Information that is essential to investors, such as a sectorial analysis or a detailed calculation of the issue price, is not legally included in the prospectus.

for every investor to collect, analyse and process all information individually. As such market efficiency resolves the initial unequal access to information because prices behave 'as if everyone knows' the relevant information.

Moreover, managers can use several market-induced signalling mechanisms to reveal inside information to the market, without disclosing valuable, confidential information to competitors. These signalling mechanisms include, among others, a certain capital structure policy, the sale of securities through investment bankers, the percentage of shares owned by insiders and share repurchase tender offers. Another device is the use of intermediaries such as financial analysts who are more knowledgeable than ordinary investors in distinguishing high-quality and low-quality securities.

It appears that the market mechanism itself can deal with solving the asymmetric information problem among market participants. Nevertheless, extensive mandatory disclosure regulation exists. Not surprisingly, studies such as Stigler and Benston in the U.S. question the value-relevancy of the introduction of mandatory disclosure rules. Although some empirical studies show that especially quarterly reports have some information value, it has not been shown that such a regulation would stand a cost-benefit test. It merely appears that such regulation favours relatively small and well-organized groups that have a high per capita stake in those regulations, at the expense of relatively large, poorly organised groups with lower per capita stake in such regulations.

CHAPTER 4
REGULATING THE DISSEMINATION OF INFORMATION DURING THE OPENING HOURS OF STOCK MARKETS – THE USE OF TRADING SUSPENSIONS

0. INTRODUCTION

When should companies disclose material information? Should they wait till market closing on the day the fact occurred or when the decision was taken? Or should companies be allowed to disclose price-sensitive information during the opening hours of the stock exchange? And what is the role of trading suspensions in this respect? This chapter looks into the dissemination of price-sensitive information during opening hours and the role of trading suspensions.

First the timing of the disclosure of price-sensitive information will be discussed in section one. Next, the use of trading suspensions to disseminate information during the opening hours of a stock exchange is analysed in section two. After distinguishing it from other regulatory measures, its pros and cons are discussed. Section three gives a review of literature on trading suspensions. Next, section four assesses the efficiency of trading halts to disseminate information among market participants on Euronext Brussels. The pattern of trading activity before and after the trading suspension is examined in order to evaluate this regulatory policy measure. Moreover, on the basis of detailed information provided by the stock exchange, the empirical analysis traces if the return behaviour surrounding the trading halt is affected by the publicly announced reason for the suspension. Conclusions are found in the final section.

1. THE TIMING OF THE DISCLOSURE OF PRICE-SENSITIVE INFORMATION

Proponents of a policy of disclosing price-sensitive information to the public after market closing argue that the disclosed information can reach all market participants simultaneously. It is argued that disclosure after market closing allows the dissemination in the broadest sense through the daily press. However, such a policy is at odds with the goal of informationally efficient stock markets. Postponing the release of the price-sensitive information until market closing will decrease the stock market's informational efficiency because the speed with which the information will be incorporated in the stock price is slowed down dramatically (Engelen, 2000). In the case of disclosure during opening hours, the stocks' trading prices are more reliable because all information is reflected in the stock price, without withholding an essential information set. In this way, the stocks' market price closely matches its fundamental value.

The comparison between disclosure of price-sensitive information during opening hours or after market closing can best be explained by means of an example (see figure 4.1). Suppose that a company can release price-sensitive information at 11 a.m. Because this is favourable new information, the stock price is expected to rise. If the news is released at 11 a.m., the stock price will adjust instantaneously in a semi-strong informationally efficient stock market. In our example, the stock price rises from EUR 100 to EUR 120. If the release of this material news is postponed until after closing, the information will only be incorporated in the stock price on the next trading day. If one takes the policy line of releasing price-sensitive information after market closing, this implies that market participants are forced to trade several hours at a market price (EUR 100) which does not reflect the fundamental value of the company's shares (EUR 120). In this way, withholding an essential information set leads to a suboptimal allocation of financial resources in the economy.

Besides the theoretical argument based on the efficient markets hypothesis, some practical arguments, which make it difficult to postpone the release of the information until after the market closes, can be mentioned. Many international companies distribute press releases just before the market opens. Moreover, a dual listing or subsidiary listing on other stock exchanges, especially in different time-zones, can complicate the policy of disclosure after closing (Engelen, 1998b). For instance, a company which is listed on Euronext, while its US-subsidiary is listed on the NYSE. Furthermore, the concept 'after closing' has relatively limited value when stock exchanges extend their opening hours or when trading round the clock becomes possible through *Electronic Communication Networks (ECNs)* or through the internet. In such a context a policy of disclosure of price-sensitive information after market closing becomes untenable.

Figure 4.1. Comparison between the disclosure of price-sensitive information during the opening or after
the closing of the stock market

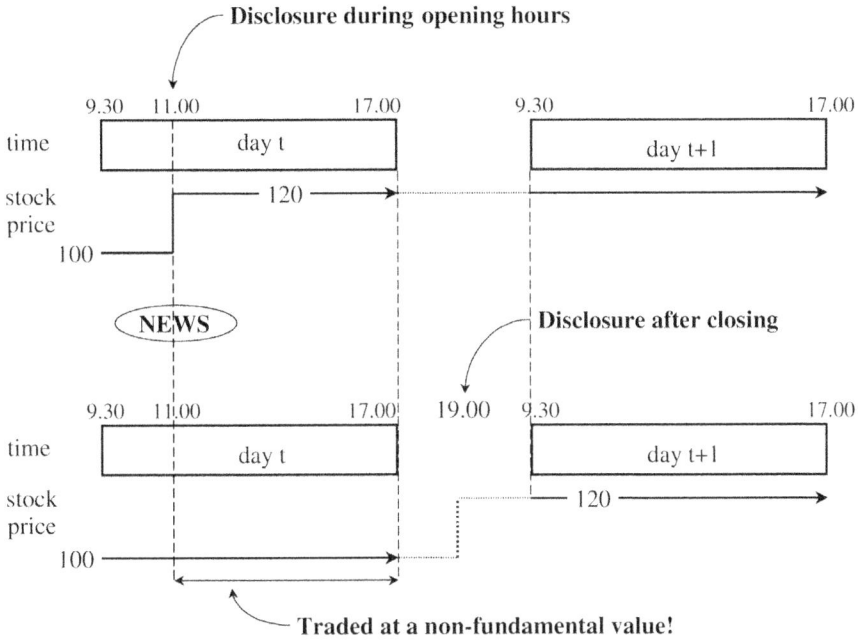

Source: Engelen (2000, p.107)

It appears that it is often difficult to control the timing of a press release and defer it until the market has closed. In such a case, the release of the information has to occur as soon as possible, meaning during the market's opening hours. In such cases the supervising market authority of the stock exchange can consider the use of a trading suspension or trading halt whenever a serious situation of information asymmetry among the different market participants occurs (Kryzanowski, 1979). A suspension of trading allows the price-sensitive information to be disseminated in a wider and more equitable manner among all investors (Hopewell and Schwartz, 1978). It is designed to decrease the possibility of some market participants acting on this information while it is not yet fully known to other market participants. A trading halt is therefore supposed to create a level playing field for all investors to evaluate the information and to consider it in making investment decisions (Kryzanowski, 1978).

2. TRADING SUSPENSIONS AS A REGULATORY MEASURE

A trading suspension (also known as trading halt) represents a temporary interruption in official trading of an individual stock on a stock exchange. Authorities usually adopt this regulatory measure to provide investors extra time to evaluate newly released information about a specific company. It is especially used when there may have been a breach of confidence in relation to inside information or market manipulation, in which case companies are required to disclose additional information. Trading suspensions are therefore said to be a crucial regulatory and supervisory measure in order to maintain a fair and orderly market in which "all investors should have simultaneous access on a timely basis to the information they require to take their investment decisions (FESCO, 2001)."

2.1. OTHER REGULATORY ACTIONS

The term 'trading halt' is often used to refer to different kinds of regulatory measures. First, it has to be distinguished from *circuit breakers,* which involves a market-wide halt of trading of all stocks because of the movement of prices (or volumes) beyond pre-set parameters in order to reduce market volatility.

Circuit breakers are slowing down mechanisms that are triggered when a stock index or an individual stock moves a certain number of points from its previous closing price.[1] For instance, the circuit breaker on the New York Stock Exchange (NYSE) based on Rule 80B was originally triggered when the Dow Jones Industrial Average (DJIA) moved 250 (or 400) points or more below its closing value on the previous day. At the moment, this circuit breaker is triggered at three levels: 10%, 20% and 30% below its previous closing value.[2] If this circuit breaker is activated, market-wide trading is halted between 30 minutes and the rest of the day, depending on the moment of the day and the magnitude of the price movement.[3]

---

[1] For an overview of the circuit breakers on the NYSE, see Engelen (1999, nos. 392-399).
[2] For the first quarter of 2005 the 10%, 20% and 30% levels are fixed at 1050, 2150 and 3200 points respectively. See NYSE, *Information Memo,* nr.05-01, January 3, 2005 and no. 98-15, April 14, 1998.
[3] Whenever a Rule 80B circuit breaker is in effect, trading in all stocks on the NYSE will halt for the time periods specified below:
Level 1 Halt (10%):
a) before 2:00 p.m. – one hour;
b) at 2:00 p.m. or later but before 2:30 p.m. – 30 minutes;
c) at 2:30 p.m. or later – trading shall continue, unless there is a Level 2 Halt
Level 2 Halt (20%):
a) before 1:00 p.m. – two hours;

Circuit breakers are supposed to control market volatility. Or, as expressed by Kahan (1992, p.985): "Circuit breakers are meant to provide cooling-off periods when herd instincts or panic overtake investors." Nevertheless, the use of circuit breakers is highly controversial. Santoni and Liu (1993) examined the impact of the circuit breaker based on Rule 80A on the NYSE. Their empirical results are not univocal. Daily volatility does not decrease after the introduction of Rule 80A. Although the intraday volatility is lower, this is not the case around the triggering of the circuit breaker, so that the causal relationship between both is unclear. Moreover, their results show that the intraday volatility on the days on which the Dow Jones moves 50 points or more, is higher since the introduction of Rule 80A. The impact of Rule 80A was also examined by Overdahl and McMillan (1998). Although this study shows that the volume of index arbitrage activity is significantly smaller, the linkage between stock markets and futures markets remains.[4] Although the short-term volatility of the stock market decreases, the volatility nevertheless increases slightly on the futures market. Moreover, the total trading volume on the stock market declines significantly. No effect of Rule 80A on the bid-ask spread is found.

Opponents of the use of drastic circuit breakers, that completely halt all trading in the market, argue that an interruption of trading undermines market liquidity and prevents buyers and sellers from completing their transactions.[5] Every time, the incorporation of new information in security prices is slowed down drastically. Moreover, the so-called '*magnet effect*' has to be mentioned as well (Naben, 1995). When the stock market index is very close to the circuit breaker limit, Subrahmanyam (1994) shows that the circuit breaker itself increases the probability of the stock market index to cross the circuit breaker trigger level and, therefore, also increases market volatility. The circuit breaker itself increases its own activation. This will especially be the case if market participants place a high value on liquidity (Ayres, 1991). If liquidity is important, certain market participants are forced to trade before the triggering of the circuit breaker makes all trading impossible (Kahan, 1992). Discretionary trading halts by the market authority therefore appear to work better than rule-based trading halts. On the one hand, the magnet effect can be avoided because market participants are less able to accurately predict these trading halts. On the other hand, the use of discretionary halts allows the market authority to include more information in the

---

b) at 1:00 p.m. or later but before 2:00 p.m. – one hour;
c) at 2:00 p.m. or later – trading shall halt and not resume for the remainder of the day.
Level 3 Halt (30%):
At any time – trading must halt and not resume for the remainder of the day.
[4]   Index arbitrage involves trading on small and short-lived price differences for the same group of stocks in the spot, futures, and options markets.
[5]   Shapiro, E., "Circuit breakers: maybe they work, maybe they don't", *The New York Times*, 29 July 1990.

trading halt than just the magnitude of the price movement because the market authority will consider more parameters than just the size of the price movement, such as market volume, liquidity, rumours in the market, market-wide circumstances, etc. (Subrahmanyam, 1995). Moreover, Subrahmanyam (1994) shows that after the activation of the circuit breaker, market participants will migrate to other stock markets, which further decreases the liquidity of the first market.

Contrary to circuit breakers which purpose is to control a price increase or decrease of securities, the aim of trading halts is quite different. These last trading suspensions are closely related to the concept of informational efficiency of financial markets. A trading halt occurs in a situation where information about one or more listed companies is insufficiently disseminated among market participants (Kabir, 1991b). In a semi-strong form informationally efficient stock market, regulatory authorities believe that market prices of securities reflect all publicly available information up to the instalment of the trading halt. Therefore, the legitimation of the trading suspension is the fact that the share's market price does not yet incorporate the new information.

Besides market-wide circuit breakers, restrictions on daily price variations of individual financial instruments also exist, such as for instance the static and dynamic volatility interruptions on Euronext. This regulation is formulated in rule 4404/1 Rule Book on volatility interruptions or extensions. If any order entered in the order book is bound to cause the price of any security to cross a defined threshold, Euronext may in continuous trading temporarily suspend ("freeze") automated execution of such orders, for the portion which would be traded outside the threshold, or in auction trading extend the call phase of the auction, as the case may be. These thresholds may be determined by Euronext in reference to a static or dynamic reference price[6]. It defines the static price range as the maximum percentage deviation (normally 10%) of the indicative price from the static reference price (usually, the previous day's closing price) in the relevant security. This device is used to detect major price movement occurring in several small steps over a relatively large time span. The dynamic price range is defined as the maximum percentage deviation (normally 5%, for the most liquid securities 2%) of the price from the dynamic reference price (usually, the last trading price) and aims at detecting large price movements between intra-day prices, i.e. in a relatively short time span.

Furthermore, it has to be distinguished from *listing suspensions* when the supervisory authority decides to suspend the listing of a particular financial instrument until the situation of non-compliance with the continuing obligations arising from a listing, has been remedied. Finally, *delisting* refers to the permanent cancellation of the listing.

---

[6]   See Euronext Instruction nr.4-01, Euronext cash market trading manual, 13 December 2004.

The terms 'trading halt' and 'trading suspension' will be used interchangeably throughout the remainder of this chapter and refers to suspension related to the dissemination of price-sensitive information.

2.2. PROS AND CONS OF TRADING SUSPENSIONS

At first sight, a trading halt seems an ideal regulatory measure to ensure wider and more equitable information dissemination among different market participants. However, there are strict working conditions. Up to the instalment of the trading halt, stock prices are supposed to correctly incorporate all publicly available information. Stock prices are expected to adjust completely over the span of the suspension period. Therefore, after the lifting of the suspension no stock price adjustment may occur in an informationally efficient stock market. This means that stock prices must adjust instantaneously to the price-sensitive information that is released during the trading halt. The difficulty of using trading halts is therefore the exact timing and the accurate assessment by the supervising market authority whether a trading suspension is necessary or not. It is clear that this requires a priori evaluation of the content of the price-sensitive information by the supervising market authority.

Moreover, the impact of a trading halt should be compared to the situation of uninterrupted trading (Kabir, 1994). Two aspects have to be mentioned. Firstly, an interruption of trading causes loss of opportunities and the cost of illiquidity during the suspension (Hopewell and Schwartz, 1978). However, it is difficult to find operational criteria to evaluate the costs and benefits of trading halts. In theory, two views are possible. Mendelson (1972) supports trading halts because they result in more efficient security pricing because it reduces investment errors made out of ignorance and speculation based on misinformation. Thus, trading halts involve a trade off between a short postponement of execution in return for more accurate pricing (Mendelson, 1972). Stigler (1964), on the other hand, lets the stock markets itself decide whether the information is price-sensitive or not and what the correct market price has to be. One could ask why willing buyers and sellers should not be allowed to transact when they both want to do so.

Secondly, the instalment of a trading halt implicitly assumes that this regulatory action is the most efficient way to disseminate information among investors. Kabir (1994) points out that the securities market itself could tackle the information dissemination efficiently. If stock prices adjust to new information instantaneously without an interruption of trading, trading halts are unnecessary as a regulatory measure. This process is illustrated in figure 4.2. Panel a shows the use of a trading halt by the supervisory body in order to disseminate price-sensitive information. At moment t=1 a company is planning to release some positive price-sensitive information during trading hours. The supervisory body decides to install a trading halt for thirty minutes. During this time frame the normal trading process is interrupted. After the lifting of the suspension at moment t=2, the security price adjusts instantaneously to the new information released during the suspension. Notice that the trading halt in this stylized example functions optimally, meaning that the supervisory body can time the instalment as well as the duration of the suspension perfectly because no abnormal price pattern occurs before or after the suspension. Panel b of figure 4.2 shows the alternative. In this case we assume that the market itself can handle the problem of disseminating the price-sensitive information among market participants. In this case, the price adjusts immediately to the new information at moment t=1. If this is the case, no regulatory action is necessary because the market does the job automatically.

However, in empirical studies it is impossible to examine the efficacy of installing a trading halt with the situation of not installing a trading halt. One exception is the empirical study by Fabozzi and Mu (1988) who examine the efficiency in the over-the-counter market during NYSE trading halts. They compare the price behaviour of stocks that are suspended on the NYSE with the price behaviour of the same stocks that were still traded at the OTC-market during the NYSE-suspension. In fact they compare panel a of figure 4.2 (NYSE) with panel b of figure 4.2 (OTC). Their empirical results are quite astonishing because they show that the first transaction price in the OTC-market during the trading halts on the NYSE immediately reflected the new information. In this way, the use of trading halts as a regulatory measure can be questioned because the market mechanism can handle the dissemination of the information itself.

To conclude, it is clear that the desirability of trading suspension is subject to debate among regulators, market participants and academics. Proponents of trading suspension argue that it provides traders extra time to evaluate newly released information so that no specific group of investors unduly obtain an advantage in stock trading. They also argue that stock prices become more informative, uncertainty is reduced and investors are protected from volatile price movements. On the other hand, critics argue that trading suspension simply delays stock price adjustments, imposes additional costs on investors who are deprived of trading opportunities and makes an exchange less attractive to investors. Ultimately, it is the supervisory authority that needs "to weigh the benefits of allowing continuous trading against the desirability of interposing processes which afford market users the opportunity to reassess a changed situation and to alter their orders accordingly."[7]

---

[7]   FESCO, *Standards for Regulated Markets* (99-FESCO-C), standard 7, paragraph 14.

Figure 4.2. Trading halts versus market mechanism

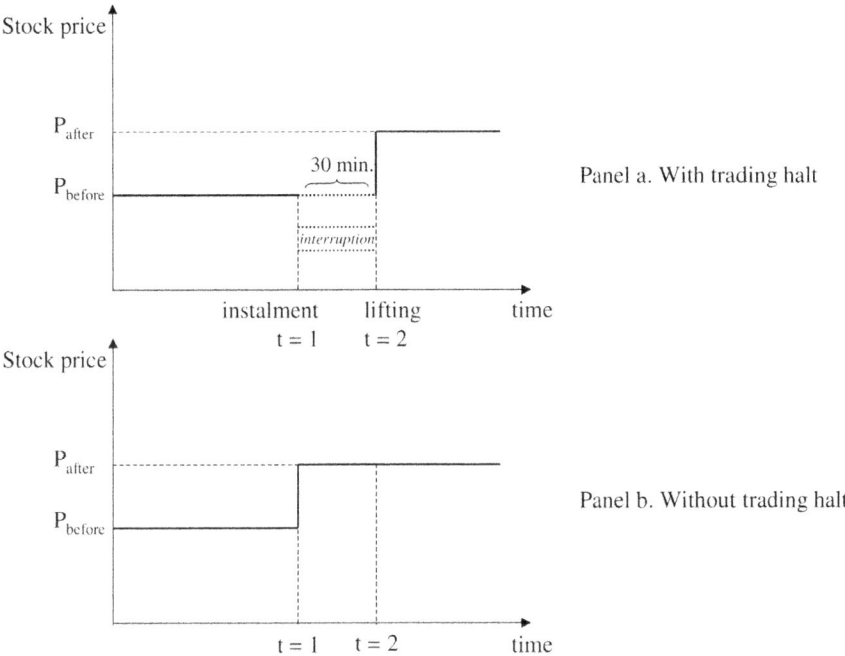

Panel a. With trading halt

Panel b. Without trading halt

3. REVIEW OF LITERATURE

Although the previous section showed that several theoretical discussions on the use of a particular regulatory measure can be held, the answer to the question on the efficiency of securities regulation is mainly an empirical one. Several empirical studies investigated the suspension of trading of a particular stock, mainly on North-American stock markets. However, the empirical results on the efficiency of trading halts show mixed results.

Hopewell and Schwartz (1978) examine NYSE-initiated trading halts from 1974 till 1975. News suspensions lasted for approximately four and one-half hours.[8] Delayed openings tended to last longer than intraday suspensions (437 minutes compared to 149 minutes).[9] Securities experience a relatively large price adjustment during a trading

---

[8] News suspensions are initiated by a pending or actual news announcement which is deemed to have a significant impact on the market price of a security. The NYSE has another event triggering a trading halt: a substantial imbalance of buy and sell orders. These trading halts are called imbalance suspensions and are requested by specialists. See Hopewell and Schwartz (1978) for more details.

[9] These are trading halts initiated some time after the opening trade.

halt, and the longer the trading halt, the larger the price adjustment. Their empirical results show that security prices adjust rapidly to the new information released during the trading halt. Post-trading halt abnormal return behaviour shows that the price adjustment is almost complete by the end of the trading halt. However, a commission-paying investor could not earn abnormal trading profits. While prices react efficiently to significant new information, pre-trading halt anticipatory price behaviour can be detected. Although their analysis cannot distinguish between the possible causes of this abnormal return behaviour, Hopewell and Schwartz suggest insider trading as a possible explanation. A distinction between bull and bear markets does not result in different conclusions (Hopewell and Schwartz, 1976).

Apart from the stock exchanges, the Securities and Exchange Commission (SEC) can also halt trading in U.S. markets. These trading suspensions are often intended to force compliance with reporting and disclosure requirements to protect investors or to promote investor equity by ensuring that sufficient information is available to make rational, informed decisions. Compared to NYSE halts, SEC-initiated trading halts are less frequent (frequency of SEC-halts is one tenth of NYSE-halts). The average length of SEC-trading halts is substantially longer: on average 12.2 weeks (Howe and Schlarbaum, 1986). It appears that SEC-trading halts should be viewed as a disciplinary measure to force compliance with securities regulation. Howe and Schlarbaum find a substantial negative abnormal return over the trading halt period. After the trading halt stock prices keep declining in the weeks thereafter. Apparently, SEC-trading halts disclose unfavourable news, to which investors react very slowly. No anticipatory abnormal return behaviour is found. The Ferris, Kumar and Wolfe (1992) study, which examines 40 SEC-initiated trading halts during 1959 and 1987, detects anticipatory price behaviour as well as no complete price adjustment to new information released during the trading halt, especially for the bad news subsample.

Other empirical studies focusing on major stock exchanges are Kryzanowski (1978, 1979) on Canadian stock exchanges and Kabir (1994) on the London Stock Exchange (LSE). Kryzanowski (1978) reports abnormal returns in the presuspension period as well as in the postsuspension period. He concludes that trading halts are not an effective mechanism to detect the exploitation of private information nor to disclose price-sensitive information during the suspension of trading. Examining a slightly different sample Kryzanowski (1979) distinguishes between good and bad new information. Both subsamples shows abnormal returns prior to the trading halts, but only the bad news subsample shows abnormal negative returns in the postsuspension period. Only the disclosure of favourable news appears to be efficient. Examining the trading halts on the LSE, Kabir (1994) confirms doubts on the efficiency of this mechanism in disseminating price-sensitive information. Anticipatory price behaviour as well as abnormal returns in the month following the month of trading reinstalment are reported.

Whereas the efficiency of trading halts on large stock exchanges such as the NYSE, the Montreal Stock Exchange or the London Stock Exchange is doubtful, empirical results on smaller stock exchanges seem more promising. Examining the trading halts on the Stockholm Stock Exchange (Sweden) De Ridder (1990) concludes that this is an effective mechanism to disseminate new information. No abnormal return behaviour is detected in the postsuspension period, so prices fully adjust over the trading halt period. Moreover, no anticipatory price behaviour is found during the presuspension period indicating that insiders did not benefit systematically from their informational advantage. Analogous conclusions can be drawn regarding trading halts on the Amsterdam Stock Exchange (the Netherlands). The market authority of the Amsterdam Stock Exchange appears to be very efficient in utilizing this regulatory mechanism in order to disclose new information. Kabir (1992) detects no anticipation of any trading halt, nor any share price behaviour in the postsuspension period indicating a possibility of abnormal profit-making. Share prices fully incorporate the information released during the trading halt. With regard to the Hong Kong Stock Exchange, Wu (1998) shows that there are no abnormal profits in the postsuspension period. However, some anticipatory price behaviour is detected.

While previous empirical studies focused on return behaviour around trading halts recent empirical studies also examine volume and volatility patterns around the suspension of trading. Examining SEC-halts, Ferris, Kumer and Wolfe (1992) observe a higher stock return volatility in the presuspension period as well as in the postsuspension period. Only several months later a significant decline of volatility is detected indicating that trading halts are not effective in immediately reducing return volatility. Analogous results are reported with regard to volume: higher than normal volume in the presuspension as well as in the postsuspension period. Only four weeks after the trading halt normal volume patterns reoccur. Also Kabir (1992) reports higher trading volume around trading halts on the Amsterdam Stock Exchange. In his study, trading volume is slightly higher than normal in the ten-day period before the trading halt and significantly higher in the ten-day period after the suspension. Lee, Ready and Seguin (1994) report increased volume and volatility after the reinstalment of trading on the NYSE. Similar results are reported by Wu (1998) with regard to the Hong Kong Stock Exchange. Kryzanowski and Nemiroff (1998) detect higher trading activity in the presuspension period on the Montreal Stock Exchange. Trading activity declines in the postsuspension period, but is still higher than in the period prior to the event window. Also increased volatility is reported in the presuspension and postsuspension period, but volatility only increases temporarily in the postsuspension period and decreases within five hours after the trading halt to its level of the pre-event window.[10]

This review of literature showed mixed results concerning the use of trading halts to disseminate information among market participants. The efficiency of this regulatory measure is doubtful on major stock markets such as the NYSE, the Canadian market and the London Stock Exchange. The efficiency on smaller stock markets as Stockholm or Amsterdam is more promising.

The remainder of this chapter analyses the efficiency of trading suspensions to disseminate information among market participants on Euronext Brussels. We examine the pattern of trading activity before and after the trading suspension in order to evaluate this regulatory policy measure. Moreover, based on detailed information provided by the stock exchange, the empirical analysis traces if the return behaviour surrounding the trading halt is affected by the publicly announced reason for the suspension. This is of major importance, because existing empirical studies mainly provide evidence for North-American stock markets, while European stock markets are barely investigated in terms of efficiency of trading suspension. This current empirical research can therefore contribute new evidence to the use of a regulatory measure on small stock exchanges by examining trading suspensions on Euronext Brussels. Moreover, it offers an opportunity to evaluate the efficiency of trading halts on an order-driven market with an electronic automated trading system without any influence of market-makers or specialists on the effect of a trading suspension, as is the case, for instance, on the New York Stock Exchange (NYSE). While trading halts on the NYSE tend to protect specialists (Howe and Schlarbaum, 1986), trading suspensions on Euronext Brussels do not appear to protect any particular member or interest group, but are intended to protect investors in general. Table 4.1 summarizes the review of literature.

---

[10]   Given the existence of specialists on the NYSE or the Montreal Stock Exchange, some empirical studies focus on the role of specialists around trading halts. See for details King, Pownall and Waymire (1991) and Kryzanowski and Nemiroff (1998). These studies focus on the price discovery process during trading halts using specialist indications (sequential forecasts of the upper and lower bounds of the security's price at the resumption of trade). See King, Pownall and Waymire (1991, 518) for an example.

Table 4.1. Overview of the empirical studies on trading halts

Study	Country	Final sample of news suspensions	Period examined in study	Who initiated the trading halt?	Anticipatory price behaviour?	Complete adjustment to new information released during trading halt?	Volume?	Volatility?
Schwartz (1976)	USA	242	Feb'74–Oct'74	NYSE[a]	–	–	–	–
Hopewell and Schwartz (1976)	USA	Bull: 201 Bear: 300	Feb'74 – June'75	NYSE	yes	yes	–	–
Hopewell and Schwartz (1978)	USA	501	Feb'74 – June'75	NYSE	yes	yes	–	–
Kryzanowski (1978)	Canada	34	Jan'67 –Dec'73	4 stock exchanges	yes	no	–	–
Kryzanowski (1979)	Canada	Good: 43 Bad: 77	Jan'67 –Dec'73	4 stock exchanges	yes	yes – good news no – bad news	–	–
Howe and Schlarbaum (1986)	USA	49	Feb'59 – May'79	SEC	no	no	–	–
De Ridder (1990)	Sweden	137	Jan'80 – June'88	SSE	no	yes	–	–
Kabir (1992)	Netherlands	59	Jan'83 – March'89	ASE	no	yes	Increases	–
Ferris, Kumer and Wolfe (1992)	USA	40	Feb'59 – Oct'87	SEC	yes	no	Increases	Increases
Kabir (1994)	UK	83	Jan'70 – March'88	LSE	yes	no	–	–
Lee, Ready and Seguin (1994)	USA	518	'88	NYSE	–	no	Increases after trading halt	Increases after trading halt
Wu (1998)	Hong-Kong	522	April'86-Dec.'93	HKSE	yes	yes	Increases	Increases
Kryzanowski and Nemiroff (1998)	Canada	412	March-Aug'88 May-Oct'89 Oct'90-March'91	MSE	–	yes	Increases	Increases temporarily

[a] NYSE: New York Stock Exchange; SEC: Securities and Exchange Commission; SSE: Sweden Stock Exchange; ASE: Amsterdam Stock Exchange; LSE: London Stock Exchange; MSE: Montreal Stock Exchange; HKSE: Hong Kong Stock Exchange.

4. RESEARCH DESIGN

This section presents the research design: data collection, sample description, description of variables and methodology. Next, the empirical results are presented.

4.1. DATA DESCRIPTION

The initial population consisted of all suspensions of common stocks of Belgian companies on Euronext Brussels from January 1992 through June 2000. This list totalled 210 trading halts. This means, on average, 2.06 trading halts per month and 0.10 trading halts per trading day or one trading halt every 10.1 trading days.[11] This list was provided by the Market Authority of Euronext Brussels. The list included for each trading halt: the company name, the date of the trading halt, the date of trading reinstatement, the last stock price before and the first stock price after the trading halt and finally, the detailed reason for suspending the trading.[12] When data was missing or incomplete, additional data was collected from the leading Belgian financial newspaper *De Financieel Economische Tijd*. Share price data were collected from *Datastream*.

4.2. SAMPLE DESCRIPTION

The initial sample consisting of 210 trading halts was further reduced in several ways. First, 12 trading halts were deleted because these companies were delisted shortly after the suspension of trading, meaning no after-suspension market price of the stock was formed. These trading halts were mainly the result of a bankruptcy, a corporate reorganisation ordered by court or a regulatory measure of the supervisory authorities for non-compliance of the disclosure regulation. Second, all related trading halts are left out of the sample. When the trading is suspended in one stock, trading in related companies is suspended as well. For example, when trading in *Petrofina* was suspended on 30 November 1998 because of the takeover bid by *Total*, trading in the stocks of the shareholders of *Petrofina* was suspended as well. In this way, seven other stocks were suspended: *Tractebel, Electrabel, Sofina, NPM, Sidro, GBL* and *Electrafina*. The trading halts of related companies are therefore left out of the final sample. Thirdly, 31 observations were lost because of lack of data. These 31 trading halts include mainly very small, thinly traded companies for which no stock price data was available. Finally, 22 observations were excluded because of overlapping event periods as well as

---

[11]   Given 250 trading days in one year.
[12]   The author thanks Mr V. Van Dessel and Mr L. Delboo of Euronext Brussels for providing this data.

overlapping pre-event periods used for the estimation of parameters to calculate abnormal returns.

In this way, the final sample consists of 102 trading halts involving 72 companies. Of these companies, 48 (66.67%) were suspended only once during the sample period, while 24 companies were suspended more than once. Eighteen companies were suspended two times and six companies three times (see panel B in table 4.2). The average number of trading halts per company is 1.42 and the median is 1.00 (see panel A in table 4.2). Of the 102 trading halts from January 1992 through June 2000, 82 are single day suspensions (80.4%), while 20 are multi-day suspensions (19.6%). The average suspension period is 2.34 days (see panel A of table 4.3). Panel B shows that 92% of all trading halts lasts two days or less.

Table 4.2. Number of trading halts per company for the final sample

Panel A. Number of trading halts	
Number of trading halts	102
Number of companies	72
Average number of trading halts per company	1.42
Median number of trading halts per company	1.00

Panel B. Distribution over number of trading halts per company	
Number of trading halts	Number of companies
1	48
2	18
3	6
4	0
5	0

Table 4.3. Single day versus multi-day trading halts of the final sample

Panel A. Single versus multiday suspensions				
single day	82	80.4%		
multi-day	20	19.6%		
average	2.34		min	1
median	1		max	65

Panel B. Duration of suspension (number of days)		
1	82	80.39%
2	12	11.76%
3	4	3.92%
≥4	4	3.92%

Legend: Final sample of 102 trading halts from January 1992 through June 2000

Table 4.4 gives more descriptive statistics for the final sample of 102 trading halts. Panel A through C give the distribution of the trading halts per year, per month and per day of the week. Except for 1997, we notice that the number of trading halts increased substantially during the last five years. There is no specific pattern of trading halts throughout the year. Most trading halts occur in October, September and May, while the least trading halts occur in August and June. Although most of the trading halts occur on Thursday, no day-of-the-week pattern is present.

Table 4.4. Descriptive statistics for the final sample

	Absolute number	Percentage
Panel A. Number of trading halts per year		
1992	15	14.7%
1993	9	8.8%
1994	5	4.9%
1995	5	4.9%
1996	19	18.6%
1997	8	7.8%
1998	14	13.7%
1999	18	17.6%
2000	9	8.8%
Panel B. Number of trading halts per month		
Jan	8	7.8%
Feb	7	6.9%
March	9	8.8%
April	8	7.8%
May	10	9.8%
June	3	2.9%
July	7	6.9%
Aug	6	5.9%

Panel B. Number of trading halts per month		
Sept	11	10.8%
Oct	16	15.7%
Nov	9	8.8%
Dec	8	7.8%

Panel C. Number of trading halts per day of the week		
Monday	18	17.6%
Tuesday	13	12.7%
Wednesday	21	20.6%
Thursday	30	29.4%
Friday	20	19.6%

Legend: Final sample of 102 trading halts from January 1992 through June 2000

Because the list provided by the Market Authority of Euronext Brussels included detailed information on the reason for suspending the trading of each particular stock, each trading halt of the final sample was categorized according to a specific type of news. A detailed list of these news categories is provided in appendix A. Table 4.5 gives a summary of this categorisation. Most trading halts occurred because of the suspended company being a takeover target (34.3%), followed by restructuring (21.6%), corporate acquisitions (18.6%) and divestitures (13.7%).

Table 4.5. Reason (news category) for the trading halt for the final sample

Reason	Absolute number	%
Corporate acquisitions	19	18.6%
Takeover targets	35	34.3%
Financial information	3	2.9%
Divestitures	14	13.7%
Restructuring except divestitures	21	21.6%
Legal issues except bankruptcy	2	2.0%
Bankruptcy	0	0.0%
Miscellaneous	2	2.0%
No news	6	4.9%

Legend: Final sample of 102 trading halts from January 1992 through June 2000

Price movements over the suspension period tend to be large indicating that significant price-sensitive information was released during the trading halt. The average raw return over the suspension period was 4.43% (median was 1.45%). The largest negative return is -47.31%, while the largest positive return is 53.68%. Similar figures are reported in other empirical studies, e.g. Schwartz (1976) reports positive returns of 52.9%, 58.8% and 75.0% and negative returns of -62.9% and -75.0%. The distribution of stock price returns over the suspension period is shown in figure 4.3. This figure shows that the majority of the trading halts cause a positive price movement over the suspension period, while 41 trading halts have a price movement equal to or smaller than zero. Furthermore, the figure shows that 33 trading halts experience a price movement of 2% (in absolute value). Half of the sample has a price movement within the 4%-range, while 28% of the suspensions have a price movement exceeding 10% (in absolute value).

Figure 4.3. Frequency distribution of the average raw return over the suspension period for the final sample of 102 trading halts

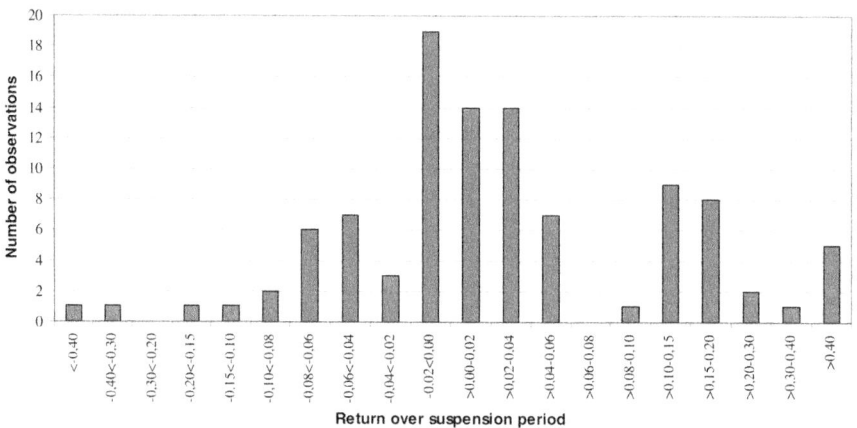

4.3. DESCRIPTION OF THE VARIABLES

In the rest of this paper the following terms are used:
$R_{i,t}$ = the logarithmic return of stock i in period t[13]
$R_{m,t}$ = the logarithmic market index return in period t
$AR_{i,t}$ = abnormal return of stock i on day t of the estimation period
$AR_{i,E}$ = abnormal return of stock i on the event day

---

[13] The logarithmic return of a stock is calculated as: $R_{i,t} = \ln\left(\dfrac{P_{i,t} + D_{i,t}}{P_{i,t-1}}\right)$, where $P_{i,t}$ is the i-stock closing price on trading day t, $D_{i,t}$ is the cash dividend paid on trading day t and $P_{i,t-1}$ is the i-stock closing price on trading day t-1, all adjusted for capital changes such as stock splits and stock dividends.

$R_{m,t}$ = market index return on day t of the estimation period

$R_{m,E}$ = market index return on the event day

$\bar{R}_m$ = average market index return during the estimation period

N = number of stocks in the sample

T = number of trading days in the estimation period

$\hat{s}_i$ = estimated standard deviation of the abnormal return of stock i during the estimation period

$SAR_{i,E}$ = standardized abnormal return of stock i on the event day

w = number of stocks in the sample with a positive abnormal return on the event date

4.4. METHODOLOGY

To evaluate the efficiency of using trading halts to disseminate price-sensitive information among market participants, an event-time study is used to analyse the impact of the trading suspension. In this case the event is the suspension of the stock and therefore day 0 is defined as the day on which the trading halt occurs, while day −1 is the trading day immediately before the suspension day and day +1 is the day immediately after the suspension day. An event study examines if the average abnormal return on the event day is equal to zero (null hypothesis) versus an alternative hypothesis of a non-zero abnormal return:

$$\begin{cases} H_0 : & AAR_E = 0 \\ H_1 : & AAR_E \neq 0 \end{cases} \qquad [4.1]$$

The average abnormal return (AAR_E) on the event day is the aggregation of the individual stock abnormal returns aligned in event time:

$$AAR_E = \frac{1}{N} \sum_{i=1}^{N} AR_{i,E} \qquad [4.2]$$

On the event day and on twenty trading days before and after the suspension, resulting in a 41-day event window, abnormal returns are calculated to examine returns behaviour around the trading halt.[14] Individual stock abnormal returns are measured as the difference between the realized or actual return on the event day ($R_{i,t}$) and the expected return $E[R_{i,t}]$, which is the benchmark normal return in the absence of the event:

$$AR_{i,t} = R_{i,t} - E\left[R_{i,t}\right] \qquad [4.3]$$

Several methods exist to estimate the expected return of the stocks. In this study the market adjusted model and the market model are used. Moreover, the market model

---

[14]   The typical length of the event period ranges from 21 to 121 days for daily studies. See Peterson (1989).

is adjusted to incorporate thin trading problems by using the Dimson (1979) methodology. These models are discussed in the next section.

Day 0 is defined as the day on which the trading halt occurs, while day −1 is the trading day immediately before the suspension day and day +1 is the day immediately after the suspension day. The return on day 0 is calculated between the last closing price before the trading halt to the first closing price after the trading halt, while the return of day +1 is calculated as the return between this first closing price and the next day's closing price. Although more precise data on raw returns is available, i.e. the return between the last market price before the trading halt and the first market price after the trading halt, the corresponding data on market index returns was lacking. Consequently, returns on day 0 are calculated from close to close. While 80% of the trading halts are single day suspensions (see table 4.2), 20 trading halts out of 102 are multi-day suspensions. In order to obtain comparable daily returns on event day 0, the multi-day returns over the suspension period are scaled by the number of suspension days.

4.4.1. Calculating the benchmark expected return

The benchmark expected return for each individual stock depends on the model used:
$E[R_{i,t}] = R_{m,t}$, for the market-adjusted model,
$E[R_{i,t}] = \hat{a}_i + \hat{b}_i \cdot R_{m,t}$, for the market model,
$E[R_{i,t}] = \hat{\alpha}_i^D + \hat{\beta}_i^D \cdot R_{m,t}$, for the Dimson model, and
$E[R_{i,t}] = \hat{\alpha}_i^{SW} + \hat{\beta}_i^{SW} \cdot R_{m,t}$, for the Scholes-Williams model.

The expected return of a stock in the market-adjusted model is the current market index return. The market-adjusted abnormal return is thus equal to:
$$AR_{i,t} = R_{i,t} - R_{m,t} \qquad [4.4]$$
This model uses no information from outside the event window to calculate abnormal returns during the event period.

Market model abnormal returns are calculated as:
$$AR_{i,t} = R_{i,t} - \left(\hat{a}_i + \hat{b}_i \cdot R_{m,t}\right) \qquad [4.5]$$
where '^' denotes the OLS-estimates from the market model:
$$R_{i,t} = a_i + b_i \cdot R_{m,t} + e_{i,t} \qquad [4.6]$$
with

$R_{i,t}$ = the return of stock i in period t; $R_{m,t}$ = the market index return in period t; a_i, b_i = intercept and slope coefficient of the market model (stock-*i*-specific and time-independent parameters); and $e_{i,t}$ = random disturbance term of the market model for stock i in period t. In order to calculate market model abnormal returns information from outside the event window is used. The parameters of the market model are estimated over a period from –21 to –140 trading days before the event day.[15]

When there is thin trading of stocks, the OLS-estimates of market model betas can be affected. Thin trading of stocks can reduce the measured correlation with the market index, and consequently the beta estimate: thinly traded stocks appear to have downward biased betas, while actively traded stocks have upward biased beta estimates. These biased beta estimates can cause biased abnormal returns and misspecified test statistics in event studies (Strong, 1992). Our sample consists of many thinly traded stocks. Therefore, the Dimson (1979)-method was used to adjust betas for the extent of thin trading.[16]

The estimation of the Dimson-beta consists of the aggregation of five estimated beta coefficients using two lead and two lag variables[17]:

$$\hat{\beta}_i^D = \sum_{k=-2}^{k=+2} \hat{b}_{k,i} \text{ , or} \tag{4.7}$$

---

[15] The typical length of the estimation period ranges from 100 to 300 days for daily studies. See Peterson (1989).

[16] An alternative procedure is Scholes and Williams (1977). However, Fowler and Rorke (1983) show that the choice between Dimson and Scholes-Williams is equivalent. The Scholes-Williams beta consists of the aggregation of three beta coefficients using one lead and one lag variable and the estimated serial correlation of $R_{m,t}$ from t=2 to t=T-1:

$$\hat{\beta}_i^{SW} = \frac{\hat{b}_{i,1} + \hat{b}_{i,2} + \hat{b}_{i,3}}{1 + 2\rho}$$

The three beta coefficients are the three OLS-estimates from:

$R_{i,t} = a_{i,1} + b_{i,1} \cdot R_{m,t} + u_{1,t}$, with t = 1, 2, ..., T

$R_{i,t} = a_{i,2} + b_{i,2} \cdot R_{m,t+1} + u_{2,t}$, with t = 1, 2, ..., T-1

$R_{i,t} = a_{i,3} + b_{i,3} \cdot R_{m,t-1} + u_{3,t}$, with t = 2, 3, ..., T

The intercept $\hat{\alpha}_i^{SW}$ is calculated as:

$$\hat{\alpha}_i^{SW} = \frac{1}{T-2} \left[\sum_{t=2}^{T-1} R_{i,t} - \hat{\beta}_i^{SW} \sum_{t=2}^{T-1} R_{m,t} \right]$$

The abnormal return using the Scholes-Williams model is therefore:

$$AR_{i,t} = R_{i,t} - \hat{\alpha}_i^{SW} - \hat{\beta}_i^{SW} \cdot R_{m,t}$$

[17] Empirical studies use a large variety of leads and lags. Brown and Warner (1985) use k=-3,...,0, ..., +3; Dimson and Marsh (1986) use k=-1,...,0,...,+5; Kabir (1994) uses k=-3,...,0,+1; O'Hanlon and Steel (1997) use k=-1,0,+1; and Ibbotson, Kaplan and Peterson (1997) use k=-1,0.

$$\hat{\beta}_i^D = \hat{b}_{-2,i} + \hat{b}_{-1,i} + \hat{b}_{0,i} + \hat{b}_{+1,i} + \hat{b}_{+2,i} \qquad [4.8]$$

The variables $\hat{b}_{k,i}$ with k = -2, -1, 0, +1, +2 are estimates of the slope coefficients in a multiple regression of the stock return in period t against the return on the market in periods t-2, t-1, 0, t+1 and t+2 (Dimson, 1979):

$$R_{i,t} = a_i + b_{-2,i} \cdot R_{m,t-2} + b_{-1,i} \cdot R_{m,t-1} + b_{0,i} \cdot R_{m,t} + b_{+1,i} \cdot R_{m,t+1} + b_{+2,i} \cdot R_{m,t+2} + w_{i,t} \quad [4.9]$$

While the OLS-estimation of beta uses the complete (-140,-21) estimation-window, the Dimson estimation uses an (-138,-23) estimation-window to allow for the two day leading and lagging. The abnormal returns are calculated as (Brown and Warner, 1985):

$$AR_{i,t} = R_{i,t} - \hat{\alpha}_i^D - \hat{\beta}_i^D \cdot R_{m,t} \qquad [4.10]$$

with

$$\hat{\beta}_i^D = \sum_{k=-2}^{k=+2} \hat{b}_{k,i} \text{, and} \qquad [4.11]$$

$$\hat{\alpha}_i^D = \frac{1}{116} \sum_{t=-138}^{t=-23} R_{i,t} - \hat{\beta}_i^D \frac{1}{116} \sum_{t=-138}^{t=-23} R_{m,t} \qquad [4.12]$$

However, the use of procedures to correct for thin trading can be questioned. Brown and Warner (1985) show that there is no evidence that these procedures improve the specification or the power of the tests. Similar results were found by Dyckman, Philbrick and Stephan (1984). These findings were also reported by Reinganum (1982), Theobald (1983) and Cowan and Sergeant (1996). Strong (1992) points out that, although OLS beta estimates can bias abnormal returns for an individual stock, these biases may average out to zero in the sample of the event study. Moreover, Bartholdy and Riding (1994) show that OLS even outperforms the use of alternative methods of beta estimation.

4.4.2. Test statistics

The traditional test procedure assuming cross-sectional independence is the Patell (1976)-test.[18] This test statistic standardises the abnormal return for each stock by its standard deviation. The resulting test statistic is given by equation [4.13].[19]

---

[18] Since the trading halts occur independent of each other and no event-date clustering is present, no correction for cross-sectional dependence is necessary. Moreover, Brown and Warner (1985, 21) point out that dependence adjustment can be harmful compared to procedures which assume independence because tests assuming cross-sectional dependence are only half as powerful and usually not better specified than test assuming independence.

[19] See section 4.3 for a description of the variables.

$$Z = \frac{\sum_{i=1}^{N} SAR_{i,E}}{\sqrt{\sum_{i=1}^{N} \dfrac{T_i - 2}{T_i - 4}}} \sim N(0,1) \qquad [4.13]$$

with

$$SAR_{i,E} = \frac{AR_{i,E}}{s_i \sqrt{1 + \dfrac{1}{T_i} + \dfrac{\left(R_{m,E} - \bar{R}_m\right)^2}{\sum_{t=-140}^{t=-21} \left(R_{m,t} - \bar{R}_m\right)^2}}} \qquad [4.14]$$

However, traditional test statistics assume stable variances, meaning that there is no change in variance between the estimation period and the event period. Event-induced variance, on the other hand, means that the variance during the event window exceeds the variance over the estimation period (Seiler, 2000). If the variance is underestimated, traditional test statistics will reject the null hypothesis too frequently, even when the average abnormal return is in fact zero (Brown and Warner, 1985; Boehmer, Musumeci and Poulsen, 1991). Several studies indeed report increases of the variance of returns when certain events occur. A parametric test that incorporates event-induced variance is offered by Boehmer, Musumeci and Poulsen (1991). This test improves the Patell-test by allowing the abnormal return variances to differ between the event and the estimation periods. They show that even a very small increase in variance is very problematic for the traditional tests. Their test statistic incorporates variance information from the estimation as well as the event window (Boehmer, Musumeci and Poulsen, 1991):

$$Z = \frac{\dfrac{1}{N} \sum_{i=1}^{N} SAR_{i,E}}{\sqrt{\dfrac{1}{N(N-1)} \sum_{i=1}^{N} \left(SAR_{i,E} - \sum_{i=1}^{N} \dfrac{SAR_{i,E}}{N} \right)^2}} \sim N(0,1) \qquad [4.15]$$

with

$$SAR_{i,E} = \frac{AR_{i,E}}{s_i \sqrt{1 + \dfrac{1}{T_i} + \dfrac{\left(R_{m,E} - \bar{R}_m\right)^2}{\sum_{t=-140}^{t=-21} \left(R_{m,t} - \bar{R}_m\right)^2}}} \qquad [4.16]$$

The main disadvantage of parametric tests is that they are based on assumptions about the probability distribution of returns. Non-parametric tests do not depend on the assumption of normality. Because non-parametric tests do not use the return variance, these tests are more appropriate in the case of event-induced variance. Two parametric tests are generally used: the sign test (see infra) and the Corrado rank test (Corrado, 1989). Corrado (1989), Corrado and Zivney (1992) and Campbell and Wasley (1993) show that the rank test performs better than the traditional test statistics in case of event-induced variance. The rank test is given by equation [4.17] (Corrado, 1989 and Corrado and Zivney, 1992):

$$Z = \frac{1}{\sqrt{N}} \sum_{i=1}^{N} \frac{\left(U_{i,0} - 0.5\right)}{S_U} \sim N(0,1) \tag{4.17}$$

with

$$S_U = \sqrt{\frac{1}{161} \sum_{t=-140}^{+20} \left[\frac{1}{\sqrt{N_t}} \sum_{i=1}^{N_t} \left(U_{i,t} - 0.5\right) \right]^2} \tag{4.18}$$

$$U_{i,t} = \frac{K_{i,t}}{\left(M_i + 1\right)} \tag{4.19}$$

with $K_{i,t}$ = rank $(AR_{i,t})$, M_i represents the number of non-missing abnormal returns for stock i and N_t represents the number of non-missing abnormal returns in the cross-section of N firms on day t in event time.

Besides event-induced variances, thin trading is another crucial problem for the event study test specification. Cowan and Sergeant (1996) point out that thinly traded stocks are characterized by numerous zero and large non-zero returns, causing non-normal return distributions. This causes traditional test statistics to be poorly specified (Campbell and Wasley, 1993). Similar results are reported by Maynes and Rumsey (1993) showing that the rank test is a good alternative for thinly traded stocks causing traditional tests to be misspecified. Cowan (1992) reports departures from normality (right skewness) causing parametric tests based on the normality assumption to be less well specified for Nasdaq stocks as compared to NYSE and AMEX stocks. Moreover, the rank test is also misspecified for Nasdaq stocks. However, the generalized sign test performs well for thinly traded stocks. The generalized sign test by Cowan (1992) is given in equation [4.20].

$$Z = \frac{\left(w - n\hat{p}\right)}{\sqrt{n\hat{p}\left(1 - \hat{p}\right)}} \sim N(0,1) \tag{4.20}$$

where w represents the number of stocks in the sample with a positive abnormal return on the event date, p represents the fraction of positive abnormal returns expected under the null hypothesis, and

$$\hat{p} = \frac{1}{N} \sum_{i=1}^{N} \frac{1}{120} \sum_{t=-140}^{t=-21} \varphi_{i,t} \tag{4.21}$$

with $\varphi_{i,t} = 1$ when $AR_{i,E} > 0$ and 0 otherwise.[20]

The poor specification of the Patell-test is also confirmed by Cowan and Sergeant (1996). Their simulations show that the best test for thinly traded stocks with no increase of the return variance on the event date is either the rank or the generalized sign test. In the case of an increase of the return variance on the event date, results are less clear. For lower-tailed tests the generalized sign test should be used. For upper-tailed tests the standardized cross-sectional test of Boehmer, Musumeci and Poulsen (1991) can be used, but it is not very powerful and it risks being misspecified if the variance increase does not occur. An alternative is the generalized sign test, but it is misspecified in a few thinly traded samples. Results are summarized in table 4.6.

Table 4.6. Best replacement of the Patell-test in case of event-induced variance or thinly traded stocks

	Tickly traded stocks	Thinly traded stocks
No variance increase on event date	– Patell-test	– Generalized sign test – Rank test
Variance increase on event date	– Standardized cross-sectional test of Boehmer et al. (1991) – Rank test of Corrado (1989) – Generalized sign test of Cowan (1992)	Lower-tailed tests: – Generalized sign test Upper-tailed tests: – Standardized cross-sectional test – Generalized sign test

Sources: Corrado (1989), Corrado and Zivney (1992), Cowan (1992), Campbell and Wasley (1993), Maynes and Rumsey (1993), Cowan and Sergeant (1996), Seiler (2000).

In the remainder of this chapter we perform both parametric and non-parametric tests to determine statistical significance. The traditional Patell t-test assuming cross-sectional independence is performed first. Next, we also use the generalised sign test of Cowan (1992) as a non-parametric test to test statistical significance of abnormal returns.

---

[20] The difference between the generalized sign test and the traditional sign test is the value of p under the null hypothesis. While the traditional sign test uses a value of 0.50, the generalized sign test uses the fraction of positive returns in the estimation period, measured across N stocks and T days as value for p.

5. EMPIRICAL RESULTS

The empirical analysis of the efficiency of trading halts on Euronext Brussels starts with an examination of the abnormal returns in section 5.1. This analysis is completed by an analysis of the abnormal trading volume in section 5.2 and the volatility of the stock returns around the suspension in section 5.3.

5.1. ANALYSIS OF ABNORMAL RETURNS

5.1.1. Complete sample

Because trading halts are a regulatory action designed to disseminate price-sensitive information among market participants, this section examines the process of the price adjustment to this new information before, during and after the suspension. Through an analysis of the valuation effects of the suspensions we can evaluate the effectiveness of trading halts as a regulatory measure. If Euronext Brussels were a semi-strong form informationally efficient stock market, the stock price would adjust instantaneously to the new information that was released during the trading halt. Moreover, semi-strong form efficiency would imply that there isn't any anticipatory price behaviour in the presuspension period, nor any significant abnormal return behaviour in the postsuspension period. In this section we examine (a) if trading halts are associated with an important release of information, (b) if there is any unusual return behaviour before the suspension and (c) if there is a complete adjustment to new information released during the trading halt.

To examine the abnormal return behaviour over the suspension period, a market adjusted model was used as the benchmark expected return. Table 4.7 contains the results for the entire sample of 102 suspensions from 1992 through 2000. The mean abnormal return over the suspension period amounts 3.31%. The cumulative abnormal returns are visualised in figure 4.4.

In order to test whether the abnormal returns in the event window are significantly different from zero, a non-parametric test was used. For, as explained above, the traditional t-test performs very poorly in case of thin trading or variance increase on event date. Because the sample in this study contains a large amount of thinly traded stocks, a generalized sign test is used to test statistical significance of the abnormal returns. The traditional t-test is merely reported for the sake of completeness.[21]

---

[21] However, the results of the t-test have to be interpreted with caution because under the conditions of this sample, the traditional t-test will reject the null hypothesis of a zero abnormal return too often while in reality there is no abnormal return present.

Figure 4.4. Market adjusted mean CARs for the entire sample from 1992 to 2000

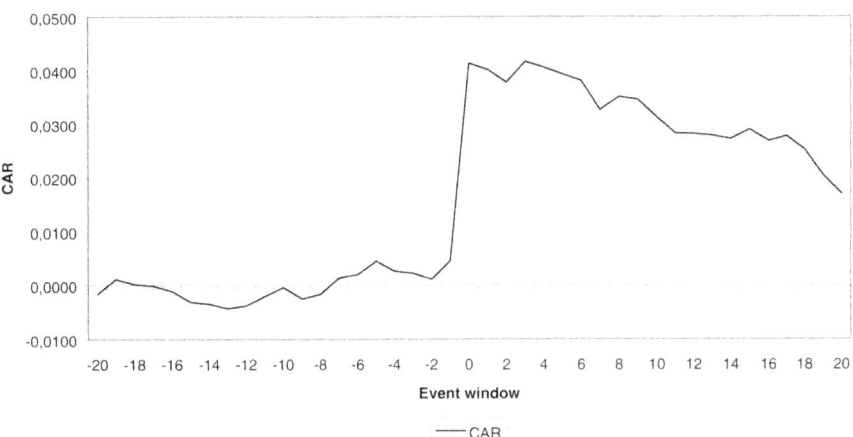

Note:
CAR = market adjusted cumulative mean abnormal returns
Sample size: n=102 suspensions

Table 4.7 shows that only the abnormal return over the trading suspension (day [0])
is significantly different from zero. It appears that there is no anticipatory price
behaviour in the presuspension period. The CAR over the presuspension period [-20,
-1] is 0.45%, although insignificant. Whilst many previous studies show anticipatory
price behaviour prior to the trading halt (see e.g. Hopewell and Schwartz, 1978;
Kryzanowski, 1979 or Kabir, 1994), our results are in line with findings on other small
stock exchanges such as Stockholm (De Ridder, 1990) or Amsterdam (Kabir, 1992).

Once the trading suspension is over, share prices do not follow any particular pattern.
Although the CAR in figure 4.4 shows a downward trend after the reinstalment of
trading, this is not statistically significant. We can conclude that share prices
instantaneously incorporate the new information released during the trading halt.
Again, these results are in line with De Ridder (1990) and Kabir (1992).

Table 4.7. Market adjusted mean abnormal returns and cumulative abnormal returns for the entire sample from 1992 to 2000

	Market adjusted (n = 102)				
	AR	CAR	t-test	p-value	Z-value Gen.Sign Test
-20	-0.0017	-0.0017	-0.85	0.3977	-0.41
-15	-0.0020	-0.0032	-1.35	0.1796	-0.21
-10	0.0017	-0.0005	1.97	0.0516	-0.01
-5	0.0025	0.0045	1.66	0.0995	1.38
-4	-0.0019	0.0026	-1.19	0.2374	0.39
-3	-0.0004	0.0022	-0.09	0.9296	-0.21
-2	-0.0011	0.0011	0.81	0.4197	0.78
-1	0.0034	0.0045	1.25	0.2154	0.39
0	0.0331	0.0377	**28.20****	0.0000	**2.96***
1	-0.0012	0.0364	0.22	0.8265	-0.01
2	-0.0024	0.0341	-0.40	0.6918	0.19
3	0.0038	0.0379	**2.30***	0.0235	1.38
4	-0.0010	0.0369	-0.64	0.5267	-1.40
5	-0.0013	0.0356	-0.38	0.7017	1.18
10	-0.0033	0.0276	-1.92	0.0572	-0.81
15	0.0017	0.0253	0.54	0.5871	-0.01
20	-0.0034	0.0132	-1.43	0.1555	-1.00

Note:
AR = market adjusted mean abnormal return
CAR = market adjusted cumulative mean abnormal returns
Sample size: n=102 suspensions
t-test and p-value: test statistics for traditional t-test
Z-value: test statistic for generalized sign test
** denotes significant at the 1% level
* denotes significant at the 5% level

5.1.2. Robustness of the benchmark model

To examine the sensitivity of the above results to the choice of the benchmark model to calculate the abnormal returns, the analysis was repeated for the market model and the Dimson model. The parameters ($\hat{\alpha}_i$ and $\hat{\beta}_i$) of the market model are calculated over the 120 days estimation period, starting with day [-140] through day [-21].

Similar to Brown and Warner (1985) we excluded all observations that did not have at least 30 daily returns in the estimation period. In this way, the sample size was reduced to 82 observations. Because our sample contains many thinly traded stocks, the beta estimate of the market model will be biased downward. We use therefore the Dimson-method to correct for thin trading, using two lead and two lag variables. Although the average beta obtained from the Dimson method (0.61) is much higher than the average beta from the OLS-estimation (0.14) it is still fairly low. The results are similar to the results obtained from the market adjusted model[22]. The mean abnormal return on day [0] is 3.43% and 3.45% for the market model and the Dimson model, respectively, compared to 3.31% using the market adjusted model. Again, the generalized sign test shows no significant abnormal returns prior to or after the trading halt.

Because the results are largely insensitive to the choice of the benchmark model, we use the market adjusted model as benchmark instead of the market model or the Dimson model in the rest of the chapter. First of all, the use of the latter would reduce the sample size from 102 to 82 observations. Secondly, the correct estimation of betas of thinly traded stocks is rather difficult. Thirdly, Fedenia, Hodder and Triantis (1994) show that the estimation of betas can seriously be distorted on stock exchanges, such as Euronext Brussels, that are characterized by the presence of holding companies and equity cross-holdings.

5.1.3. Subsamples based on news categories

Because the above results include the entire sample, it is difficult to interpret these price adjustments. Because the entire sample includes both positive and negative news, as well as different news categories (e.g. corporate acquisitions, restructuring or legal issues), aggregation across securities makes the results difficult to interpret because of potential offsetting price impacts of the different subsamples. We therefore divide the total sample of trading halts in three subsamples according to the reason for the suspension. The first subsample contains 54 trading halts for news concerning corporate acquisitions and takeover targets.[23] This subsample is labelled "mergers and acquisitions". The second subsample includes all trading halts with regard to divestitures, such as the sale of business segments, participations and spin-offs. This group includes 14 observations. Finally, a subsample of 21 trading halts is used for news related to other restructurings.[24] Although a finer partitioning of the data, according to the detailed scheme in appendix A, would be very useful, it is not possible because of the small sample size.

---

[22]   Results available upon request.
[23]   See appendix A for the different new categories.
[24]   News categories 41 to 45 in appendix A.

Figure 4.5. Mean CARs for the three subsamples based on the reason for the suspension

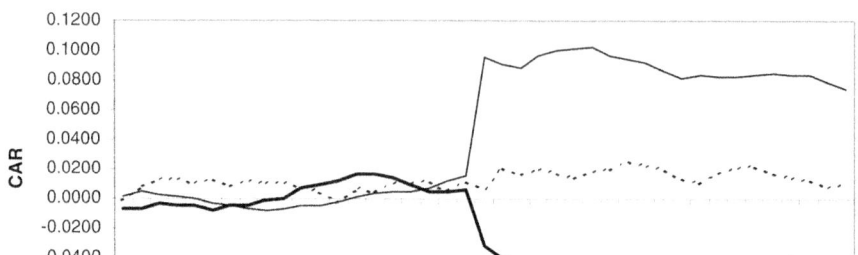

Note:
CAR = market adjusted cumulative mean abnormal returns
Sample size: n=54 (Mergers and acquisitions), n=14 (Divestitures) and n=21 (Restructuring)

The results for the three subsamples are reported in table 4.8. Figure 4.5 contains a graphic representation of the CARs. None of the three subsamples shows any anticipatory price behaviour. It appears that there is not any information leakage to the market with regard to mergers and acquisitions, divestitures or restructuring plans. Over the suspension period the mean abnormal return of the mergers and acquisitions subsample is 8.03%, which is significant at the 1% level. The mean abnormal return for the divestitures and restructuring subsamples are –0.4% and –3.66% respectively, although not statistically significant. Notice that figure 4.5 shows that the mergers and acquisitions subsample have, an average, a positive price impact, while the restructuring subsample has a negative price impact. If one compares figure 4.5 and figure 4.4, it is clear that the mergers and acquisitions subsample dominates the results of the total sample. Similar findings are reported by De Ridder (1990) for the Swedish stock market. Furthermore, table 4.8 shows that there is no significant abnormal return behaviour after the reinstalment of trading. It appears that stock prices adjust completely to the new information released during the trading suspension.

Table 4.8. Abnormal returns and cumulative abnormal returns over the event window for three subsamples

	Mergers and acquisitions (n=54)					Divestitures (n=14)					Restructuring (n=21)				
	AR	CAR	t-test	p-value	Z-value	AR	CAR	t-test	p-value	Z-value	AR	CAR	t-test	p-value	Z-value
-20	0.0016	0.0016	0.24	0.81	0.72	-0.0017	-0.0017	-0.53	0.60	-0.78	-0.0065	-0.0065	-0.92	0.37	-0.83
-15	-0.0036	-0.0035	-1.62	0.11	-0.37	0.0018	0.0125	0.62	0.54	0.29	-0.0031	-0.0074	-1.30	0.21	-0.83
-10	0.0022	-0.0045	1.91	0.06	0.45	-0.0028	0.0082	-0.21	0.84	-1.31	0.0068	0.0071	1.58	0.13	0.48
-5	0.0015	0.0047	0.80	0.43	0.99	0.0050	0.0103	1.76	0.10	0.83	-0.0013	0.0139	0.72	0.48	-0.39
-4	0.0000	0.0047	-0.74	0.46	0.99	0.0008	0.0110	0.91	0.38	0.83	-0.0046	0.0094	-1.00	0.33	-0.83
-3	0.0026	0.0074	0.99	0.33	1.27	0.0012	0.0122	0.14	0.89	-0.78	-0.0052	0.0042	-1.00	0.33	-1.70
-2	0.0047	0.0120	0.93	0.35	0.72	-0.0061	0.0062	0.35	0.73	0.29	0.0002	0.0044	1.12	0.28	0.92
-1	0.0027	0.0148	0.76	0.45	-0.37	0.0054	0.0115	1.89	0.08	-0.78	0.0017	0.0061	1.20	0.24	0.92
0	0.0803	0.0951	39.75**	0.00	3.72**	-0.0040	0.0075	3.24**	0.01	0.83	-0.0366	-0.0304	-1.69	0.11	0.48
1	-0.0048	0.0903	-1.84	0.07	0.17	0.0136	0.0211	2.59*	0.02	0.29	-0.0079	-0.0384	-0.30	0.77	-0.83
2	-0.0019	0.0884	-0.62	0.54	0.99	-0.0042	0.0169	-1.09	0.30	-1.31	-0.0039	-0.0423	-0.13	0.89	-0.39
3	0.0080	0.0964	3.41**	0.00	2.36*	0.0033	0.0202	-1.70	0.11	-0.24	-0.0145	-0.0568	-1.40	0.18	-1.26
4	0.0031	0.0995	0.34	0.73	0.45	-0.0029	0.0174	-0.71	0.49	-1.31	-0.0069	-0.0637	-1.93	0.07	-1.70
5	0.0011	0.1006	0.02	0.98	0.17	-0.0037	0.0137	-1.03	0.32	-0.24	0.0006	-0.0631	0.72	0.48	3.11*
10	-0.0056	0.0861	-2.00	0.05	-0.92	-0.0032	0.0195	-1.22	0.25	-1.31	0.0001	-0.0604	0.07	0.94	0.48
15	0.0014	0.0832	-0.13	0.90	-0.10	0.0002	0.0219	0.37	0.72	0.29	0.0077	-0.0403	0.87	0.39	0.48
20	-0.0039	0.0746	-1.59	0.12	-1.73	0.0010	0.0089	0.45	0.66	0.83	-0.0044	-0.0500	-1.12	0.28	-0.39

Legend: n = number of trading halts in the sample; AR = market adjusted mean abnormal return; CAR = market adjusted cumulative mean abnormal return; t-test & p-value = test statistic resp. p-value for the traditional t-test; Z-value = test-statistic for the generalized sign test; ** denotes significant at the 1% level and * denotes significant at the 5% level

5.1.4. Price impact over the span of the suspension period

Regardless of the sign of the price movement (positive or negative), figure 4.6 represents the magnitude of the abnormal returns over the event window [-20, +20]. It is clear that a trading halt is associated with the release of important price-sensitive information, resulting in an abnormal return over 8% (in absolute value) on day [0]. This is not surprising because the trading halts on Euronext Brussels are generally associated with the release of non-routine and extremely price-sensitive information such as mergers and acquisitions or restructurings. Routine announcements of earnings or dividends are in general not released during a trading halt. Only three cases out of the total sample of 102 trading halts concern the release of financial information such as earnings or dividend announcements. Similar results are reported by King, Pownall and Waymire (1991) for the US: 79.3% of their sample is related to disclosures about corporate takeovers and leveraged buyouts, which cannot be predicted by investors, but which have large price impacts.

Figure 4.6. Magnitude of the abnormal returns over the event window

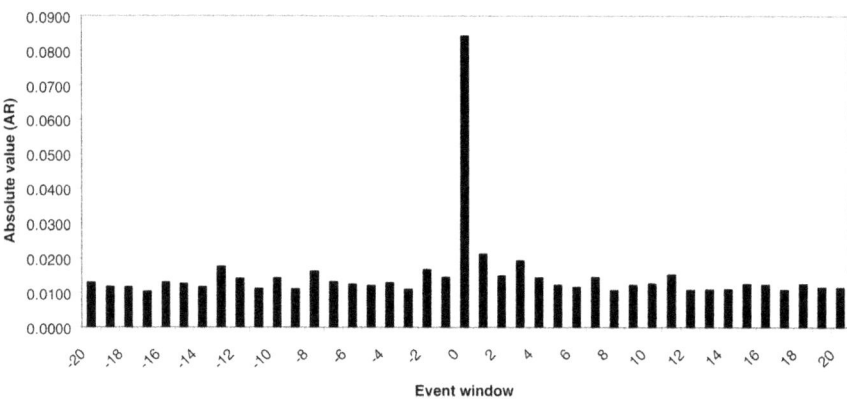

Note:

ABS(AR) = absolute value of the market adjusted mean abnormal returns

Sample size: n=89 (Mergers and acquisitions, divestitures and restructuring)

Figure 4.7. Median CARs for the three subsamples based on the reason for the suspension

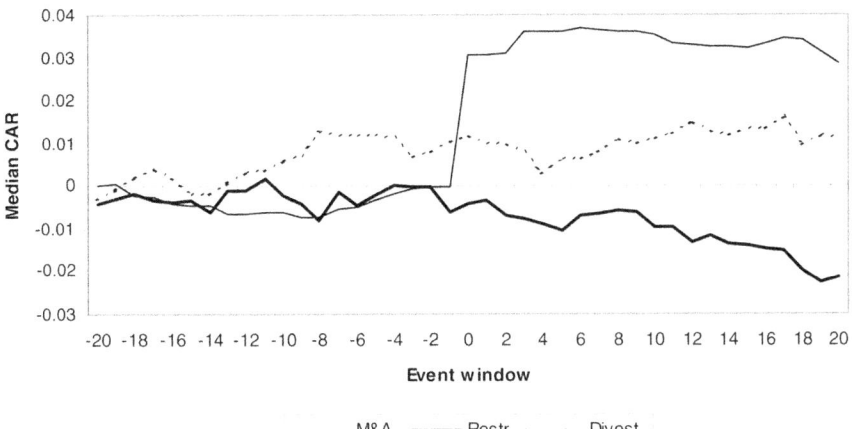

Note:
median CAR = market adjusted cumulative median abnormal returns
Sample size: n=54 (Mergers and acquisitions), n=14 (Divestitures) and n=21 (Restructuring)

5.1.5. The impact of outliers

To test the impact of outliers on the mean abnormal returns, median abnormal returns
are calculated as well. The median abnormal returns for the three subsamples are
3.11%, 0.19% and 0.16% for the mergers and acquisitions, divestitures and restructuring subsamples, respectively. In general, the conclusions of the median abnormal
return analysis are similar to the mean abnormal returns. No anticipatory stock price
behaviour and complete price adjustment over the trading suspension (see table 4.9
and figure 4.7).

Table 4.9. Median abnormal returns and cumulative abnormal returns over the event window for three subsamples

	Mergers and acquisitions			Divestitures			Restructuring		
	AR	p-value	CAR	AR	p-value	CAR	AR	p-value	CAR
-20	0.0003	0.4207	0.0003	-0.0042	0.4263	-0.0042	-0.0030	0.1349	-0.0030
-15	-0.0003	0.2025	-0.0046	0.0005	0.6698	-0.0033	-0.0040	0.1491	-0.0018
-10	0.0000	0.5156	-0.0062	-0.0039	0.2412	-0.0021	0.0025	0.3377	0.0061
-5	0.0016	0.3263	-0.0035	0.0023	0.4631	-0.0024	-0.0001	0.9861	0.0117
-4	0.0015	0.7962	-0.0020	0.0025	0.7064	0.0001	-0.0001	0.4340	0.0116
-3	0.0014	0.2056	-0.0006	-0.0003	0.9749	-0.0002	-0.0048	0.0885	0.0068
-2	0.0003	0.3705	-0.0002	0.0001	0.9515	-0.0001	0.0013	0.8649	0.0081
-1	-0.0002	0.6512	-0.0005	-0.0059	0.8077	-0.0060	0.0022	0.4041	0.0103
0	0.0311**	0.0000	0.0306	0.0019	0.7609	-0.0041	0.0016	0.5315	0.0119
1	-0.0001	0.4409	0.0305	0.0006	0.5830	-0.0035	-0.0019	0.5663	0.0100
2	0.0005	0.7664	0.0310	-0.0036	0.0580	-0.0070	-0.0002	0.7281	0.0099
3	0.0050**	0.0053	0.0360	-0.0007	0.7775	-0.0078	-0.0021	0.1790	0.0078
4	0.0001	0.7962	0.0361	-0.0010	0.3151	-0.0088	-0.0050	0.2722	0.0028
5	-0.0001	0.8228	0.0360	-0.0018	0.3792	-0.0105	0.0034*	0.0290	0.0062
10	-0.0009	0.1643	0.0352	-0.0035	0.4263	-0.0097	0.0013	0.6091	0.0111
15	-0.0001	0.6920	0.0323	-0.0003	0.8260	-0.0139	0.0016	0.3133	0.0133
20	-0.0028*	0.0453	0.0285	0.0013	0.5830	-0.0214	-0.0003	0.3754	0.0115

Note:
AR = market adjusted median abnormal return
CAR = market adjusted cumulative median abnormal returns
Sample size: n=54 (Mergers and acquisitions), n=14 (Divestitures) and n=21 (Restructuring)
p-value: test statistics for the Wilcoxon signed rank test
** denotes significant at the 1% level
* denotes significant at the 5% level

5.1.6. Good news versus bad news subsamples

Besides subsamples based on the news categories of appendix A, another two subsamples are formed: a good news and a bad news subsample. In order to categorize a trading halt in one of the two subsamples, the tick sign test of Kraus and Stoll (1972), Hopewell and Schwartz (1976, 1978) and King, Pownall and Waymire (1991) was used. The tick sign is the sign of the price movement over the suspension span. This method permits the classification of those securities experiencing favourable and unfavourable developments such as good and bad news (Hopewell and Schwartz, 1976). If the return was positive, the trading halt was classified as good news (61 observations); if it was

negative, it was classified as bad news (33 observations).[25] The mean abnormal returns
and CARs for the good and bad news subsamples are reported in table 4.10 and
visualized in figure 4.8.

Figure 4.8. Mean CARs for the bad and the good news subsample

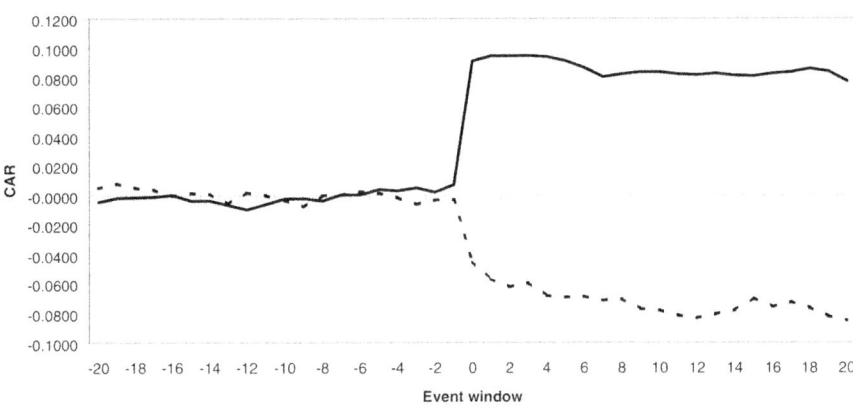

Note:
CAR = market adjusted cumulative mean abnormal returns
Sample size: n=33 (bad news) and n=61 (good news)

Again, both subsamples are in line with the predictions of a semi-strong form
informationally efficient stock market. No anticipatory price behaviour is detected
and a complete and instantaneous price adjustment over the trading suspension is
observed. The mean abnormal return for the good news subsample is 8.42%, while
the mean abnormal return for the bad news subsample is –4.18%. The CARs for the
good news subsample remain stable in the postsuspension period, while the CARs for
the bad news sample show a downward trend, which is, however, not statistically
significant. In contrast to Kryzanowski (1979) and Howe and Schlarbaum (1986) we
do not find lags and frictions in the downward adjustment of security prices to the
release of unfavourable information during a trading suspension.

---

[25]   Eight zero tick suspensions are excluded from the analysis.

Table 4.10. Abnormal and cumulative abnormal returns for the bad and good news sample

	Bad news sample (n = 33)					Good news sample (n=61)				
	AR	CAR	t-test	p-value	Z-value	AR	CAR	t-test	p-value	Z-value
-20	0.0047	0.0047	1.17	0.250	1.66	-0.0046	-0.0046	-1.63	0.108	-1.62
-15	0.0018	0.0011	0.74	0.467	0.97	-0.0040	-0.0040	-2.38*	0.021	-0.85
-10	-0.0032	-0.0034	-0.06	0.955	-1.13	0.0036	-0.0026	2.19*	0.032	0.18
-5	-0.0012	0.0012	-0.15	0.883	0.27	0.0035	0.0038	2.14*	0.037	1.71
-4	-0.0030	-0.0018	-1.01	0.320	1.32	-0.0011	0.0027	-0.76	0.450	-0.34
-3	-0.0048	-0.0065	-1.35	0.187	-1.48	0.0021	0.0048	0.89	0.377	0.69
-2	0.0032	-0.0033	1.07	0.294	0.27	-0.0029	0.0019	0.07	0.942	0.18
-1	0.0002	-0.0031	-1.73	0.092	-0.43	0.0051	0.0070	2.48*	0.016	0.43
0	-0.0418	-0.0449	-13.91**	0.000	-2.87**	0.0842	0.0912	45.88**	0.000	5.81**
1	-0.0123	-0.0572	-1.57	0.126	-0.08	0.0033	0.0945	0.80	0.428	0.69
2	-0.0054	-0.0626	-0.80	0.430	-0.78	0.0000	0.0945	0.13	0.893	1.71
3	0.0030	-0.0595	2.69*	0.011	1.66	0.0003	0.0947	-0.15	0.881	-0.08
4	-0.0090	-0.0686	-2.09*	0.045	-1.48	-0.0007	0.0940	0.05	0.960	-0.59
5	-0.0011	-0.0697	-0.11	0.916	1.32	-0.0028	0.0912	-0.29	0.773	0.43
10	-0.0008	-0.0784	0.34	0.733	-0.43	-0.0002	0.0834	-0.64	0.527	-0.34
15	0.0081	-0.0703	1.57	0.125	0.97	-0.0003	0.0808	-0.64	0.522	-0.59
20	-0.0030	-0.0855	-0.11	0.910	1.66	-0.0069	0.0772	-2.14*	0.036	-3.16**

Note:
AR = market adjusted mean abnormal return
CAR = market adjusted cumulative mean abnormal returns
t-test and p-value: test statistics for traditional t-test
Z-value: test statistic for generalized sign test
** denotes significant at the 1% level
* denotes significant at the 5% level

5.2. ANALYSIS OF ABNORMAL TRADING VOLUME PATTERNS

Being a 'close to the market' supervisor, the Market Authority of Euronext Brussels monitors price as well as volume patterns of shares traded on the exchange. In some cases abnormal price or volume patterns indicate a possible unequal distribution of price-sensitive information among market participants and, in this way, a potential danger for insider trading. If abnormal volumes are detected and if there is a danger of unequal distribution of price-sensitive information, then the Market Authority can halt trading in this share.[26] Besides analyzing the abnormal returns around trading halts on Euronext Brussels, the behaviour of abnormal trading volume around the suspensions is therefore investigated as well in this section. Moreover, as pointed by, for instance, Kabir (1992), Holthausen and Verrecchia (1990) and Stickel and Verrecchia (1994), a simultaneous price and volume study is necessary in order to assess the information content of an event more accurately. If trading halts show abnormal trading volumes, than these trading suspensions are likely to be associated with major information content.

Kabir (1992) reports higher than average trading volumes around suspensions, especially in the postsuspension period. The highest trading volume occurs on day [+1] and shows a decreasing trend from day [+1] through day [+10]. Also, Ferris, Kumar and Wolfe (1992) report higher abnormal trading volumes around the trading suspension. Their results show that trading volume returns to normal levels four weeks after the trading halt. An increase of trading volume after the trading suspension is found by Lee, Ready and Seguin (1994). Furthermore, the empirical results of Kryzanowski and Nemiroff (1998) and Wu (1998) show an increase of trading volume as well.

To analyse the abnormal trading volumes around the trading halt, we follow the methodology of Michaely, Thaler and Seguin (1994) and Wu (1998). First, the normal trading turnover for each stock was calculated over the estimation period from day [-100] to day [-21]. The normal trading turnover is defined as the number of traded shares by the number of outstanding shares of stock i:

$$TURN_{it} = \frac{VOLUME_{it}}{SHARES_i} \text{ , with i = 1, 2, ..., N and t = -100, ..., -21} \qquad [4.22]$$

where $VOLUME_{it}$ is the number of traded shares of stock i on date t, and $SHARES_i$ is the number of outstanding shares of stock i. Next, on each trading day, the average trading turnover is calculated across firms:

$$TURN_t = \frac{1}{N} \sum_{i=1}^{N} TURN_{it} \text{ , with t = -100, ..., -21} \qquad [4.23]$$

where N is the number of trading halts in the sample. Because of data availability the sample size was reduced from 102 trading halts to 61 trading halts. The average trading turnover is then calculated across all days in the estimation period [-100, -21]:

$$\overline{TURN} = \frac{1}{80} \sum_{t=-100}^{t=-21} TURN_t \qquad [4.24]$$

---

[26]   Interview with Mr V. Van Dessel, President of the Market Authority of Euronext Brussels, in June 2000.

Finally, the abnormal trading volume, measured as abnormal trading turnover, can be calculated over the event window $[-20, +20]$[27]:

$$AV_E = \frac{TURN_E}{\overline{TURN}}, \text{ with } E = -20, \ldots, +20 \qquad [4.25]$$

Table 4.11. Abnormal trading volume patterns around trading halts on Euronext Brussels

Event period	Abnormal trading turnover	t-statistic	p-value
-20	0.87	-0.40	0.6930
-15	1.21	0.68	0.5005
-10	0.89	-0.36	0.7220
-5	0.90	-0.33	0.7452
-4	1.08	0.25	0.8020
-3	1.19	0.60	0.5524
-2	1.32	1.00	0.3229
-1	1.16	0.51	0.6097
1	6.32	16.76**	0.0000
2	3.70	8.51**	0.0000
3	3.27	7.15**	0.0000
4	2.90	5.98**	0.0000
5	1.93	2.93**	0.0048
10	1.57	1.81	0.0757
15	1.40	1.25	0.2150
20	1.22	0.69	0.4902

Note:
Abnormal trading volume is measured as the abnormal trading turnover, i.e. the ratio between the daily trading turnover in the event period $[-20, +20]$ and the daily average trading turnover across firms and across trading days in the estimation period $[-100, -21]$; Sample size: n=61 trading halts in the period 1992-2000
t-test and p-value: test statistics for t-test
** denotes significant at the 1% level
* denotes significant at the 5% level

The abnormal trading volume is reported in table 4.11 and figure 4.9. Before the trading suspension no abnormal trading volume pattern is present. On the first trading day after the suspension the average daily trading turnover is six times as high as

---

[27] Note that the standard deviation can be calculated as:

$$STDEV_t = \frac{1}{79}\sum_{t=-100}^{t=-21}\left(AV_t - \overline{AV}\right)^2, \text{ with } \overline{AV} = \frac{1}{80}\sum_{t=-100}^{t=-21} AV_t.$$

normal (significant at a 1% level). On day [+2] and [+3] the abnormal daily trading
turnover is 3.70 and 3.27 (t-values are 8.51 and 7.15 respectively). Table 11 shows that
abnormal volumes are found during the first five trading days after the suspension.
Figure 9 clearly shows that the trading volume has a decreasing trend from day [+1]
to day [+20]. It appears that the trading volume returns to its normal levels after ten
trading days. A similar volume pattern is reported by Wu (1998). The increase of the
trading volume during the first trading days after the suspension confirms the findings
from the abnormal return behaviour, indicating that trading halts are associated with
an important release of information. Moreover, our results confirm the results of prior
empirical studies such as Kabir (1992), Ferris, Kumer and Wolfe 1992), Lee, Ready
and Seguin (1994), Wu (1998) and Kryzanowski and Nemiroff (1998).

Figure 4.9. Abnormal trading volume pattern around trading halts

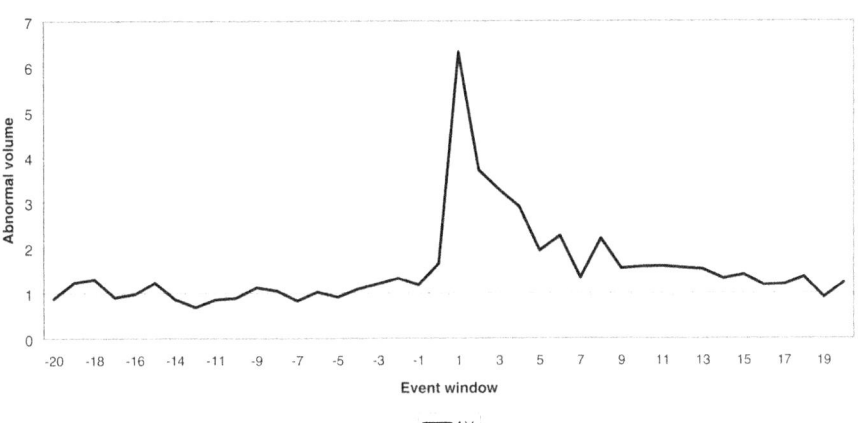

5.3. ANALYSIS OF STOCK RETURN VOLATILITY

Besides analysing abnormal return and trading volume behaviour around trading halts,
recent empirical studies also examine stock return volatility around suspensions (see
e.g. Lee, Ready and Seguin, 1994 and Wu, 1998). This is a parameter which can be of
interest for supervisory bodies in order to install a trading halt or not, and is closely
related to the objectives of circuit breakers. This section investigates the impact of
trading halts on stock return volatility. In fact, it is analysed if a sudden information
flux causes abnormal volatility around the trading halt. The stock price volatility is
measured as the variance of daily stock returns. To obtain a benchmark estimate of
normal volatility, the variance of daily returns over the historical period [-140, -81]

was calculated.[28] Analogously, the variances for the complete suspension period [-20, +20], for the presuspension period [-20, -1] and for the postsuspension period [+1, +20] were calculated.

Skinner (1989) shows that the median is more representative of the true change in volatility than the mean. Therefore, table 4.12 tests whether the median variance around the suspension increases compared to the median historical variance (VAR hist). It appears that the median variance of the complete event period [-20, +20] is about twice that of the historical variance. To test if these medians are significantly different from each other, a Wilcoxon signed rank test was used. The Z-score for the Wilcoxon signed rank test that the median variance is the same in the two periods is –4.30, which is significant at the 1% level. This means that the variance in the event period [-20, +20] is higher than the historical variance. However, the higher variance in the event period is solely due to the large price jump over the trading halt. This can be seen when the event window is broken up into a presuspension and a postsuspension period. Although the variance of the presuspension period (VAR pre) slightly increases compared to the historical variance (VAR hist) and slightly declines in the postsuspension period (VAR post compared to VAR pre), the Z-values of the Wilcoxon signed rank test are insignificant. This means that the variances are not significantly distinct in the different periods (see table 4.12). Similar results are found if we use abnormal instead of raw returns.

In conclusion, therefore, it seems that volatility does not increase prior to or after the instalment of a trading halt. This evidence contradicts the results of Ferris, Kumar and Wolfe (1992) and Lee, Ready and Seguin (1994) for US markets and Wu (1998) for the Hong Kong stock exchange. This is an important finding because it implies that the Market Authority does not have to worry about increasing volatility around suspensions. Consequently, the Market Authority should not focus on volatility as a parameter for their regulatory policy towards the dissemination of price-sensitive information. Our findings are especially interesting because the key issue in the decision by the Market Authority to halt trading is the expected price impact of the news, not the expected volatility.[29]

---

[28] Similar to Ferris, Kumar and Wolfe (1992) a conservative choice of the historical period to calculate the normal volatility was used, by opting for a distant period [-140, -81] compared to the event period [-20, +20]. Ferris, Kumar and Wolfe (1992) use a historical period [-210, -151] compared to an event period [-60, +60].

[29] Interview with Mr V. Van Dessel, President of the Market Authority of Euronext Brussels, in June 2000.

Table 4.12. Volatility patterns around trading suspensions

	RAW RETURNS			ABNORMAL RETURNS		
	MEDIAN	Z-value	p-value	MEDIAN	Z-value	p-value
VAR hist (-140, -81)	0.000269	-4.30**	0.0000	0.000237	-4.42**	0.0000
VAR susp (-20,+20)	0.000598			0.000485		
VAR hist (-140, -81)	0.000269	-0.30	0.3837	0.000237	-0.12	0.4522
VAR pre (-20,-1)	0.000280			0.000238		
VAR pre (-20,-1)	0.000280	-0.19	0.4248	0.000238	-0.70	0.2411
VAR post (+1, +20)	0.000277			0.000256		
VAR hist (-140, -81)	0.000269	-0.43	0.3336	0.000237	-1.22	0.1111
VAR post (+1, +20)	0.000277			0.000256		

Note:
VAR hist refers to the stock return variance calculated over the estimation period [-140, -81]; VAR susp refers to the stock return variance calculated over the event period [-20, +20]; VAR pre refers to the stock return variance calculated over the presuspension period [-20, -1] and VAR post refers to the stock return variance calculated over the postsuspension period [+1, +20]
Sample size: n=82 trading halts in the period 1992-2000
Z-value and p-value: test statistics for the Wilcoxon signed rank test that the variance is the same in the two periods
Abnormal returns are calculated using a market adjusted model
** denotes significant at the 1% level
* denotes significant at the 5% level

6. CONCLUSIONS

Because investors care about the quality of the financial markets, it is of the upmost importance for the growth and development of European financial markets as a financing source for companies to exhibit the highest levels of market quality and market integrity. This is especially the case with respect to the ad-hoc disclosure of price-sensitive information during the opening hours of the stock exchange. This chapter empirically examines trading suspensions on the Euronext Brussels. The study is of particular interest because of three reasons.

First, these suspensions occur in order to compel firms to disclose new information to the market. This is different from suspensions of stock trading at times of imbalances in buy or sell orders and extreme volatility. In particular, this chapter analysed the use of trading halts to disseminate new information. If a situation arises of unequal distribution of price-sensitive information among market participants because of an information leakage prior to a press release and there is danger of insider trading, the Market Authority of Euronext Brussels can halt trading in the shares of the company at issue. This chapter examined the efficiency of trading halts to disseminate price-sensitive information among market participants on Euronext Brussels in order to maintain a high level of market quality.

Secondly, prior studies show conflicting results on the effectiveness of trading suspensions. Both efficient and inefficient stock price adjustments are documented. Although previous empirical studies on the NYSE, the Canadian stock market and the London Stock Exchange show mixed results on the efficiency of trading halts, the use of trading suspensions on smaller stock exchanges such as Stockholm or Amsterdam seemed more promising. This chapter analyses whether the empirical results of Euronext Brussels are in line with these smaller stock exchanges.

Thirdly, this empirical study adds to the debate whether an exchange can add value by ensuring market integrity, compared to a single central, administrative regulatory authority which is promoted by the European Commission.

In this study, we focus on three different parameters: stock return, trading volume and return volatility to determine in a robust way the efficiency of trading suspensions. After examining the entire sample of trading halts we find that there is not any anticipatory or unusual return behaviour before the suspension. Nor is there any significant abnormal return pattern in the postsuspension period, meaning that there is a complete and instantaneous adjustment to the new information released during the trading halt. It seems that the Market Authority was very effective concerning the correct timing of installing a trading suspension. Moreover, the results also indicate the semi-strong form informationally efficiency of Euronext Brussels. Our results furthermore show that trading halts are associated with an important release of information. This is not surprising because trading halts on Euronext Brussels are generally associated with the release of non-routine information, which is extremely price-sensitive, such as mergers and acquisitions or restructurings. On average, the magnitude of the abnormal return over the span of the trading halts was over 8%.

An analysis of three subsamples based on the news categories shows similar results. On average, mergers and acquisitions have a positive price impact (+8.03%), while restructurings have a negative price impact (-3.66%). Our investigation shows that there is no anticipatory or unusual return behaviour before the suspension. Nor is there any significant abnormal return pattern in the post-suspension period. It indicates that there is a complete and instantaneous adjustment to the new information released during trading halts. It seems that the Exchange was successful concerning the correct timing of installing a trading suspension as well as reinstating trading. Also, an analysis of the good news and the bad news subsamples confirms these results.

Next, the abnormal trading volume was examined as well. We find an increase of the trading volume during the first five trading days of the trading halts. The trading volume pattern shows a decreasing trend returning to normal levels approximately ten trading days after the suspension. The abnormal volume analysis confirmed the results of the abnormal return analysis. Finally, the analysis of stock return volatility shows that volatility does not increase prior to or after the instalment of a trading halt.

Overall, our results confirm the efficiency of trading halts to disseminate price-sensitive information among market participants on Euronext Brussels. It appears that, in line with other small stock exchanges such as Stockholm or Amsterdam, this regulatory action of the Market Authority on Euronext Brussels to disseminate price-sensitive new information among market participants is very efficient. One explanation why small stock exchanges are more efficient in using trading halts as a regulatory measure is the 'closeness' of supervisory bodies of the exchange. The exchange is more familiar with its trading system and its screening devices, it has closer contact with market participants and it can react more timely when market irregularities are detected. With respect to the dissemination of price-sensitive information and the instalment of trading halts, the empirical results show that an allocation of regulatory powers 'close to the market' operates efficiently.

APPENDIX 4.A. NEWS CATEGORIES

1. Corporate acquisitions
10. Preliminary negotiations
11. Acquisition: formal proposal or agreement reached
12. Merger: formal proposal or agreement reached

2. Takeover targets (suspended firm = target)
20. Rumour or preliminary disclosure of possible takeover
21. Formal takeover-bid
22. Substantial change in ownership, followed by formal bid or price maintenance
23. Proposal rejected or withdrawn or negotiations terminated
24. Leveraged buyouts

3. Financial information
30. Earnings announcements (negative news)
31. Management or analyst earnings forecast
32. Dividend announcement (dividend reductions)

4. Restructuring

40. Divestitures (sale of business segments, participations and spin-offs)

41. Announced intent to repurchase stock

42. Capital structure changes (stock/debt issues)

43. External restructuring plans (initiated plans or announced progress of restructuring)

44. Internal restructuring (e.g. new management, personnel cut)

45. Announcement of financial difficulties, corporate reorganization ordered by court (creditors) or liquidation of the company

5. Legal issues

50. Announced start of a legal action

51. Legal decisions in favour of the firm

52. Legal decisions against the firm

53. Legal decision concerning the firm

54. Announcement and status of bankruptcy

55. Involvement in criminal procedure

56. Other regulatory measure (e.g. by Banking and Finance Commission)

6. Miscellaneous

60. Important contract

61. Trading halt on other stock exchange

7. No news

70. Unknown or no news

71. Abnormal price behaviour (insider trading, stock price manipulation)

CHAPTER 5
REGULATING THE USE OF PRIVATE INFORMATION ON STOCK MARKETS – INSIDER TRADING

0. INTRODUCTION

Chapter two showed that empirical research mostly confirms semi-strong form market efficiency. However, no empirical evidence is found on strong-form market efficiency. Based on non-public information, it is therefore possible to earn a better return than the market. Examining legal insider trading, Jaffe (1974), Finnerty (1976), Baesel and Stein (1979), Keown and Pinkerton (1981), Penman (1982), Givoly and Palmon (1985), Seyhun (1986, 2000) and Heinkel and Kraus (1987), Rozeff and Zaman (1988), Lin and Howe (1990) and Jeng, Metrick and Zeckhauser (1999) show clearly that insiders earn abnormal returns.[1] Some empirical studies also focused on illegal insider trading using detailed data on illegal inside trades. Cornell and Sirri (1992) report an abnormal return of 5.4% during the month insiders were trading. Also Meulbroek (1992) finds an abnormal return realized by insiders of 3.06% on the day of the insider trade and a cumulative abnormal return of 6.85% for an insider trading episode.

Although there seems to be broad consensus for prohibiting the use of private information by a ban on insider trading, especially among supervising authorities and market professionals, the debate on insider trading still has not been settled defini-

---

[1] Legal insider trading refers to the transactions by corporate insiders that have to be reported to the SEC. In the U.S. 'officers', 'directors' and beneficial owners of more than ten percent of any class of stock have to disclose their fraction of share ownership and their transactions in shares of their company (Section 16a-3 (a) Securities Exchange Act of 1934). Within ten days of obtaining their insider status, insiders have to disclose their initial fraction of ownership in the company via a Form 3. Subsequent changes in their fraction of ownership have to be disclosed via a Form 4 by the tenth day of the month following on the month of the transaction. Moreover, insiders have to disclose their fraction of ownership within 45 days after the fiscal year-end via a Form 5. The SEC distributes these notifications to the investment public through the publication 'Official Summary of Security Transactions and Holdings'. This legal insider trading has to be distinguished from illegal insider trading prohibited by section 10(b) of the Securities and Exchange Act of 1934 and SEC rule 10b-5.

tively. The question whether insider trading is harmful or not is still an active one. Within the law and economics framework, insider trading should only be prohibited if it harms the prosperity of other members of society (Becker, 1968). Therefore, this chapter analyses the pros and cons of a ban on insider trading. After balancing the costs and benefits of allowing insider trading it is argued that the current ban lacks a rational financial economic basis. Using a property rights perspective, this chapter proposes a model according to which insider trading is allowed as a default rule, but companies are given the option to exclude the use of inside information by its agents.

The chapter is organized as follows. Section one starts with the traditional perspective of analysing the pros and cons of insider trading. The section starts by outlining the traditional arguments against insider trading. The next subsections will refine or rebut some of these arguments. In this way, the section analyses price formation and market efficiency, examines the impact on market liquidity, and demystifies the alleged damage to the insider's counterpart. The next subsection examines the use of insider trading as a compensation scheme. The section ends by analysing the optimal amount of deterrence and the effectiveness of a ban on insider trading. A public choice perspective focusing on the private interest versus public interest aspects of a ban on insider trading is outlined in section two. Finally, using a property rights perspective in section three, it is argued that the choice of a ban on insider trading depends on the type of shareholders. The final section contains the conclusions.

Before analysing the pros and cons of banning insider trading, some attention must be paid to the definition of insider trading. What exactly is insider trading? Although numerous publications on this subject exist, Fletcher (1991) pertinently points out that this question cannot be answered easily. It appears that it is quite difficult to give an exact definition of the phenomenon of insider trading. Besides, a distinction must be made between inside information from an economic point of view and from a legal (criminal) point of view. Firstly, it is clear that it involves a situation of asymmetric information. In general, a situation of symmetric information occurs when no market participant disposes of useful individual information that other market participants do not possess. In the opposite case, a situation of asymmetric information arises.

Therefore, from an economic point of view, inside information refers to all situations where some market participants are better informed and others are less well informed about the relevant aspects of the valuation of a share of a certain company. A situation where market participants subsequently trade on the stock exchange based on the superior knowledge arising from this information asymmetry can be labelled as 'insider trading'. Insider trading in an economic sense is therefore not automatically reprehensible or punishable.[2] As informational disparity is inevitable in the stock markets, the legal definition of insider trading should be more restrictive because otherwise no trading could occur. In general, we can define insider trading as trading on the basis of non-public information of a certain company-specific event that can influence the stock price of a company. The precise legal interpretation of insider trading then depends on the legal system that is being analysed.[3]

1. THE TRADITIONAL PERSPECTIVE – PROS AND CONS OF INSIDER TRADING

After the enumeration of the traditional arguments against insider trading, the next sections will refine or rebut some of these arguments, leading to the conclusion of the optimal amount of deterrence at the end section one.

1.1. TRADITIONAL ARGUMENTS AGAINST INSIDER TRADING

Most of the (legal) literature on insider trading is based on the premise that insider trading is always harmful, or offers only very concise argumentation against it. Traditional arguments against insider trading are (Schotland, 1967; Mendelson, 1969; Brudney, 1979; Haft, 1982 and Levmore, 1982): (1) insider trading causes a wrong price formation of securities and undermines confidence in the capital market; (2) it decreases liquidity; (3) it harms the non-informed counterpart of the insider; (4) it is not in the interest of small investors and (5) it diverts part of the firm's earnings that would otherwise go to shareholders. The next sections analyse these possible harmful effects of insider trading. Both arguments for and against insider trading can be found.

1.2. PRICE FORMATION AND INSIDER TRADING

Two aspects of the price formation process are considered. First, the relationship between insider trading and market efficiency is examined. Next, the impact on investor confidence is analysed.

---

[2]   See Engelen (1999, nos. 323 and 331) for examples of insider trading in an economic sense that are not criminally punishable.

[3]   See Engelen (1999) for a comparison between the legal interpretation of insider trading in the U.S. and in Belgium/Europe. His analysis shows that the legal formulation of insider trading is rather difficult to encapsulate within one closed definition.

1.2.1. Market efficiency

As we saw in chapter two, the two major goals of securities regulation are market efficiency and liquidity. Both companies and investors value efficient and liquid stock markets because it allows a quick and cheap disposal of their securities and gives them low-cost access to information in such a way that they can rely on current market prices. This section will analyse the relation between insider trading and market efficiency, while the next section will focus on the impact of insider trading on market liquidity.

Capital markets are a major financing source for companies because they allocate scarce financial resources to various securities. Given a specified degree of risk, investors will select (portfolios of) securities with the highest possible return. This return is determined by the future cash flows that investors expect, based on all currently available information. A security market is efficient if security prices instantaneously and fully reflect all relevant available information. In such a world security prices are a reliable criterion for the optimal allocation of scarce financial resources at a 'fair' price. Empirical research mostly confirms semi-strong form market efficiency.

Because security prices in a semi-strong efficient stock market only reflect all publicly available information but not non-public information, the transactions of insiders will reveal the private information component to the market. Precisely due to the transactions of insiders security prices will better and faster reflect the real fundamental value by incorporating the private information (Manne, 1966). In this way insider trading adds to market efficiency and financial resources will be allocated more optimally on the security market.

The relationship between insider trading and market efficiency is illustrated in figure 5.1. Assume a price-sensitive event occurs at moment t=0. If there is no insider trading, the stock price will remain at its pre-event level until the news is announced at moment t=1 (panel a of figure 5.1). If insider trading were allowed, the informed trading by the insider at t=0 signals to the market that some value relevant event has occurred and the stock price will adjust according to the solid line (n°1) in panel b of figure 5.1. If insiders facing criminal charges try to disguise their trading, the signal will be less clear and stock prices may adjust according to the dashed line (n°2) in panel b of figure 5.1. Hence, by allowing insider trading, the allocation-efficiency of the security market will definitely improve. By reducing insider trading, security prices will deviate from their real fundamental value for a longer period (compare panel a and c in figure 5.1). Analogously, Vermaelen (1986) concludes that "reduction of insider trading will reduce, rather than increase market efficiency because it will slow down the speed with which information will be reflected in security prices."

Figure 5.1. The impact of insider trading on security prices

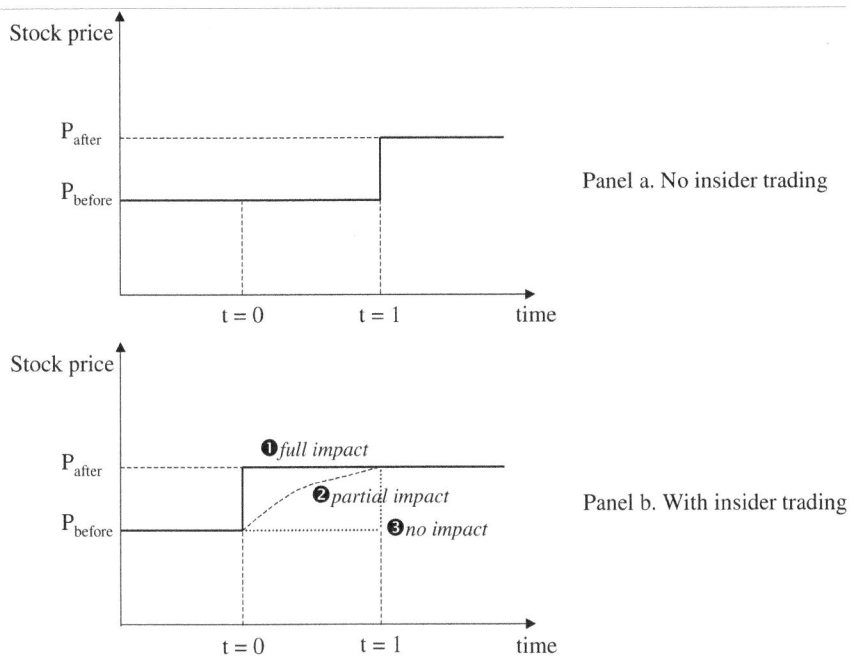

Panel a. No insider trading

Panel b. With insider trading

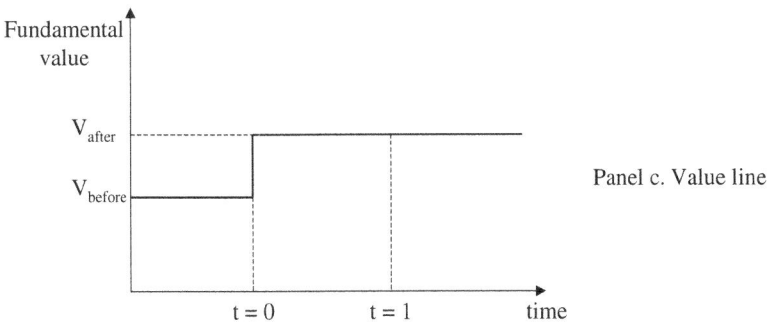

Panel c. Value line

A traditional counter-argument is that insider trading postpones the disclosure of information and therefore reduces market efficiency (Schotland, 1967). However, this argument has to be strongly refined. Mostly, insiders cannot control the timing of the release of some news because most of the disclosure is not voluntary but mandatory. In most countries companies have to make a public announcement of price-sensitive information. In such a case the moment t=1 in figure 5.1 is fixed. Moreover, even if insiders could control the timing of disclosure, the news has to be disclosed shortly after the insider trading to make any profit. Each additional minute, hour or day the probability of a new event occurring to cause a price movement in the opposite direction rises rapidly (Manne, 1970). Using a theoretical model Leland (1992) also shows that stock prices more quickly reflect information when insider trading is permitted. After examining cases, Dooley (1980) finds that insider trading did not delay the public disclosure of information.

The improved informational efficiency is empirically confirmed by Meulbroek (1992) who examined the transactions of 320 individuals charged with insider trading by the SEC during the period of 1980 to 1989. The empirical results show that insider trading led to quick price changes and in 81% of the cases stock prices moved in the same direction as they do on the day of the public announcement of the price-sensitive event, hereby confirming the increased informational efficiency of securities markets because of insider trading. In this way, this empirical study supports the arguments of Manne (1966).

Another empirical study supporting the proposition that insiders' trades incorporate a large fraction of private information into security prices before the information is made public through an official announcement is offered by Cornell and Sirri (1992). They examine insider trading cases in Anheuser-Busch's 1982 tender offer for Campbell Taggart by using the court records to isolate individual insider transactions from the other trades. Because there was no direct leak of information to the market, the only information available to the non-informed market participants was the one that could be inferred from the insider's trades. Their empirical results show that the abnormal returns on Campbell Taggart occur only on days when insiders purchase shares. The substantial price run-up before the tender offer announcement caused by insider trading in Campbell Taggart is thus consistent with an increased informational efficiency.

Similar results are reported by Chakravarty and McConnell (1997). This study examines insider trading activity prior to the announcement of the acquisition of Carnation Company by Nestlé S.A. in 1984. In this period Ivan Boesky bought 1,711,200 shares of Carnation stock spread over 24 trading days (approximately 5% of the total outstanding shares of Carnation stock). Their empirical results show that Boesky's trades led to subsequent price increases. Again, this study confirms that insider trading leads to more rapid price discovery.

Chakravarty and McConnell (1999), however, question the informational efficiency of insider trading. Their results show that insider trades did have an effect on the stock price, but using a χ^2 test of equality of the regression coefficients for the insider buy volume and the non-insider buy volume, they are unable to statistically distinguish between insider and non-insider trades.

Another aspect of the efficiency-argument is the fact that insider trading creates an additional method for communicating information (Carlton and Fischel, 1983). Insider trading incorporating new information in security prices can therefore be an alternative way to communicate information to the financial markets, which could not be disclosed effectively through an official public announcement because investors wrongly perceive the information as incredible or implausible. This is especially the case with diffuse, complex information that is not readily encapsulated in a public announcement (King and Roell, 1988). In this way, insider trading acts as a replacement for public disclosure of the information to incorporate a particular set of information in the market price of the security, while the company does not have to reveal its confidential information.

Healy and Palepu (1995) offer an excellent example of the difficulties concerning investor communication issues, in particular the case of the company CUC International that had serious difficulties convincing investors of its profitable investments. The profitability of the services that this company provided depended heavily on the renewal rates of its customers. Although management communicated its estimates for new services, investors did not believe these figures, even though the firm's auditors accepted them. This caused a 35% decline in the stock price. Management perceived its stock to be heavily undervalued, mainly because of an information problem in communicating its profitability to investors[4]. In order to overcome this problem management first changed its accounting policy to a more conservative method of reporting its marketing costs. However, this clinical study suggests that accounting policy choices and accounting reports were not viewed by investors as credible signals[5]. Subsequently, management used some financing policy decisions to signal its profitability to investors. The capital structure change by means of a leveraged recapitalization, i.e. the payment of a large special dividend financed with debt, had mixed results. Initially market price declined even further because it was viewed with suspicion by investors. Only two months later investors fully appreciated this positive signal. Only the accelerated repayment of debt and the announcement of a stock repurchase programme had more immediate credibility. The case study of Healy and Palepu (1995) shows that it is sometimes difficult to disclose value-relevant informa-

---

[4]   The spectacular stock price increase in the four following years after the recapitalization can be viewed as proof of this.
[5]   Even though the auditing process and management's legal liability is generally viewed as a means to ensure that earnings reports are credible and therefore a relevant source of information for valuation.

tion effectively through an official public announcement. In such cases, insider trading can act as a replacement for public disclosure.

1.2.2. Investor confidence

It is often argued that small investors are reluctant to invest on the stock market unless they believe they are competing on a level playing field. In the absence of a credible investor injury story (see below), Bainbridge (2000) points out that it is difficult to see why insider trading should undermine investor confidence in the integrity of the securities markets. As insider trading improves the efficiency of the security market, the confidence of a rational investor in the security market will not be damaged. It is irrelevant to him whether an insider can earn abnormal profits, because the investor can always buy or sell the security at a fair price, namely its fundamental value. In an efficient market an investor can rely on the accuracy of market prices because every piece of information is already reflected in security prices, without the necessity to collect and process the information himself. If all information is reflected in security prices, investors can *trust* market prices[6].

Nevertheless, the argument of confidence is frequently used to prohibit insider trading. Moreover, prohibiting insider trading will not produce a level playing field as will be explained in section two. In fact, small investors will always be in a position in which they are at an informational disadvantage compared to market professionals. Finally, one can ask if small investors actually prefer such a level playing field. Later sections will show that small investors benefit from allowing insiders to trade on their privileged information. It merely appears that the investor's confidence argument is used by market professionals to maintain their private interests if insiders are banned from trading (see section two).

No empirical study has ever shown a decrease in investor confidence when insider trading is allowed. For instance, Young (1985) points out that the number of small individual investors on the U.S. stock markets sharply increased during the 1980s, despite the many cases of insider trading during the same period. Carlton and Fischel (1983) point out that in Japan insider trading was considered proper and "there has never been a reported case under the limited insider trading prohibition currently in effect (p.860)." This has not limited the development of the Japanese stock market. Macey and Kanda (1990) point out that the Tokyo Stock Exchange is highly automated, enjoys high liquidity, is the same size as the New York Stock Exchange and has higher price-earnings ratios than the NYSE. Bainbridge (2000) therefore concludes that insider trading does not seriously threaten investors' confidence.

---

[6]   This is the difference between insider trading and market manipulation. While insider trading moves stock prices closer to their fundamental value, market manipulation moves stock prices away from their fundamental value, thereby decreasing the allocative efficiency of market prices.

Historically, insider trading on stock markets outside the U.S. has not been regulated at all. One of the reasons why other countries adopted rules on insider trading is the "export" of U.S. legal rules to the rest of the world (Kitch, 2000). During the 1980s the U.S. has persistently pressured European countries to adopt legal rules prohibiting insider trading, especially with regard to Switzerland (Haddock and Macey, 1986b). Switzerland adopted such a regulation in 1988. Examining 103 countries Bhattacharya and Daouk (1999) show that most European countries enacted insider trading regulations in the early 1990s, such as Italy and Denmark in 1991, Austria in 1993 and Spain and Germany in 1994. Figure 5.2 shows an explosion of the number of countries adopting insider regulations since the 1990s.[7] By the end of 1999, 87 countries had an insider trading regulation, although only enforced in 38 countries. Also Grundfest (1998) points out that insider trading prohibitions have spread worldwide at the urging of the U.S. and are now supported by a complex web of 'memoranda of understanding'. A plausible explanation for the export of insider trading rules can be found in the private interest theory of regulation. Market professionals benefiting the most from a ban on insider trading, would then prefer a worldwide playing field to capture all trading opportunities based on new information arriving to the markets.[8]

Figure 5.2. The number of countries with insider trading regulations

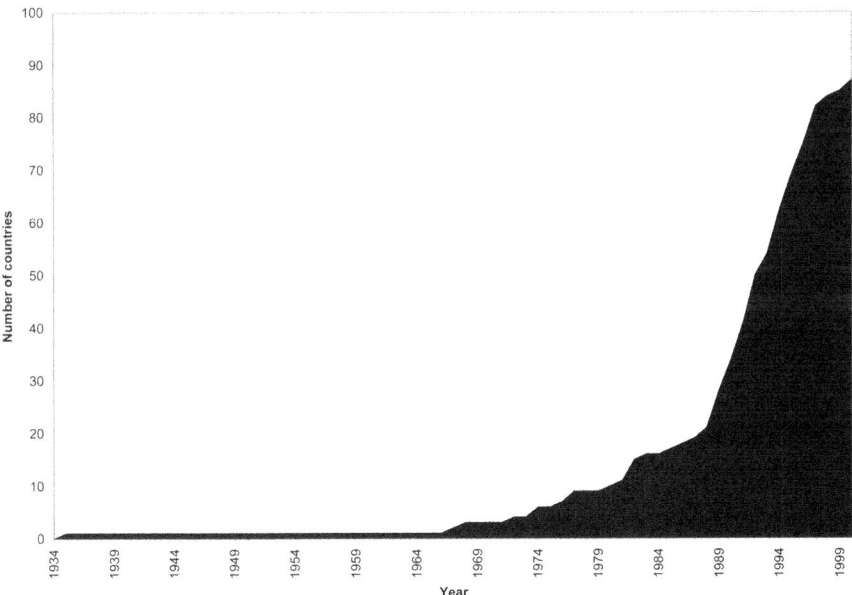

Source: Bhattacharya and Daouk (1999)

---

[7]   Before 1966 the U.S. was the only country banning insider trading. Not surprisingly, Canada was second.

[8]   See also section three.

1.3. LIQUIDITY

Besides market efficiency, chapter two showed that the second major goal of securities regulation is liquidity. Investors value liquid stock markets because it allows a quick and cheap disposal of their securities. Therefore the impact of insider trading on market liquidity is an important issue to be examined. This section will analyse the relation between insider trading and market liquidity.[9]

There exist several theoretical models making predictions about market liquidity in case of insider trading, though these predictions differ widely. Different assumptions about the relative importance of insiders, liquidity traders, noise traders or market makers lead to different outcomes.[10] For instance, Kyle (1985) predicts less liquid stock markets, while Grossman (1986) and Holden and Subrahmanyam (1992) predict just the opposite, i.e. an increase of market liquidity. The argument that banning insider trading increases liquidity ignores the liquidity enhancing role of the insiders themselves and of some noise traders (Kabir and Vermaelen, 1996). Ultimately, the question of the impact on liquidity is an empirical issue.

Kabir and Vermaelen (1996) examined the effect of the introduction of insider trading restrictions on the liquidity of the Amsterdam Stock Exchange. On January 1, 1987 a Model Code prohibited insiders from trading in the company's stock and stock options during the two months preceding the announcement of annual earnings

---

[9] The analysis focuses on liquidity effects of insider trading on order-driven or auction markets and not on quote-driven or dealership markets. The price formation of a security market can be organized in two ways. A security market is order-driven when there is a periodic or continuous matching of buy and sell orders. Demand and supply are confronted with each other until an equilibrium price is reached. On a quote-driven security market all trading of securities goes through market-makers who buy at a certain bid-price and sell at a certain ask-price. These market-makers quote bids and asks throughout the day. Market-makers make a part of their profit on this bid-ask spread. While our analysis does not show that insider trading decreases market liquidity, some studies on quote-driven markets, such as Benston and Hagerman (1974) and Copeland and Galai (1983) show that market-makers quote a wider bid-ask spread if insider trading occurs than in a situation where no insider trading occurs. This causes an increase of transaction costs for the other market participants which affects security returns in a direct way because transaction costs are not diversifiable in a portfolio. This negative effect of insider trading only occurs on security markets which are quote-driven and cannot be used as an argument against insider trading on security markets which are order driven as Euronext (Schmidt, 1991). However, it is also important to note that Cornell and Sirri (1992) and Chakravarty and McConnell (1997) do not report wider bid-ask spreads. So empirical studies on the effect of insider trading on bid-ask spreads in quote-driven markets show mixed results. A complete analysis and comparison between order-driven and quote-driven markets is however not within the confines of this book. See Stoll (1992), Pagano and Roëll (1993) and Degryse (1995).

[10] Noise traders are investors who trade on the basis of what they believe, falsely, is special information. See Black (1986). In this case, they are investors who trade on fundamentals and who fail to recognize the extent of the inside information reflected in security prices and thus incorrectly believe they have superior information.

reports.[11] This study clearly shows that liquidity (as measured by trading volume) decreases after the introduction of these restrictions on insider trading, while the amount of company-specific information did not change. The authors conclude that this is an example of 'regulatory overkill' because market liquidity decreased while the main objective was to increase liquidity by eliminating insiders trades.

Examining a clinical case of insider trading surrounding the acquisition of Campbell Taggart by Anheuser-Bush, Cornell and Sirri (1992) also report that insider trading did not reduce market liquidity nor did it cause the bid-ask spread to widen, mainly because of the increase in uninformed trading volume.

Chakravarty and McConnell (1997) who examine Boesky's trades around the acquisition of Carnation by Nestlé report that his trades had no significant adverse effect on either quoted or effective bid-ask spreads, nor on bid and ask depths. So measuring market liquidity by the bid-ask spread and by the market depth, it appears that insider trading does not decrease market liquidity.[12]

Although there are few empirical studies on the issue of market liquidity, the current studies show that a ban on insider trading could cause stock markets to become less liquid.

1.4. THE ALLEGED DAMAGE TO THE INSIDER'S COUNTERPART

An argument that is often used to ban insider trading is the fact that it allegedly harms the insider's counterpart. This section demonstrates that insiders do not harm the counterpart. On the contrary, he is better off than in a situation in which insiders do not use their privileged information. This will be illustrated by means of an example. Suppose an event occurs which has a negative impact on the value of the firm. In such a case of bad news on the security price, insiders can realize a profit based on their inside information by selling the security before the news is announced (see figure 5.3). The security price p_1 will decrease between the price-sensitive event date t_1 and the announcement date t_3 (see the dashed line AC). If no insider trading occurs, the price will move along the solid line ABC and fall to price p_3.

---

[11] Insiders are defined as top management and any other person connected with the company who can have access to private information, like employees, stock exchange members, and financial journalists with access to the exchange floor.

[12] Market depth is measured as the number of shares available at each bid and ask price.

Figure 5.3. The alleged damage to the outsider in case of negative news with regard to the stock price

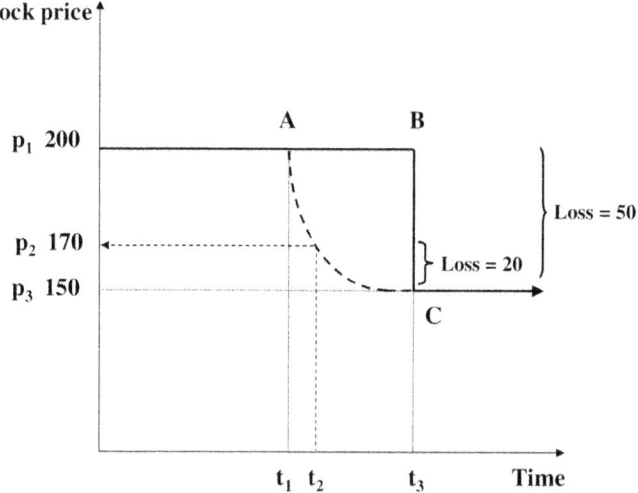

Source: based on Haddock and Macey (1986a)

Suppose the original price at moment t_1 amounts to EUR 200. Because of the bad news insiders sell their securities so that the stock price falls as a result of the extra supply. Suppose an insider sells his security to the outsider-buyer for EUR 170. The price falls to EUR 150 and the outsider-buyer loses EUR 20. But without insider trading this buyer would have bought the security for EUR 200 and he would have suffered a loss of EUR 50. Due to the insiders' extra supply buyers are better off than buying without the insiders' transactions.

Analogously, the price of a security will rise in the case of good news (see figure 5.4). Without insider trading the security price will move along the solid line ABC until it reaches the new equilibrium price p_3. In the case of insider trading the security price will already change before the announcement date t_3 along the dashed line AC. Again it can be demonstrated that "if insider trading increases share prices before the announcement, all current shareholders who were planning to sell before the announcement are better off, (while the others are not worse off) than if no such insider trading occurred" (Vermaelen, 1986, p.439).

Figure 5.4. The alleged damage to the outsider in case of positive news with regard to the stock price

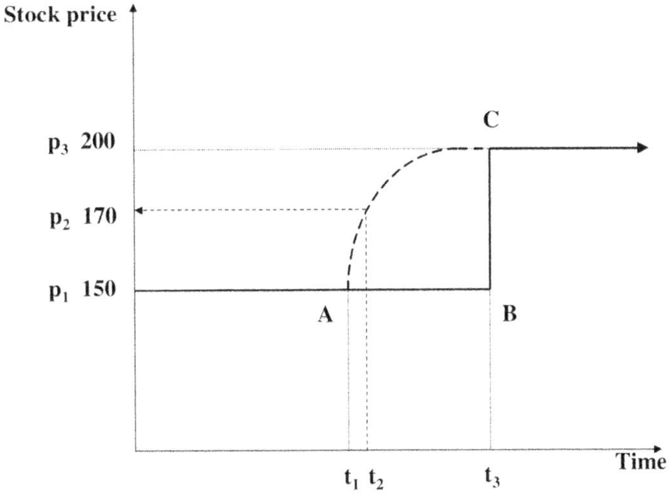

Source: based on Haddock and Macey (1986a)

1.5. INSIDER TRADING AS A COMPENSATION SCHEME

One of the arguments for prohibiting insider trading is the fact that it diverts part of the firm's earnings that would otherwise go to shareholders. When one situates this argument in a corporate governance context, it is clear that it is erroneous. As the corporate governance issue originates from the separation between ownership and control in publicly traded companies, agency problems may occur (Jensen and Meckling, 1976). Driven by their personal utility function, managers will not act automatically in the interest of shareholders when adopting investment and financing policies (Fischel, 1982 and Coffee, 1999). This might lead to actions, e.g. in terms of investment decisions, that diverge from those that maximize shareholders' value. However, several corporate governance mechanisms exist to align the interests of shareholders and managers. Moerland (1995a, 1995b) distinguishes four corporate governance mechanisms depending on their functioning (direct or indirect) and the type of residual rights (cash flow rights or voting rights) (see table 5.1).[13]

---

[13]   Other mechanisms may include the managerial labour market (Fama, 1980) and competitive pressures in the product market (Hart, 1983).

Table 5.1. Classification of corporate governance mechanisms

	Cash flow rights	Voting rights
Direct	Remuneration scheme	Supervisory board
Indirect	Stock market	Market for corporate control

Source: Moerland (1995a)

The stock market exercises discipline through the stock price.[14] Another corporate governance mechanism is the market for corporate control (Manne, 1965, Renneboog, 1996). The third corporate governance mechanism is the supervisory board. It deals with issues such as the relation between the board of directors and the executive board, the optimal number of directors in the board of directors, the separation of the chairmanship of the executive board and of the board of directors, as well as the selection of independent directors in the board of directors.

The use of remuneration schemes which link compensation to the creation of shareholder value (as measured by the evolution of the stock price) to align the interest of shareholders and managers is another mechanism to align interests of shareholders and managers (Brindisi, 1985; Baker, Jensen and Murphy, 1988). Morck, Shleifer and Vishny (1988) found that the higher the shareholdership of management in the firm, the more management acts in accordance with shareholders' interests. Other studies on the relationship between stock price evolution and the introduction of equity-linked compensation systems include Brickley, Bhagat and Lease (1985), Murphy (1985), Mehran (1995), Mishra, McConaughy and Gobeli (2000), Core, Guay and Larcker (2003), Murphy (2003) and Tian (2004). By substituting a part of the fixed wage by a variable equity-linked part, interests of shareholders and managers are better aligned.

An overview of equity-linked compensation schemes is always limited to bonuses, stock options, shares, etc. Insider trading by corporate insiders is always excluded a priori. As nobody would argue seriously that salaries, options, bonuses and other compensation schemes allow insiders to profit at the expense of shareholders, why should insider trading be treated differently (Carlton and Fischel, 1983)? This section will show that insider trading can be an alternative way of compensating managers for creating shareholder value. Several objections can be made to using insider trading as a compensation scheme. However, no remuneration device works perfectly.

---

[14] Warner, Watts en Wruck (1988) find a negative relationship between stock price return and the probability of dismissal of top management. Several empirical studies confirm this disciplinary mechanism: Coughlan and Schmidt (1985), Weisbach (1988), Kaplan (1994), Franks, Mayer and Renneboog (1996).

Therefore, from an efficiency point of view, insider trading as a compensation scheme can only be excluded if other remuneration schemes yield the same benefits at a lower cost.

1.5.1. The working of insider trading as a compensation scheme

In order to better understand the use of insider trading as a compensation scheme, it will be compared with the nowadays well established use of executive stock options (ESOs). As this section shows, most arguments against insider trading as a remuneration device can also object to the use of ESOs. Using insider trading as a compensation scheme allows management to receive a market-based remuneration for its efforts, because wages are linked directly and automatically to the size of the stock price increase.

Because a company can be viewed as an open financial system, which constantly interacts with financial markets, investors will continuously evaluate the management's projects and investment policy (Brealey and Myers, 1999). This evaluation is then reflected in the share's market price. In an efficient market stock prices reflect all relevant and available information concerning the value of the company. In such a market stock prices are a reliable criterion for the value of the company. If the efforts of management increase the company's value, the stock price will rise. Insofar as the remuneration of management is linked to this increase in stock price, managers are more inclined to increase shareholder value. By using insider trading there is a direct link between the value of the company and the stock price that is the basis for rewarding management.

As such, insider trading is particularly suited for rewarding corporate insiders for innovative value-increasing projects, for instance, R&D-projects of high-tech companies. As the shareholder value of such innovative projects is difficult to predict ex-ante, the use of traditional remuneration devices such as ESOs will be rather difficult. If managers are granted ESOs, the following characteristics have to be determined: How many options have to be granted? What expiration date should these options have? When can these options be exercised? Which strike price should be adopted? It is almost impossible to determine all these features ex-ante in such a way that managers will receive correct remuneration for the shareholder value they create. According to Manne (1966) only insider trading is therefore suited to reward innovative managers or entrepreneurs.

Because traditional compensation schemes cannot predict in advance correct remuneration for innovative efforts by corporate insiders, periodic renegotiations between the company and management must occur to adjust the remuneration package. However, repeated renegotiations about the compensation of management are costly (Carlton and Fischel, 1983). Moreover, these adjustments to remuneration will be quite slow.[15] The benefit of insider trading as a compensation scheme is the fact that such renegotiations are unnecessary, because the remuneration is adjusted automatically to the shareholder value creation by management. An automatic market-based adjustment of management compensation will therefore be more efficient than slow and costly renegotiations between the company and its managers. Given that stock markets are efficient and that the creation of shareholder value is the company goal, this conclusion must be drawn. Table 5.2 summarizes the working of ESOs and insider trading as a compensation scheme (see panel a and b).

When a company grants ESOs to its management, it in fact writes call-options on its own shares. This is an open position necessitating adequate risk management to avoid future losses (Kabir, Duffhues and Mertens, 1999). It can be hedged by e.g. buying back own shares in the stock market.[16] However, the company's position only remains hedged for a relatively short period of time because the amount of shares to close the open position continuously alters. The hedge therefore has to be adjusted or rebalanced periodically (Hull, 2000). Such continuous risk management can be avoided by allowing insider trading as a compensation scheme (see panel c in table 5.2).

Table 5.2. The working of ESOs and insider trading as a compensation scheme

	ESOs	Insider trading
a. Correct compensation for shareholder value added?	No, difficult to predict ex-ante	Yes, because automatically linked to stock price
b. Renegotiation necessary?	Yes 1. Slow 2. Expensive	No, because automatically linked to stock price
c. Appropriate risk management necessary?	Necessary	Not necessary

1.5.2. Arguments against insider trading as a compensation scheme

Traditional counter-arguments concerning insider trading as a compensation scheme include (Scott, 1980 and Easterbrook, 1981):

---

[15]   The adjustment speed can be increased by raising the frequency of the wage renegotiations. However, at the same time, the costs will also increase. See also Smith and Watts (1982).

[16]   The amount of shares necessary to hedge an open call-option position is expressed by the "delta" of an option. Expressed mathematically, delta (Δ) is the partial derivative of the call price (C) with respect to the underlying stock price (S): $\Delta = \dfrac{\partial C}{\partial S}$.

1. Managers can also trade on negative inside information. In this case they are rewarded for value-decreasing investment strategies, while the company goal is precisely the opposite, i.e. the creation of shareholder value;
2. Managers will focus on short-term stock price movements to exploit insider trading opportunities. In this way, the alignment of the long-term interest of shareholders and managers will be poorly realized;
3. Managers can create false information to induce stock price movements to capture profits based on inside information at the expense of shareholders;
4. Managers will choose risky projects to increase the volatility of stock prices in order to increase profits based on inside information; and
5. The general meeting of shareholders will lose control over the amount of compensation for management if insider trading were allowed.

This section will show that each of these arguments can be rebutted or refined and that they are also relevant with regard to ESOs. Table 5.3 gives an overview of objections to the use of insider trading as a compensation scheme compared to the use of ESOs.

Table 5.3. The drawbacks of equity-linked compensation schemes

	ESOs	Insider trading
Objection 1:	Managers can exploit negative news	
Solution	No put-options allowed	Managerial labour market Market for corporate control Legal liability of directors No short-selling
Objection 2:	Managers will focus on short-term stock price movements	
Solution	Minimum holding period	No short swing profits
Objection 3:	Managers will create false information	
Solution	Regulation on market manipulation	Regulation on market manipulation
Objection 4:	Managers will choose risky projects	
Solution	No problem for well-diversified shareholders	No problem for well-diversified shareholders
Objection 5:	General meeting of shareholders will lose control	
Solution	Is the GMS really in control? Corporate governance-problems!	No loss of control; GMS only chooses for an equity-linked compensation scheme

The first objection to the use of insider trading as a compensation scheme is the fact that managers can also exploit negative news. With regard to ESOs this objection is solved by prohibiting put-options. Can this objection also be solved with respect to the use of insider trading? Several mechanisms exist to prevent the exploitation of negative news using insider trading such as the managerial labour market and the market for corporate control. The managerial labour market will prevent value-decreasing strategies by management (Fama, 1980). Such behaviour affects their managerial reputation and consequently the value of their human capital. Next, the market for corporate control will prevent such strategies as well. If managers try to exploit negative news by deflating the stock price, the company becomes a potential target for a hostile takeover (Manne, 1965). Renneboog (1996) finds a market in share stakes in poorly performing companies with shareholders selling out to other companies rather than exercising control themselves. Subsequent to the sale, the management is being replaced by the new shareholders. The disciplinary mechanism of a market for corporate control will prevent management from decreasing the value of the company. Furthermore, value-decreasing strategies are also prevented by the legal liability of directors. Finally, the exploitation of negative news by management through insider trading is prevented in a direct way by prohibiting short-selling by management.[17]

The second objection that insider trading as a compensation scheme will urge management to focus on short-term stock price movements, holds as well for granting ESOs. In the case of ESOs this problem is solved by granting European call-options or Bermudan call-options, which can only be exercised on the expiration date, respectively, during a particular time frame of the duration of the option. Granting American call-options, which can be exercised at any time up to the expiration date, is avoided. Such a restraint on short-term behaviour by management can also be constructed in case of insider trading. The legislator could, by analogy with section 16(b) of the U.S. Securities Exchange Act of 1934, prohibit so-called 'short swing profits'.[18] Section 16 (b) is directed at 'officers', 'directors' and beneficial owners

---

[17] See e.g. section 16 (c) of the U.S. Securities Exchange Act of 1934.

[18] Section 16(b) of the U.S. Securities Exchange Act of 1934: *"For the purpose of preventing the unfair use of information which may have been obtained by such beneficial owner, director, or officer by reason of his relationship to the issuer, any profit realized by him from any purchase and sale, or any sale and purchase, of any equity security of such issuer (other than an exempted security) within any period of less than six months, unless such security was acquired in good faith in connection with a debt previously contracted, shall inure to and be recoverable by the issuer, irrespective of any intention on the part of such beneficial owner, director, or officer in entering into such transaction of holding the security purchased or of not repurchasing the security sold for a period exceeding six months. Suit to recover such profit may be instituted at law or in equity in any court of competent jurisdiction of the issuer, or by the owner of any security of the issuer in the name and in behalf of the issuer if the issuer shall fail or refuse to bring such suit within sixty days after request or shall fail diligently to prosecute the same thereafter; but no such suit shall be brought more than two years after the date such profit was realized. This subsection*

holding more than 10% of the shares of the company, who realize profits from any purchase and sale (or vice versa) of stocks within a period of less than six months (Phillips and Zutz, 1984). Short-term trading by such insiders is prevented by giving individual shareholders and the company a cause of action to recover profits made from these transactions. Notice that section 16(b) applies irrespective if the trades were based on inside information or not (Wu, 1968). By making such transactions profitless, the danger disappears that management will focus on short-term price movements. Such a regulation can also be used with regard to insider trading as a compensation scheme. The time period of six months can, if necessary, be extended to say twelve months.

The third objection alleges that managers can create false information and subsequently exploit it based on inside information. Again the same objection can be made with respect to ESOs. But one has to distinguish clearly between the phenomena of insider trading and stock price manipulation.[19] The difference is subtle, but important. Contrary to insider trading, stock price manipulation is improper because in this case the fundamentals of the company do not change, while they do change in an insider trading case. While insider trading moves the stock price closer to its fundamental value, stock price manipulation artificially moves the stock price away from its fundamental value, thereby decreasing the allocative efficiency of an economy. As such, it is perfectly possible to allow insider trading as a compensation scheme, while, at the same time, prohibiting stock price manipulation. If enforced, such a (criminal) prohibition can prevent managers from creating false information. Moreover, such strategies will also be prevented by the managerial labour market and by legal liabilities.

The fourth allegation of insider trading as a compensation scheme is the fact that it will induce management to select more risky projects than shareholders would prefer. By selecting risky projects the range of future outcomes will be wider, increasing future insider trading profits for management (Bebchuk and Fershtman, 1994). However, the same goes for ESOs (DeFusco, Johnson and Zorn, 1990). Because of their asymmetric payoff, stock options increase in value if the volatility of the underlying share price increases (Hull, 2000). However, an increase of volatility is not an objection for well-diversified shareholders. In reality managers tend to be risk-averse. This is because managers care about the total risk of the company, while shareholders only

---

shall not be construed to cover any transaction where such beneficial owner was not such both at the time of the purchase and sale, or the sale and purchase, of the security involved, or any transaction or transactions which the Commission by rules and regulations may exempt as not comprehended within the purpose of this subsection."

[19] For an overview of mechanisms involving stock price manipulation or market manipulation, see e.g. Lee (1993), Soderquist (1994, chapter 14), de Vauplane and Simart (1997) and Cerfontaine (1997).

look at the systematic or market risk because shareholders can eliminate the non-systematic risk by holding a well diversified portfolio (Elton and Gruber, 1995). Managers, however, cannot diversify the human capital that they invested in a specific company because more risky projects will also increase the probability of bankruptcy, which is a real threat to the value of their (company-specific) human capital and their remuneration (Coffee, 1986). Therefore, granting options or allowing insider trading will be beneficial to shareholders, because risk-averse managers will be induced to select risky projects that maximize shareholder value instead of opting for a conservative investment policy that does not maximize shareholder value (Bebchuk and Fershtman, 1994). In this way, the interests of shareholders and managers are again aligned.

The fifth objection states that the general meeting of shareholders loses all control over the amount of remuneration for management if insider trading were allowed as a compensation scheme. This objection is irrelevant because insider trading as a remuneration device implies an automatic and market-based reward for the creation of shareholder value by management without any slow and costly negotiations or renegotiations about correct compensation (see above). Moreover, the general meeting of shareholders does not 'lose' control. It only decides to compensate management with a fixed part and with a variable part on the basis of inside information. Thus, it only decides to use a market-based remuneration device. Furthermore, the general meeting can always alter this decision by prohibiting management to trade on inside information and opt for whatever compensation scheme it feels appropriate. Finally, one can question the control of granting ESOs by the general meeting of shareholders in practice, which gives rise to additional corporate governance problems.

To conclude, this section showed that insider trading can be a valid way of compensating management. It is therefore a valuable alternative to more traditional forms of remuneration such as ESOs. The above analysis furthermore showed that insider trading as a compensation scheme has some clear benefits compared to these traditional remuneration devices. The automatic and market-based compensation for the creation of shareholder value by management avoids slow and costly negotiations or renegotiations between the company and its management about the correct amount of remuneration. As long as one does not show that other remuneration schemes yield the same benefits at a lower cost, insider trading can therefore not be excluded as a valid compensation scheme.

1.6. THE OPTIMAL AMOUNT OF DETERRENCE

The above sections examined whether insider trading is harmful or not. After analysing the pros and cons of a ban on insider trading, this section determines the optimal amount of deterrence. In general, crime imposes two basic kinds of costs on society. The first cost component is the net total social harm caused by the crime (van Velthoven and van Wijck, 1997). It is the harm suffered by the victim of the crime minus the benefits gained by the criminal. For instance, a thief shatters a car window costing EUR 100 to steal a car radio worth EUR 75. The loss of the victim amounts EUR 175, while the gains of the criminal amounts EUR 75. Therefore, the net harm caused by the crime equals EUR 100 (Cooter and Ulen, 1997). The net total social harm is represented in figure 5.5 by curve A. The social harm is an increasing function of the level of crime. If the level of crime rises, the resulting social harm is expected to increase.

Figure 5.5. The net social harm of a crime versus the costs of preventing a crime

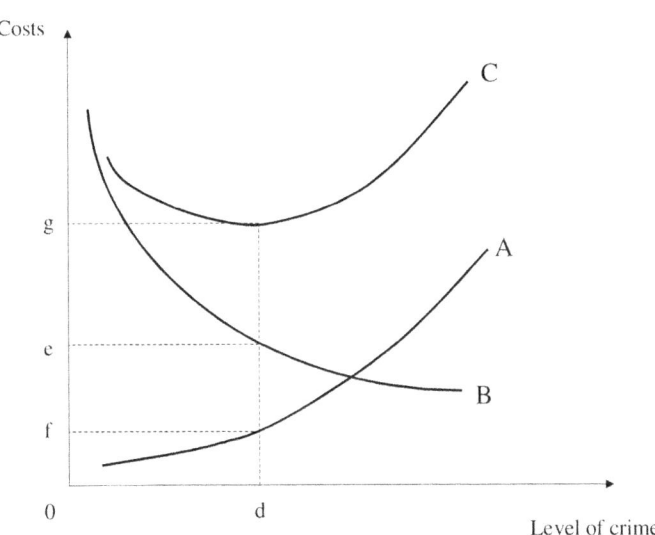

Source: van Velthoven and van Wijck (1997, p.395)
Legend: A – net total social harm caused by the crime; B – total costs to prevent the crime; C – total social cost of the crime

The second cost component is the total cost of preventing the crime. These are the resources spent by the state on police, courts, public prosecutors and prisons. The cost of preventing a crime is represented by curve B in figure 5.5. This curve takes the other direction compared to curve A. This can be explained by the fact that achieving additional reductions in crime becomes increasingly costly. For instance, reducing a crime by an additional 1% is more costly if it has already been reduced 90% than when it only has been reduced 10% because the state first undertakes easy deterrence before moving to harder deterrence (Cooter and Ulen, 1997).

The sum of both cost components equals the total social cost of a crime and is represented by curve C, which has a U-shape. Efficient deterrence implies balancing the net social harm caused by the crime and the costs to prevent it. The policy-maker can therefore use the minimization of the total social cost of crimes as a goal for criminal law enforcement (Cooter and Ulen, 1997 and van Velthoven and van Wijck, 1997). The optimal amount of deterrence in figure 5.5 is therefore given by $0d$. In point d the level of crime minimizes the sum of the net social harm and the costs of prevention. It is not useful to spend more resources on preventing crime than the amount $0e$. Spending less on prevention is inefficient because the net social harm outweighs the resources necessary for prevention, while the opposite is true when spending more on prevention.

Expressed mathematically, the total expected social cost of a crime can be represented as (Cooter and Ulen, 1997):

Total expected social cost $= (h - b)P(z) + z$ [5.1]

in which the variable h represents the harm caused by the crime, including direct costs as well as indirect cost such as the private resources spent by potential victims such as a car alarm to prevent the crime.[20] The variable b represents the gains obtained by the criminal.[21] The difference between h and b is the net social cost of the crime. However, the probability of occurrence of the crime, $P(z)$, has to be taken into account as well. This probability in turn depends on the cost of deterrence z. The variable z represents the resources spent on police, courts, public prosecutors, prisons and so on. $P(z)$ or the probability of the crime is a decreasing function of expenditure on deterrence. The net social cost of the crime multiplied by the probability $P(z)$ is the expected net social cost of the crime. Summing the expected net social cost and the cost of deterrence yields the total expected social cost of the crime. For the criminal law to be efficient, the policy-maker has to spend the cost of deterrence z that minimizes total expected social costs.

Balancing the pros and cons of insider trading, one has to observe from the analysis in this chapter that it appears that there is very little harm caused by insider trading. The confidence of investors is not expected to decline, empirical studies showed no decrease of market liquidity and it was shown that the non-informed counterpart of the insider was not harmed, on the contrary. Therefore, the variable h will likely take a value close to nil.

---

[20] The loss of the EUR 175 suffered by the victim of the theft in the above example is an example of a direct cost.

[21] Such as the EUR 75 obtained by the thief of the car radio.

On the other hand, the variable b will take a positive value. Besides the capital gains realized by the insider, the social gains from informationally efficient capital markets must be stressed. The more accurately prices reflect information, the better prices guide capital investment in the economy. Moreover, it creates an additional signaling device for management to communicate complex news in a credible way. Another important social benefit from insider trading is the market-based compensation scheme, which also makes it possible to reward the innovative and entrepreneurial inputs of corporate insiders.

Given the fact that h is close to nil and b takes a positive value, it is quite astonishing to see that the amount of net social harm (h-b) is negative. Besides the net social harm, there is also the (substantial) cost of deterrence z. Moreover, as chapter seven will clearly demonstrate, current criminal sanctions are insufficient to restrict insider trading. As minimizing the expected net social cost of crimes is the goal of the policy-maker, an economist has to conclude that social welfare will increase: (1) either by reducing enforcement effort, or (2) by eliminating insider trading regulation.

2. PUBLIC CHOICE PERSPECTIVE: PRIVATE INTEREST VERSUS PUBLIC INTEREST

Most authors believe that small individual investors benefit from a prohibition of insider trading. However, by stating that insider trading is not in the interest of small investors two implicit assumptions are made. First, it is implicitly assumed that there are only two groups involved on securities markets: insider-managers and outsider-investors. Prohibiting insider trading is then viewed as a solution to the information asymmetry between insiders and outsiders. Second, the implicit assumption is made that profits on the security market are equally and randomly distributed among all market participants if insider trading is banned. However, both assumptions do not match reality.

2.1. MARKET PROFESSIONALS

The group of outsiders is not as homogeneous as is implicitly assumed. It has to be subdivided into, at least, small individual investors and market professionals such as arbitrageurs, brokers, portfolio managers and financial analysts.[22] Consequently, insider trading regulations involve at least three distinct groups: (1) corporate insiders, (2) small investors and (3) market professionals. Moreover, as chapter two already showed, the idea of equal access to information for these three groups is a non-realistic

---

[22]   Further refinements are possible to include for instance large shareholders or market makers.

presumption. It is clear that corporate insiders, because of the nature of their employment, are better informed about their own company than market professionals, which in turn are better informed than small investors and the public in general. Market professionals are specialized in obtaining new information in order to differentiate themselves from other market participants and obtain a higher profit. Haugen (2001) accurately describes market professionals as "an army of intelligent, well-informed security analysts, arbitrageurs, and traders, who literally spend their lives hunting for securities that are mispriced based on currently available information. These professionals are armed with computers, and they subscribe to database management services that are tied into their computers. They have at their fingertips up-to-date information on thousands of companies, and they process this information using state-of-the-art analytical techniques. These people can access, assimilate, and act on information very quickly (p.573)." Therefore, market professionals are in a position to respond faster to new information than the average market participant by executing stock market transactions before other market participants have collected and processed the new information.

By prohibiting corporate insiders to trade on their firm-specific inside information about the present value of the future cash flows of their company, the market participant who is next in line of the information processing channel will take the gains of the valuable new information. In companies with widely dispersed share ownership, the next fastest group are market professionals (see figure 5.6). By banning corporate insiders from trading on inside information, it will be mainly those market professionals, and not the small investors, who benefit from a prohibition of insider trading. Or as Haddock and Macey (1986a) put it: "When market professionals are the next-best information processors, from the shareholders' perspective a ban on insider trading is the equivalent of a rule requiring insiders to throw money out of the window of the firm's corporate headquarters. The market professionals who happen to be passing by at the time the money flutters down certainly benefit. But shareholders who have other productive uses for their time have no chance of grabbing any of these funds and inevitably lose (p.1463)."

Figure 5.6. Information processing channel

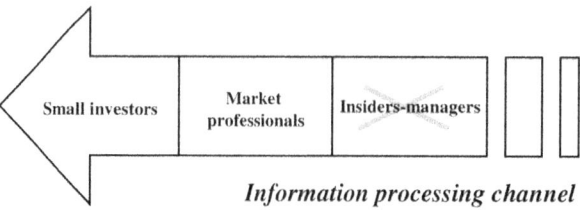

Information processing channel

Insider trading regulation is a nice example of the economic theory of regulation (Stigler, 1971 and Posner, 1974) that explains regulation as a process by which interest groups seek to promote their private interests.[23] If the economic theory of regulation is valid, insider trading regulation tends to favour relatively small and well-organized groups that have a high per capita stake in this regulation, at the expense of relatively large, poorly organized groups with a lower per capita stake. It is clear that market professionals and insiders are well organized, while small investors are poorly organized. Because small investors lack any political organization to lobby for insider trading laws, it is expected that market professionals or insiders influence this regulation. Because there are two well organized interest groups, insider trading regulations is expected to depend on the relative efficiency of each group in exerting political pressure and influence (Becker, 1983, 1985). Haddock and Macey (1987) present a private interest model in which insiders and market professionals compete for regulatory favor. According to this model the SEC chooses the level of regulation that maximizes political support from interest groups.

The model of Haddock and Macey (1987) is visually represented in figure 5.7. The circle represents the objective function of the supervisory authority (SEC), i.e. to maximize the political support for the agency. In this way, the agency can enlarge its jurisdiction, its prestige and its budget (Bainbridge, 2000). By choosing certain policy positions, the SEC will attract the support of a specific interest group, while another position will cause opposition from this group. In figure 5.7 the political support or opposition for an insider trading policy by insiders and market professionals is represented on the horizontal and vertical axes, respectively. The magnitude of the circle represents the SEC's policy selection opportunity set as defined by courts and by U.S. Congress. The SEC can choose any policy within the boundaries of the circle. However, it will adopt a policy on the circle, thereby receiving more political support from both insiders and market professionals (e.g. moving from A to B in figure 5.7). To maximize its political support, the policy in point D has to be selected.[24] However, market professionals will prefer point B, while insiders will prefer point C. After the U.S. Supreme Court decisions in Chiarella[25] and Dirks[26], market professionals were almost free to trade as long as there was no fiduciary duty not to trade.[27] This court decision caused the SEC to move its policy in the direction of point B, thereby receiving

---

[23]   See in detail chapter one.
[24]   In D the forty-five degree tangent intersects the opportunity set: another unit of support from one group can only be gained by sacrificing a unit support from the other group.
[25]   445 U.S. 222 (1980), *Federal Securities Law Reports*, 1980, nr.97-309.
[26]   463 U.S. 646 (1983), *Federal Securities Law Reports*, 1983, nr.99-255.
[27]   Both decisions rejected the equal access to information doctrine and replaced it by a fiduciary duty to disclose. Absent of any fiduciary duty to shareholders, one was free to trade. In this way, market professionals were largely immune to ordinary insider trading sanctions.

more political support from market professionals. Market professionals subsequently lobbied for more severe penalties and more enforcement by the SEC of insider trading violation. Subsequently, penalties were enhanced by the Insider Trading Sanctions Act of 1984. The increased enforcement by the SEC is given in table 5.4. After the decision in Dirks, enforcement efforts were increased, leading to more insiders being prosecuted. Moreover, 80% of the cases were directed to insiders only. Increased enforcement effort to ban insiders from trading on their inside information is beneficial for market professionals, being the next fastest information processors.[28]

Figure 5.7. Maximizing the political support given the policy opportunity set of the SEC

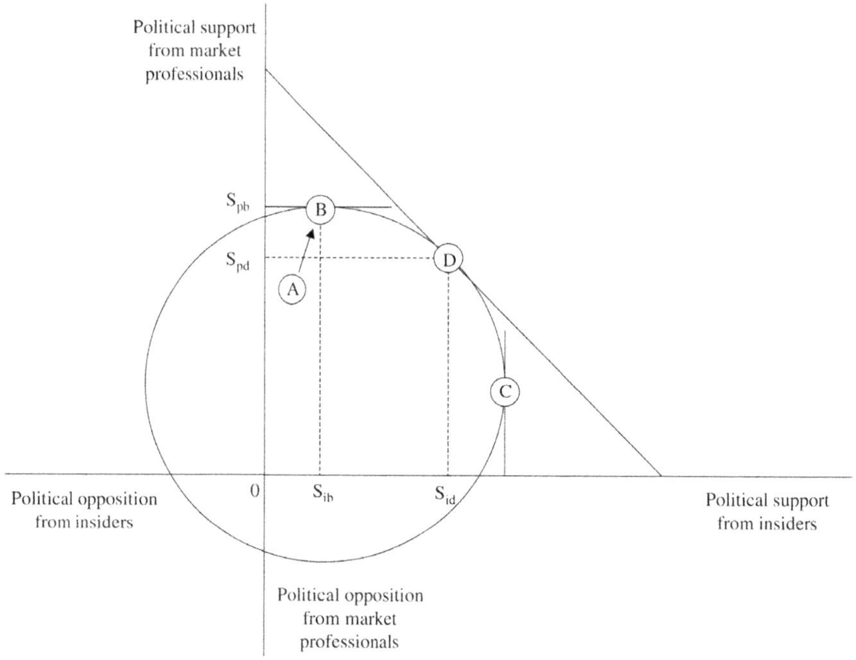

Source: Haddock and Macey (1987)

---

[28]   Insiders have pressured SEC to restrain market professionals acting on inside information surrounding hostile takeovers. Subsequently the SEC promulgated Rule 14e-3.

Table 5.4. Prosecution of insider trading in the U.S. between 1968 and 1987

Case against:	Only insiders	Only market professionals	Both	Total
Before 1980 (12 years)	18 (49%)	14 (38%)	5 (13%)	37 (100%)
After 1983 (4.6 years)	63 (80%)	5 (6%)	11 (14%)	79 (100%)
Total	81	19	16	116

Source: Haddock and Macey (1987) and Dooley (1980)

The above analysis shows that insider trading regulation reflects the relative power of market professionals and insiders as competing interest groups and the resulting legal framework has little to do with the public interest. In the end, the prohibition of insider trading does not solve the informational asymmetry or the 'unfair' situation; it merely rearranges the ranking of 'winners' and 'losers'. As such, the so-called 'fairness' argument is in reality a problem of distributing insider trading profits. Insider trading thus redistributes resources. However, competing for insider trading profits against market professionals the small investor will fight a losing battle. Extending the model of Haddock and Macey (1987), Tighe and Michener (1994) clearly show that, instead of transferring trading profits from corporate insiders to small investors (as is generally assumed), the largest gains are earned by market professionals. The current ban on insider trading only serves private interest and is therefore not in the public interest. By banning corporate insiders from trading, market professionals obtain the benefits of the insider trading regulation, while imposing the cost on a large number of small investors, who will not seriously challenge the current rules because these costs are distributed at a low per capita rate (Wilson, 1974, 1980). By allowing corporate insiders to trade based on their inside information, small investors will benefit, i.e. the enhanced shareholder value creation because of the equity-linked compensation of management (see above). However, as this group is poorly organized and has a low per capita stake, it is unable to influence insider trading regulation.

2.2. AN EXAMPLE OF THE IMPACT OF INTEREST GROUPS: THE REGULATION IN BELGIUM

As the SEC exported its rules on insider trading to Switzerland and the European Union during the eighties (Kitch, 2000), this was clearly beneficial for market professionals operating worldwide. So, indirectly the European regulation was influenced by interest groups. In Belgium, an additional interest group succeeded in influencing the Belgian insider trading laws. The Belgian regulation had an exception for holding companies. Article 181 paragraph 2 of the Belgian Statute of December 4, 1990 on Financial Transactions and Financial Markets[29] stated that the information which portfolio companies possess by virtue of their role in the management of the companies in which they own a participation, is not considered as inside information, provided that the information does not have to be publicly announced according to the Royal Decree of July 3, 1996.[30] According to the Royal Decree Occasional Information, listed companies in Belgium have to disclose within the shortest possible term, all information with regard to the rights connected to the possession of financial instruments and disclose promptly to the public all facts and decisions that the issuer has knowledge of and that can affect the value of the securities of the issuer significantly if the information were to be disclosed to the public.[31]

Given the concentrated stock ownership in Belgium (Engelen, 1997b), the holding exception was not surprising. In the information processing channel large shareholders are the fastest group after insiders but before market professionals because they monitor the company's investment policy very closely, among others by its board members. Compared to market professionals they are the next-best information processors who benefit the most from a prohibition on insider trading by corporate insiders in Belgium.

In the Belgian legal literature there was some discussion whether this exception for holding companies was a real or apparent exception. The answer to this question depends on the fact if there is a set of information that does not have to be disclosed according to the Royal Decree Occasional Information, but which is nevertheless privileged according to article 181 SFTFM. While some legal scholars such as Lambrecht (1991), Philippe (1991) and Devos (1991) answer in the negative (see panel a of figure 5.8), the majority view answers this question positively (Geens, 1991a, Krekels, 1992 and Engelen, 1999). There is a real application field on which those holding companies are exempted from the prohibition of insider trading. Panel b of figure 5.8 shows that some information does not have to be publicly announced according to the Royal Decree Occasional Information, but which falls within the scope of the Statute of December 4th, 1990 concerning privileged information. For instance, a proposal that the board of directors has not been accepted yet. Although this proposal

---

[29] *Belgian Gazette*, 22 December 1990, erratum, *Belgian Gazette*, 1 February 1991, modified by the Statute of 6 April 1995 on the Secondary Markets, the Status and Supervision of Investment Firms, Intermediaries and Advisers, *Belgian State Gazette*, 3 June 1995 [*in short: SFTFM*].

[30] Royal Decree of 3 July 1996 on the obligations with regard to occasional information of issuers whose securities are listed on the first market or on the new market of a public stock exchange, *Belgian Gazette*, 6 July 1996, modified by the Royal Decree of 13 January 1997, *Belgian Gazette*, 25 January 1997 and Royal Decree of 9 June 1997, *Belgian Gazette*, 2 July 1997, errata, *Belgian Gazette*, 12 September 1997 [*In short: Royal Decree Occasional Information*].

[31] Articles 4 §1 and 5 §1 Royal Decree Occasional Information.

does not have to be publicly announced according to the Royal Decree Occasional Information, if it is sufficiently clear and price-sensitive it falls under the prohibition of insider trading. All privileged information that is not yet a "fact" or a "decision" does not have to be publicly disclosed according to the Royal Decree Occasional Information (Geens, 1991b).

Figure 5.8.Two views in legal literature with respect to the holding exception

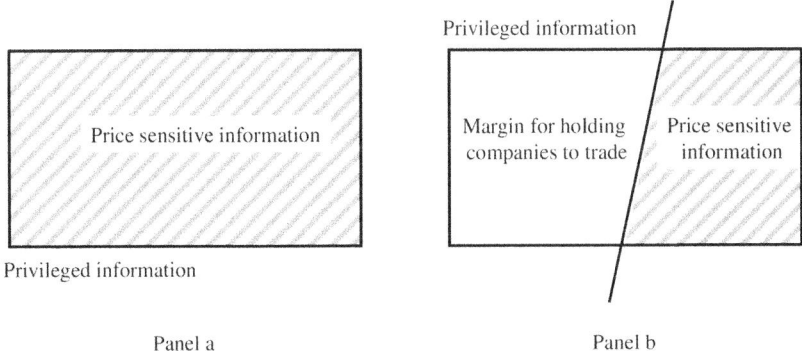

Panel a   Panel b

Suppose we represent the amount of information available to the portfolio companies, by virtue of their role in the management of the companies in which they own a participation, by the variable Φ. The margin in which they can trade depends on the precision of the information, going from perfectly precise information ($\Phi = 1$) to information with no content ($\Phi = 0$). We define the critical value of information to be considered as inside information as Φ_{IT}. As long as $\Phi < \Phi_{IT}$, investors are allowed to trade on that information. In the opposite case, they are (criminally) prohibited from trading. Next, we define the critical value of information to be considered price-sensitive under the Royal Decree Occasional Information as Φ_{RDOI}. Information has to be disclosed promptly to the public when $\Phi \geq \Phi_{RDOI}$. As can be seen in figure 5.9 the critical value of the Royal Decree is less strict than the critical value of the SFTFM: $\Phi_{IT} < \Phi_{RDOI}$. Within this margin portfolio companies can trade on their private information obtained in the management of the companies in which they own a participation. Moreover, portfolio companies can pursue an active strategy to legally exploit this margin to the maximum. If portfolio companies only stay 'vaguely informed' about profitable investment opportunities in their participations and avoid as much as possible 'facts' and 'decisions', they enlarge their trading possibilities on privileged information as much as possible. They can thus legally trade on information they acquire about participations, without the need to disclose it.

Figure 5.9.The margin for holding companies to trade on privileged information

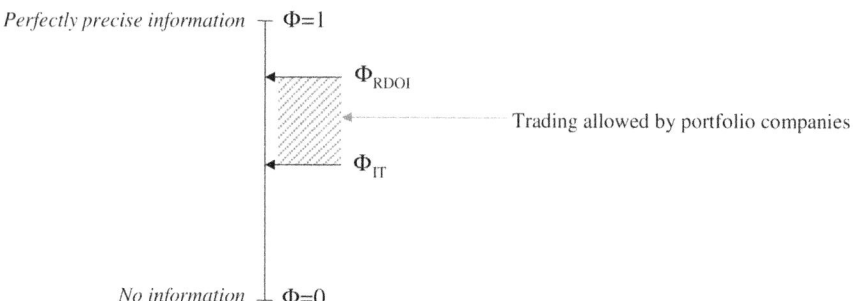

Holding companies in Belgium clearly succeeded in influencing the insider trading laws by giving them a margin in which they can trade completely immune to insider trading sanctions. Being the next-best information processors holding companies capture most trading benefits in companies in which they own a participation compared to other market participants. Again, this is a nice example of private interest groups influencing regulations, hereby confirming that insider trading laws are in reality a device to distribute resources, i.e. valuable information, among competing interest groups. In its activity report of 1997 also the Market Authority questioned the so-called holding exception.[32]

This is a legally formalized version of the 'grey zone' in the current insider trading regulation in the European Union, where some private information can be traded on. Because of its narrow definition of inside information, which ought to be "precise", the EU Insider Dealing Directive created a grey zone, where information is private but cannot be classified as inside information and can, therefore, be traded on. In Belgium holding companies succeeded in formalizing this grey zone in the legal definition of inside information. According to Maug (2000), the reason for the precision require-ment is that insider trading laws in the EU are enforced mainly through criminal courts, demanding a high standard of proof. He points out that the legal framework in the US does not share this handicap and that such a focus on precision is absent from US Law, where civil penalties are used more frequently.

With respect to the holding exception, the First Instance Criminal Court of Ghent referred to the European Court of Justice for a preliminary ruling whether Article 181 SFTFM is compatible with Article 6 of the Directive which states that a member state

---

[32] *Activity report of the Market Authority of the Brussels Stock Exchange 1997*, Brussels Stock Exchange, 1998, p.37.

can adopt more stringent provisions provided that such provisions are applied generally.[33]

In 2001 the European Court of Justice ruled on this case.[34] The three questions for a preliminary ruling can be found in consideration 17. The Court stated that "it is for the national court to determine whether or not the additional elements included by the national legislature in article 181 [...] result in making the information regarded as inside information in the case of holding companies more restricted than the information regarded as inside information for the purposes of the general definition contained in article 181." In fact, the national court must determine "whether or not holding companies [...] are more favourably treated than other participants in the financial market [...] insofar as concerns the provisions of the 1990 Law that are more stringent than those set out in the directive (consideration 34)." If the national court determines the provisions to be incompatible with Article 6 Directive, "the national court must disapply those more stringent provisions with regard to all persons to whom they might otherwise apply (consideration 38)." Because the SFTFM does not require that an insider use inside information in his possession with full knowledge of the facts, it is more stringent than the Directive.[35] According to Article 6 of the Directive, such provisions are permitted provided that they are applied generally. In a legal technical sense, the question was whether the holding exception is compatible with the Directive.

Based on the ruling of the European Court of Justice, the First Instance Criminal Court of Ghent judged the holding exception not to be in line with the European Directive.[36] As a result of the ruling of the European Court of Justice, the new Belgian insider trading regulation no longer mentions the holding exception.[37]

---

[33] First Instance Criminal Court of Ghent [27 January 1999], TRV, 1999, 47-49.

[34] European Court of Justice [3 May 2001], Case C-28/99 [2001] ECR I-3399.

[35] It has to be noted that in the proposal of the New Directive, the expression 'with full knowledge of the facts' is suppressed in article 2. The explanatory memorandum argues that primary insiders by nature may have access to inside information on a daily basis and are aware of the confidential nature of the information they receive. See the Proposal for a Directive of the European Parliament and of the Council on insider dealing and market manipulation (market abuse), 30 May 2001, COM(2001) 281 final, 27 p.

[36] First Instance Criminal Court of Ghent [18 December 2002], *Bank- en Financieel Recht*, 2003, 53-57. For a legal analysis of this case, see Engelen (2003b).

[37] As a consequence of a European Directive (Directive 2003/6/EC of the European Parliament and of the Council of 28 January 2003 on Insider Dealing and Market Manipulation (Market Abuse), *OJ*, L96/16, 12 April 2003 – in short: the *Market Abuse Directive* or *MAD*), the insider trading regulation was rewritten in Article 40 of the Statute of 2 August 2002 on the Supervision on the Financial Sector and the Financial Services, *Belgian Gazette*, 4 September 2002 (edition 2). The Statute came into force on 1 June 2003. See Article 1 of the Royal Decree of 3 April 2003, *Belgian Gazette*, 29 April 2003.

3. PROPERTY RIGHTS PERSPECTIVE: CHOICE PER COMPANY

One thing is clear about insider trading: information has value. Privileged corporate information can therefore be seen as a valuable, intangible property right. The existence of property rights in intangibles such as patents, copyright, trademarks, trade secrets and information, is well-established (Kitch, 1980, Easterbrook, 1981, Bainbridge, 2000). Consequently, Easterbrook (1981) sees the right to trade on some piece of information about a company as a part of the larger question of whether and how to allocate property rights in intangible assets. Just as other property rights in intangible assets, the property rights perspective to regulating insider trading treats inside information as a valuable property right within the firm. In general, property rights refer to a bundle of exclusive rights of use (van Velthoven and van Wijck, 1997). In particular ownership of a right means that a person controls at least a three-element bundle of rights in which each of the rights can be separated from the others (Demsetz, 1998). First, the bundle of rights includes the right to use a scare resource. Second, it includes the right to exclude others from exercising this right of use without permission. Finally, it includes the right to transfer control of the three-element bundle to other potential owners.

Intellectual property laws such as patent law deal with the tension between encouraging valuable creative activity and the restricting of competition and monopolistic pricing (Dnes, 1996). By granting an exclusive right to freely use an invention for a maximum of twenty years, patents give the inventor the possibility to recover his research and development costs. Without this possibility, competitors facing similar marginal production and marketing costs are able to set a market price at which the inventor cannot recover the R&D costs. If an inventor expects such a situation ex-ante he will have little or no incentive to invent (Dnes, 1996). The patent gives the inventor this possibility and, at the same time, encourages information revelation. Analogously, copyright laws protect the property rights of authors, composers and artists and give them an exclusive right to collect royalties from copying up to seventy years after their decease. Insider trading regulation has a similar rationale by protecting the economic incentive to produce socially valuable information (Bainbridge, 2000).

As the regulation of insider trading can be seen as an allocation of property rights within the company, the relevant question is how these property rights should be allocated efficiently. A rule allowing insider trading assigns the property right to the insider, while a rule prohibiting insider trading assigns this right to the company (Bainbridge, 2000). Depending on whether the property right in inside information is more valuable to the managers or to the shareholders, allowing insider trading will be beneficial (Carlton and Fischel, 1983). It should therefore be allocated to the party that values it most. No uniform legal rule is a solution to this allocation, because it depends on who is the next-best information processor after the insiders.

In such a situation the best legal rule is contractual in nature (Macey, 1991).[38] Coase (1960) has shown that property rights will be allocated to their highest value user (absent of transaction costs). It is thus irrelevant to which party the property rights are allocated initially, because the parties can engage in a value-maximizing exchange by allocating the property right to its highest value user (Haddock and Macey, 1986b). As long as parties are free to contract around the initial rule, they can allocate the property rights in a way that increases the total value of the firm. Of course this depends upon the level of transaction costs. The cost of including provisions specifying the preferred insider trading rule in the corporate charter or in employment contracts is insignificant (Carlton and Fischel, 1983). One could argue that the enforcement costs of such contracts are high, but this is a separate issue unless one can show that all companies have attempted to limit insider trading by contract. Otherwise, a uniform legal rule banning inside trading displaces efficient private contracts with inefficient regulatory solutions (Carlton and Fischel, 1983). First, the cost-effectiveness of enforcement by a governmental body is never shown. Second, even if it is more efficient to enforce a ban on insider trading by such a supervisory authority, this does not prevent individual companies from customizing their own rules (Haddock and Macey, 1986b).

Being a simple application of the Coase theorem, companies and managers have the strong incentive to allocate the property right in valuable information to its highest value user (Fischel, 1984). As such the distribution of the gains from inside information should be a matter of contract (Macey, 1999). In this way, regulating the use of inside information is simply an applied executive compensation problem[39]. Regulating the use of inside information in a contractual nature, allows companies to specify which 'insiders' may trade on private information and which not, because a company might want to prohibit some individuals, but not others, from trading on the same information (Fischel, 1984). For instance, a company might want managers to trade, but not lawyers, accountants or consultants. Or, it might choose to exclude members of the board of directors to trade on inside information. Moreover, it allows companies to specify in the contract on what type of private information insiders may trade or

---

[38] Historically, companies have made little or no attempt to prohibit insider trading (Carlton and Fischel, 1983). Or as Manne (1985, 940) puts it: "Clearly the overwhelming number of companies, when they were perfectly free to contract their way into such a rule, did not do so. This failure of corporations to design internal rules against insider trading could not have been an accident or oversight." The behaviour of companies suggests that insider trading may be beneficial (Fischel, 1984). However, this does not mean that insider trading will be beneficial in all situations (see infra).

[39] As we have shown earlier problems of using insider trading as an executive compensation scheme are no more severe than they are with other forms of aggressive compensation devices such as ESOs.

not. For instance, a company might want managers to trade on private information, except on information related to an impending merger or acquisition.

Haddock and Macey (1986a) show that allocation to the highest valued user depends on the identity of the next-best information processor. As we have seen in the previous section, four market actors have to be distinguished: corporate insiders, market professionals, dominant shareholders and small shareholders. Depending on who is the next-best information processor after the insiders determines whether the property rights are assigned to the corporate insiders or to the shareholders. So, again, the key question is who captures the benefits when insiders cannot. As we already saw in the previous section, in companies with widely dispersed share ownership, it will mostly be market professionals who will capture the gains from the new information when insider trading is banned. Neither the insiders nor the small shareholders will benefit from this rule. So a ban on insider trading is not beneficial to small shareholders. It is therefore better to allocate the property rights to the corporate insiders. Allowing them to trade benefits shareholders in the form of reduced fixed salary obligations to the corporate insiders and the enhanced shareholder value creation and innovation by the equity-linked compensation scheme (Haddock and Macey, 1986b).[40] Similar conclusions can be drawn from the model in Zhang (2001), which suggests that insiders can be allowed to trade on private information so long as this trading also brings benefits to shareholders. These benefits result from a better shareholder control over corporate decisions because insider trading is a useful mechanism to convey managerial private information. In order for this mechanism to operate properly, two conditions must be satisfied. First, the insider is required to report his trading activity, and second, he is prohibited from profiting by making short-term reversals of his trading position.

However, Haddock and Macey (1986a) indicate situations where it is more likely to assign the property rights to the shareholders instead of the insiders.[41] Such a situation arises when shareholders are the next-best information processors. This is the case of dominant shareholders who closely monitor the company. When profits from trading on inside information (when insiders are banned) is likely to exceed the benefits from fixed salary reduction, dominant shareholders will prefer a ban on insider trading by corporate insiders. They show that this will be especially the case if insiders are more risk-averse because the inside trading profits are less certain, thereby more unwilling to give up a fixed salary. So, depending on the next-best information processor,

---

[40] This substitution effect between explicit fixed salaries of managers and insider trading opportunities is also reported in the model of Noe (1997). Thus by allowing insider trading shareholders provide lower fixed compensation packages.
[41] The model of Hu and Noe (2001) also predicts situations where shareholders and insiders will benefit from insider trading.

insiders and shareholders will reach an arrangement that would make both sides better off.

However, one aspect is ignored by Haddock and Macey (1986a) when assigning property rights to dominant shareholders when they are the next-best information processors. Dominant shareholders can opt for a ban on insider trading at the expense of small shareholders. In this way, corporate governance problems between dominant and small shareholders may arise. This aspect is also recognized in the model of Maug (2000), where dominant shareholders and managers collude at the expense of small shareholders.[42]

Given the property rights perspective, a default rule that allows insider trading by corporate insiders could be considered. Realizing that sometimes shareholders would prefer a more efficient arrangement, i.e. a ban on insider trading, companies can contract around this default rule. In this way companies can opt out of this default rule and ban trading on private information by its corporate insiders. Ultimately, it is up to the companies to decide whether they want to allow or prohibit insider trading. Given the contractual nature of this agreement, it allows maximum flexibility to determine which insiders under what conditions may trade on private information. To make this system transparent to investors, companies should be obliged to disclose whether they allow their insiders to trade on private information and under what conditions.

4. CONCLUSION

Insider trading has a bad reputation. It is often blindly assumed that insider trading is harmful and should therefore be banned. However, balancing the pros and cons of insider trading, an economic analysis of trading on private information reveals that the detrimental effects, attributed by this dogmatic view, are questionable, to say the least.[43] The social gains from informationally efficient capital markets must be stressed. The more accurately prices reflect information, the better prices guide capital

---

[42] Although not in the same context and in my opinion leading to erroneous conclusions. This paper alleges that a uniform rule banning insider trading is in the interest of small investors because otherwise, dominant shareholders and managers will collude at the expense of small shareholders. However, the crucial assumption of his models rests on the premise that information is equally distributed among all market participants if insider trading is banned. As we have shown extensively, this is an unrealistic assumption. Furthermore, the role of market professionals is ignored. Once one recognizes the models' shortcomings, the conclusions no longer hold.

[43] Are small investors brainwashed to believe that a prohibition of insider trading benefits them, while in reality some private interest groups capture the benefits? As Haddock and Macey (1987) put it: "One might suspect that the barrage of public statements and news stories emanating from the SEC are intended in part to discredit and deflect ordinary citizens' attention from the ongoing academic debate about [legalizing] insider trading (p.324)."

investment in the economy (allocative efficiency). Moreover, it creates an additional signalling device for management to communicate complex news in a credible way. Another important social benefit from insider trading is the market-based compensation scheme, which enables innovative and entrepreneurial inputs of corporate insiders to be rewarded. Moreover, investor confidence is not expected to decline; empirical studies revealed no decrease of market liquidity and it was shown that the insider's non-informed counterpart was not harmed.

If insider trading is not harmful, why isn't it allowed? Legalization seems to be in the public interest. The public choice perspective offers a possible explanation. A ban on insider trading is beneficial to market professionals because they are the market participants who are next in line for the information processing channel and will benefit from the valuable new information at the expense of small shareholders. Insider trading laws are in reality a device to distribute resources, i.e. valuable information, among competing interest groups.

Given our goal for efficient deterrence, being the minimization of expected net social cost of a crime, an economist will be eager to conclude that social welfare will increase either by reducing enforcement effort, or by eliminating insider trading regulation. It appears that we do not need a uniform rule banning insider trading. However, we do not support a uniform rule allowing insider trading, because it all depends on the identity of the next-best information processor.

Given the above conclusions and the property rights perspective in this chapter, a default rule that allows insider trading by corporate insiders could be considered. Realizing that sometimes shareholders would prefer a more efficient arrangement, i.e. a ban on insider trading, companies would be permitted to contract around this default rule. If companies chose to do so they could opt out of this default rule and ban trading on private information by its corporate insiders. Companies have to disclose this choice publicly. If dominant shareholders and managers would collude at the expense of small shareholders, the latter can vote 'by their feet' and alter their portfolios in favour of companies that did not opt out of the default rule. Once companies opt for a ban of insider trading, the choice of private (by the company itself) or public (by a governmental body) enforcement is a practical one based on cost efficiency grounds.

CHAPTER 6
DETECTING INSIDER TRADING –
A CLINICAL STUDY

0. INTRODUCTION

While the previous chapter analysed the pros and cons of prohibiting insider trading, this chapter analyses problems of detecting insider trading. This chapter will illustrate several difficulties in prohibiting and prosecuting insider trading by using a clinical study of the Belgian industrial company *Bekaert, NV*.[1] Up to now, no economic analysis of this case has ever been conducted in literature. Although a clinical study cannot resolve all aspects of regulating and prosecuting insider trading, several interesting conclusions can be drawn which were previously undocumented.

On February 22, 1994, Belgian national television reported on criminal prosecutions in the very first Belgian insider trading case. The suspicious transaction in 1992 included shares of the Belgian industrial company *Bekaert, NV*. Being the first insider trading case in Belgium, the financial press in particular paid a lot of attention to it. Insider trading has been prohibited in Belgium since 1989.[2]

---

[1]   First Instance Criminal Court of Ghent [27 September 1995], *Bank- en Financiewezen*, 1995, vol. 9, 535-538. Besides the Bekaert case only one other criminal insider trading case was pronounced in Belgium, i.e. the Bemat case. An accountant of the Bemat company acting on inside information was convicted to 50,000 Belgian francs. See: First Instance Criminal Court of Charleroi [27 September 1995], *Bank- en Financiewezen*, 1995, vol.9, 539. Being a very small case with little or no legal or economic aspects, we chose Bekaert as a case-study. Recently a third insider trading case was pronounced. See First Instance Criminal Court of Ghent [18 December 2002], *Bank- en Financieel Recht*, 2003, 53-57. For a legal analysis of this case, see Engelen (2003b).

[2]   Incorporation of Article 509-4 into the Belgian Criminal Code. See Article 27 of the Statute of 9 March 1989 modifying the Commercial Code and the Royal Decree No.185 of 9 July 1935 on Bank Control and on the Issuance of Transferable Securities, *Belgian Gazette*, 9 June 1989, erratum, *Belgian Gazette*, 27 June 1989. In consequence of European Directive 89/592/EEC of 13 November 1989 for the Coordination of the Regulations of Insider Trading, OJ, L334/30, the regulation of insider trading was rewritten in Part V (Art.181-193) of the Statute of 4 December 1990 on Financial Transactions and Financial Markets, *Belgian Gazette*, 22 December 1990, erratum, *Belgian Gazette*, 1 February 1991, modified by the Statute of 6 April 1995 on the Secondary Markets, the Status and Supervision of Investment Firms, Intermediaries and Advisers, *Belgian Gazette*, 3 June 1995 [*in short: SFTFM*]. This Statute, which came into force on 1 January 1991, replaced the former insider trading regulation of Article 509-4 of the Belgian Criminal Code. Again, as a consequence of a European Directive (Directive 2003/6/EC of the European Parliament and of the Council of 28 January 2003 on Insider

The chapter is organized as follows. Section one contains a brief overview of the Bekaert company, while section two summarizes the facts. Section three contains a brief legal analysis of the Bekaert case. The next section analyses this case from an economic point of view. We will demonstrate that by acquitting both accused the Court of Appeal correctly decided on this insider trading case, although for the wrong reasons. We will show that despite the fundamental difference between the First Instance Criminal Court and the Court of Appeal, both courts have much in common, i.e. they appear to have a complete lack of knowledge about the financial markets. Section four will therefore provide an economic analysis of this case. We will demonstrate that it is impossible to formulate legal rules on insider trading without some understanding of the economic consequences of different kinds of actions. Without a clear understanding of financial economics, there is a good chance that the courts' legal analysis will be reduced to a recitation of clichés lacking any analytical content such as "the information was privileged because the stock price increased after the public announcement of the interim dividend".[3] Because both criminal courts seem to lack a good understanding of the nature of financial markets, it is doubtful that their decisions give much guidance to future litigants. Section four will therefore offer such a framework. It examines the privileged character of the information and analyses the problem of the burden of proof. Section five contains the conclusions.

1. THE BEKAERT COMPANY

Formed in 1880 by Leo Leander Bekaert, Bekaert N.V. quickly became the largest independent manufacturer of wire, wire products and steel cord.[4] It started its international expansion in the 1920s, first in Western Europe, and after World War II, in Latin America (1950s) and North America (1970s). By 1992 the company exploited 48 manufacturing facilities in fifteen countries, such as the United States, Brazil, Australia, the U.K., Ecuador and Japan.[5] Besides manufacturing facilities, Bekaert also had 28 worldwide sales offices, including China, Canada and the U.S. Since the 1950s, steel cord for rubber reinforcement, used chiefly in radial tyres, has been a major determinant of company growth. In 1992 the Bekaert group, compromising the consolidated companies and participating interests, achieved a turnover of

---

Dealing and Market Manipulation (Market Abuse), *OJ*, L 96/16, 12 April 2003 – in short: the *Market Abuse Directive* or *MAD*), this regulation was recently rewritten in Article 40 of the Statute of 2 August 2002 on the Supervision on the Financial Sector and the Financial Services, *Belgian Gazette*, 4 September 2002 (edition 2). The Statute came into force on 1 June 2003. See Article 1 of the Royal Decree of 3 April 2003, *Belgian Gazette*, 29 April 2003.

[3]   First Instance Criminal Court of Ghent [27 September 1995], *Bank- en Financiewezen*, 1995, vol. 9, 537.

[4]   Bekaert Group, *Annual report*, 1992, p.3.

[5]   Bekaert Group, *Annual report*, 1991, p.19.

EUR 1.31 billion and a consolidated profit of EUR 67.23 million. By the end of 1992 the Bekaert group had a workforce of 11,087 employees. The key figures of the company for that period are summarized in table 6.1.

Table 6.1. Key financial figures for Bekaert, NV (consolidated), in million euro[a]

Year (31/12/XX)	1992	1991	1990
Total assets	1,501	1,477	1,488
Equity	632	585	589
Turnover	1,319	1,313	1,413
Operating result	57	10	31
Net result	67	(16)	(11)
Net dividend per ordinary share	6.20	2.48	2.48
Price of ordinary share on 31 Dec.	334.66	226.33	185.18

[a] except the net dividend and the stock price
Source: Bekaert Group, Annual report, 1992, 1991, 1990

By the end of the 1980s and the early 1990s market conditions aggravated as a result of the recession in the United States (especially due to the decreasing demand for cars and increasing competition among tyre manufacturers) and Europe, the collapse in demand from the former Eastern bloc, decline in demand in the Middle-East because of the Gulf War and difficulties in the Brazilian economy.[6] The combination of these factors brought about a net loss of EUR 11 and EUR 16 million in 1990 and 1991 respectively (compared to net positive result of EUR 100 and EUR 91 million for 1988 and 1989 respectively). To turn around these financial difficulties, the company announced major restructuring programmes such as the 'breakthrough'-programme in its steel cord division and the restructuring of its wire division in Europe.[7] To finance these restructuring programmes without an increase of its capital, Bekaert was forced to cut back its dividend from EUR 7.44 in 1989 to EUR 2.48 in 1990, promising to raise the dividend back to its normal level as soon as possible.[8]

Being of crucial importance for the success of Bekaert since the 1950s, the company invested heavily in the manufacturing of steel cord for rubber reinforcement in radial tyres. It therefore established a joint venture with *Bridgestone*, a local Japanese player at that moment, to manufacture steel cord for the tyre industry. After the acquisition

---

[6] Bekaert Group, *Annual report*, 1990, p.2, 1991, p.8.
[7] Bekaert Group, *Annual report*, 1991, p.9.
[8] Bekaert Group, *Annual report*, 1990, p.7 and testimony of Karel Vinck, CEO, during the Bekaert trial. See also "Karel Vinck getuige op proces Storme-Bekaert" [*Eng.: Karel Vinck, CEO, witness at Storme-Bekaert trial*], *De Financieel Economische Tijd*, 23 February 1995.

of *Firestone*, Bridgestone became the third most important tyre manufacturer worldwide. Because the production of steel cord for tyres accounted for 80% of Bekaert's production and because other tyre manufacturers objected to the collaboration between Bekaert and Bridgestone, the company already decided on its 1991 General Meeting of Shareholders to review its collaboration with Bridgestone.[9] In order to maintain its independence and competitive position vis-à-vis all tyre manufacturers, Bekaert and Bridgestone decided to list their joint-venture (*Bridgestone-Bekaert Steel Cord Co., Ltd.*) as an independent company on the second market of the Japanese stock exchange.[10] Bekaert would sell a stake of 12.75% to Japanese investors in 1992 and sell its remaining shares afterwards on the stock exchange during 1993. The sale of the 12.75% stake in Bridgestone-Bekaert Steel Cord realized capital gains of EUR 26 million.[11] Because of this extraordinary profit, the company decided to distribute an interim dividend of EUR 2.48 in December 1992. It was precisely around the announcement of this interim dividend that the alleged insider trading occurred. The account of the facts is outlined in the next section.

2. THE ACCOUNT OF THE FACTS

There were two suspects in this criminal insider trading case. The first accused, being a great-granddaughter of the company founder, had been a member of the board of directors of Bekaert since 1991. Her spouse was the second accused. Because the company realized a capital gain of EUR 26 million on the sale of their Bridgestone-Bekaert Steel Cord stocks, the board of directors discussed the possibility of distributing an interim dividend for the first time during the board meeting of November 20, 1992.[12] The formal decision to distribute an interim dividend of EUR 2.48 was taken on December 18, 1992 by the board of directors, of which the first accused was a member. News that this interim dividend would be distributed was released on December 21 after the closing of the Brussels Stock Exchange and appeared in the financial press on the following day. On December 21 the stock price rose from its opening price of EUR 312.97 to its closing price of EUR 337.14, being 3.17% higher than its opening price or 3.37% higher than its previous close. The next day, Bekaert stock opened at EUR 330.94 and closed at EUR 337.14, while the total volume accounted 5,410 and 5,640 stocks on December 21 and December 22 respectively.

---

[9] Bekaert Group, *Annual report*, 1991, p.9.

[10] "Bekaert stapt uit Japanse joint venture met Bridgestone" [*Eng.: Bekaert leaves its Japanese joint venture with Bridgestone*], *De Financieel Economische Tijd*, 21 March 1992 and Bekaert, *Annual report*, 1992, p.19-20.

[11] The realized capital gains accounted for over 56% of the extraordinary profits (EUR 46 million) in 1992. Excluding these capital gains the net result would decrease by 27.3%. See consolidated profit and loss statement of 1992 in Bekaert, *Annual report*, 1992, p.36-37.

[12] Testimony of Karel Vinck, CEO, during the Bekaert trial. See also Court of Appeal of Ghent [30 April 1997] (1997) *Bank- en Financiewezen*, 414.

The Belgian Banking and Finance Commission (BFC), being the supervisory authority on the Brussels Stock Exchange in 1992, continuously monitored price and volume patterns and apparently started an investigation because of the price and volume behaviour of the Bekaert stock.[13] Investigating a period of three weeks before the announcement of the distribution of the interim dividend, the BFC detected a stock order of 400 Bekaert shares on December 21 for EUR 128,859 on the account of *NV Batibo*.[14] In this company, the second accused is the delegated director and holds the majority of the shares. Because the purchase by the second accused occurred one day before the official announcement of the distribution of the interim dividend and because he was married to the first accused, who was a member of the board of directors that decided on the interim dividend, insider trading was suspected and both faced criminal prosecution. The alleged information processing channel is summarized in figure 6.1.

Figure 6.1. Alleged information processing channel

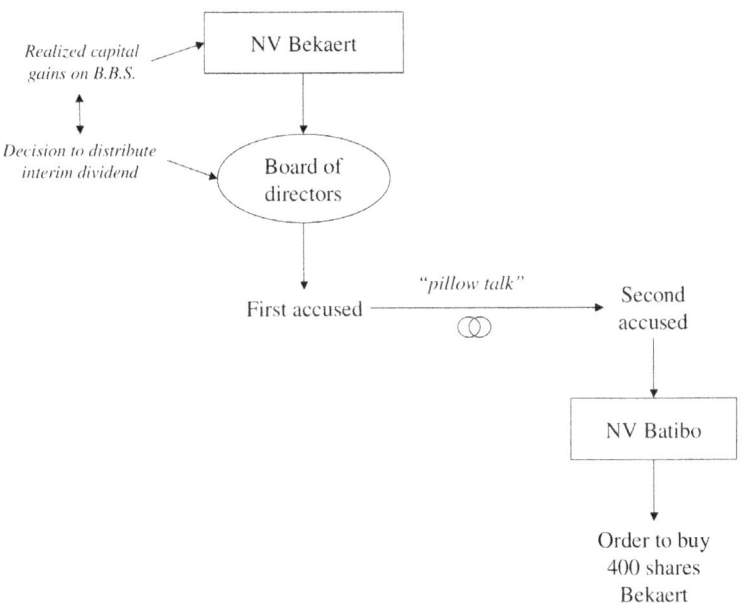

13 Court of Appeal of Ghent [30 April 1997], *Bank- en Financiewezen*, 1997, 413.
14 First Instance Criminal Court of Ghent [27 September 1995], *Bank- en Financiewezen*, 1995, vol.9, 536.

3. BRIEF LEGAL ANALYSIS OF THE BEKAERT CASE

The first accused faced criminal charges based on articles 182 and 183 SFTFM.[15] Article 182 SFTFM prohibits persons who, by virtue of their membership of the administrative, management or supervisory bodies of the issuer, possess information that they know or could reasonably be expected to know that it is privileged (the so-called primary insiders) to acquire or transfer, for their own account or for the account of a third party, either directly or indirectly, securities or other financial instruments relating to this information. Moreover, article 183 SFTFM also prohibits the disclosure of the privileged information to third parties (unless such disclosure is made in the normal course of the exercise of their employment, profession or duties) or recommendations to third parties to acquire, dispose of, or make a third party acquire or dispose of securities or other financial instruments on the basis of that privileged information. The first accused was therefore charged with the crime of tipping the privileged information to her spouse, the second accused.

The second accused who made the actual purchase of the Bekaert shares based on the alleged privileged information, could not be qualified as a primary insider according to article 182 SFTFM. The second accused did not possess any privileged information either by virtue of membership of the administrative, management or supervisory bodies of Bekaert, by virtue of a holding in the capital of Bekaert or by virtue of the exercise of any employment, profession or duties (Engelen, 1999). Consequently, the second accused had to be prosecuted on the grounds of article 184 SFTFM that states that the prohibition laid down in articles 182 and 183 SFTFM is applicable to any person, other than those referred to in these articles, who with full knowledge possesses information that he knows or is reasonably expected to know that it is privileged and comes directly or indirectly from a person referred to in article 182 or 183 SFTFM. For the second accused to be liable to criminal prosecution under article 184 SFTFM as a secondary insider, three conditions must be satisfied: (1) to possess the information with full knowledge, (2) to know or reasonably be expected to know that the information is privileged and (3) to know or reasonably be expected to know that the information comes directly or indirectly from a primary insider.

The two accused were convicted by the First Instance Criminal Court of Ghent because the first accused by virtue of her membership of the board of directors of Bekaert clearly knew or could reasonably be expected to know that the announcement of the

---

[15] Statute of 4 December 1990 on Financial Transactions and Financial Markets, *Belgian Gazette*, 22 December 1990, erratum, *Belgian Gazette*, 1 February 1991, modified by the Statute of 6 April 1995 on the Secondary Markets, the Status and Supervision of Investment Firms, Intermediaries and Advisers, *Belgian Gazette*, 3 June 1995 [*in short: SFTFM*].

distribution of an interim dividend was privileged information and that it was abundantly clear that the first accused had communicated this privileged information to the second accused, who subsequently bought Bekaert shares with full knowledge of information that he knew or was reasonably expected to know to be privileged. The criminal court therefore imposed the following sanctions: an imprisonment of three months with delay, professional restrictions on board functions, a fine of EUR 12,395 and a triple disgorgement of EUR 44,620.

However, the Court of Appeal acquitted both accused.[16] According to the Court of Appeal it is not sufficient to identify the persons involved with insider trading; the link between the trader and the information has to be demonstrated as well. In this case, the Court of Appeal applied a very difficult burden of proof. Although both the First Instance Criminal Court and the Court of Appeal demonstrated that a member of the Board of Directors of Bekaert possessed material non-public information and demonstrated that her husband bought stocks of this company, both courts reached a different conclusion. While the First Instance Criminal Court judged that the link between the trader and the information was proven, the Court of Appeal reversed this decision. According to the Court of Appeal, "this was a serious presumption, but this presumption in itself is insufficient to satisfy the burden of proof of insider trading, unless this was supported by other facts or presumptions."[17]

4. AN ECONOMIC ANALYSIS OF THE BEKAERT CASE

While the previous section contains a legal analysis of the Bekaert case, this section analyses this case from an economic point of view, for one cannot avoid the impression that both courts had a complete lack of knowledge of the functioning of financial markets. Section 4.1 starts with examining the privileged character of the information. Next, section 4.2 analyses the problem of the burden of proof.

4.1. PRIVILEGED CHARACTER OF THE INFORMATION

According to criminal law, if one of the constituent parts of the criminal offence is lacking, the accused can be acquitted of the charge of insider trading by the court without further investigation of any other elements of the criminal case (Van den Wyngaert, 1999). Consequently, the court's first task is to determine whether the

---

[16]   Court of Appeal of Ghent [30 April 1997], *Bank- en Financiewezen*, 1997, 413.
[17]   Court of Appeal of Ghent [30 April 1997], *Bank- en Financiewezen*, 1997, 414.

information is privileged or not. The accused's acts should only be investigated when this question has been answered affirmatively by the court. However, neither the First Instance Criminal Court, nor the Court of Appeal explicitly investigated the privileged character of the information. This is truly a lost opportunity because financial economics offers a clear theoretical framework and adequate empirical instruments to assess explicitly whether the information is privileged or not.

By using an event study approach, one can determine how security prices react to new information. In this way event study methodology clearly fits the definition of the criminal offence. According to article 181 SFTFM, 'privileged information' is any information of a sufficiently precise nature relating to one or several issuers of securities or other financial instruments, which has not been made public and, if it were made public, *would be likely to have a significant effect on the price listed* for these securities. By examining the causal connection between the information that the first accused possessed by virtue of her membership of the board of directors and the purchase by the second accused, both courts implicitly assumed the information on the distribution of an interim dividend had a significant effect on the listed price. Because an explicit investigation of the privileged character of the information is a necessity, this section offers theoretical as well as empirical instruments for determining whether there was any privileged information or not.

The question if any piece of information is price-sensitive cannot be answered on an a priori basis and can never be answered in the abstract. As the current legal literature offers little guidance for determining whether the information is price-sensitive or not, there is a danger that some information may at first sight appear to be important to investors when in fact it is not. Only a clinical analysis of the case can show whether the information is price-sensitive or not.

4.1.1. Theoretical considerations

From an economic point of view, information can be considered to be privileged if it has a significant effect on the market price of the security once the information is made public. Chapter two showed that if security prices are semi-strong informationally efficient with regard to some pieces of information, stock prices will reflect all publicly available information and react instantaneously to the disclosure of new non-public information (Fama, 1970 and 1991). Consequently, the relevant question is whether the announcement contained some value-relevant information to investors. What piece of *new* information was disclosed by announcing the distribution of an interim dividend of EUR 2.48?

Section one showed that Bekaert decided to distribute an interim dividend of EUR 2.48 in December because of the realization of the extraordinary profit on the sale of its participation in Bridgestone-Bekaert Steel Cord (BBS). However, as section one showed, the company already decided at its 1991 General Meeting of Shareholders to review collaboration with Bridgestone in order to maintain its independency and competitive position vis-à-vis all tyre manufacturers. Following this decision Bekaert announced the sale of its participation in Bridgestone-Bekaert Steel Cord on March 21, 1992 (see BBS-news in figure 6.2). Because these facts were publicly known well before the announcement of the distribution of the interim dividend on December 21, this information could be expected to have already been incorporated in the security price of Bekaert. Although one could argue that the exact capital gain was not known before the announcement, financial markets had a very good idea of the value of the participation based on the financial statements of Bridgestone-Bekaert Steel Cord. Furthermore, Bekaert had already sold a 12% participation in Bridgestone-Bekaert Steel Cord to its Dutch daughter *Bekaert Holding B.V.* in 1990 realizing a capital gain of EUR 42 million at that time.[18] All this information was available in public documents and therefore already reflected in security prices.

Figure 6.2. Daily closing stock prices and volumes for Bekaert from January 1992 to June 1993

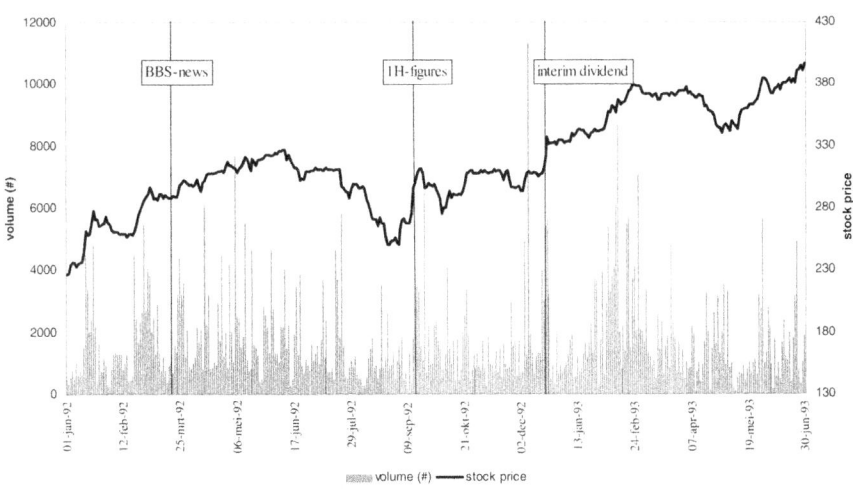

Moreover, a companies' dividend policy is irrelevant with respect to the value of a company (Brealey and Meyers, 2000)[19]. Distributing a dividend therefore creates no

---

[18]   Bekaert, *Annual report*, 1990, p.3 and 1991, p.16.
[19]   Assuming perfect and efficient capital markets, Miller and Modigliani (1961) show that the dividend policy does not affect the company's value. Dividend policy is therefore said to be irrelevant. So the dividend controversy comes down to the existence of market imperfections such as taxes or

value to investors. This can be illustrated by means of an example. Assume a company starts with a capital of EUR 1,000,000, represented by 1,000 shares. After one year, the company realizes after-tax earnings of EUR 200,000. The company has several options: distribute the profits as a cash dividend, retain the earnings inside the company, distribute the earnings by way of a stock dividend or repurchase some of its own shares. If the company decides to distribute all of its earnings as a cash dividend, the shareholders as a group receive EUR 200,000, while the value of the company is EUR 1,000,000 at the end of the year. If it retains all of the earnings, the company's value increases from EUR 1,000,000 at the beginning of the year to EUR 1,200,000 at the end of the year. In an efficient market the stock price will rise from EUR 1,000 to 1,200. As can be seen, shareholders will be indifferent about receiving a cash dividend of EUR 200 or a capital gain of EUR 200.[20]

Alternately, the company can distribute a stock dividend to its shareholders, e.g. issue 200 new shares to its existing shareholders. In this case, the value of the company is still EUR 1,200,000, represented by 1,200 shares with a stock price of EUR 1,000. Finally, the company can decide to repurchase its own shares, e.g. at an offer price of EUR 1,200. Using the earnings of EUR 200,000 it would be possible to buy back 166.67 shares. In this way, a shareholder will realize a capital gain of EUR 200, while the company value is equal to 833.33 times EUR 1,200 or EUR 1,000,000. Again, this is the same value as the cash dividend case. Therefore, the choice between retaining the realized capital gains inside the company and the distribution through an interim dividend is basically irrelevant to Bekaert shareholders. Announcing the decision to distribute of the interim dividend had no value-relevance.

---

transaction costs. Proponents of the personal tax hypothesis argue that dividend policy does matter. They argue that shareholders will prefer companies not to pay dividends as long as the personal tax rate on income received in the form of dividends is greater than the personal tax rate on capital gains. It is more beneficial for shareholders to realize capital gains or to be paid out through share repurchases. This means that for a given company, stock prices will be higher than a situation in which they pay out dividends. Put differently, high-dividend yield stocks tend to sell at lower prices (Brealey and Myers, 2000). See on the tax hypothesis also Farrar and Selwyn (1967), Brennan (1970), Litzenberger and Ramaswamy (1979) and Litzenberger and Ramaswamy (1982). Shareholders who need cash can always sell off a fraction of their holdings. If anything, investors in Belgium would prefer capital gains over dividends, given the tax rates in Belgium. In that case, distributing a dividend would be bad news. However, several studies such as Black and Scholes (1974), Miller and Scholes (1978) and Miller (1986) demonstrate that, in equilibrium, the dividend payouts of companies match the preferences of investors, and no company would be able to affect its share price by altering its dividend policy. Therefore, even with taxes, dividend policy is irrelevant.

[20] Ignoring tax effects and transaction costs, although see supra the remarks in previous note.

Figure 6.3. Net dividends per share of Bekaert, NV

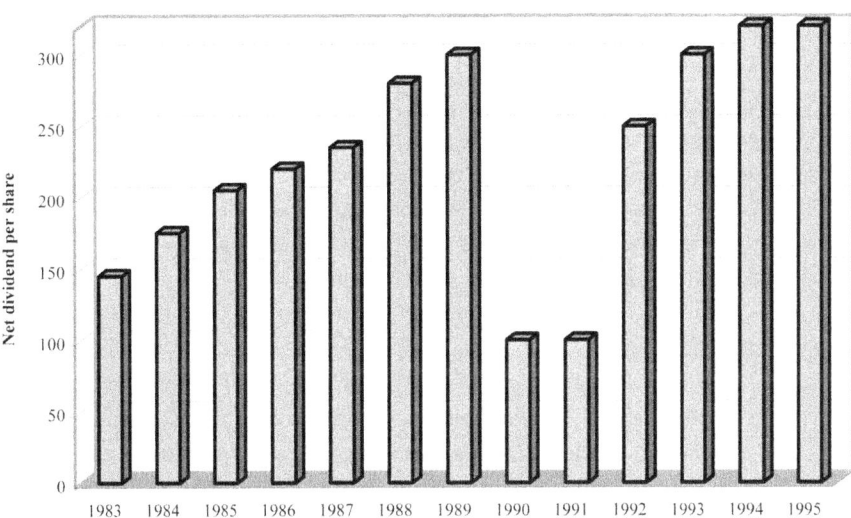

Source: Bekaert Group, *Annual reports*

As the choice of distributing the extraordinary profits is irrelevant, the only news the announcement of the interim dividend could contain is that it signals better future performances.[21] As put forward in section one, Bekaert decided to cut back its dividend from EUR 6.20 in 1989 to EUR 2.48 in 1990 because of financial difficulties and, at the same time, it promised to raise the dividend back to its normal level as soon as possible.[22] The announcement to distribute an interim dividend of EUR 2.48 could therefore signal that Bekaert's performance was improving. Again, this does not seem to be the case because Bekaert already released the information on improved performance during the announcement of its half-year figures on September 14, 1992 (see 1H-figures in figure 6.2).[23] Besides, an extraordinary one-time dividend would signal little about the evolution of ordinary profits[24].

Finally, the interim dividend, being equal to EUR 2.48 for common stocks, was only a fraction of the realized capital gains on the sale of the participation. Given a total of 2,245,732 outstanding shares, the realized capital gain per share amounts EUR 11.60.

---

[21]   A number of empirical studies report that increases in dividends lead to positive abnormal returns, while decreases lead to negative abnormal returns. See Eades, Hess and Kim (1985), Healy and Palepu (1988), Lang and Litzenberger (1989), Kao and Wu (1994) and Michaely, Thaler and Womack (1995).

[22]   Bekaert Group, *Annual report*, 1990, p.7.

[23]   "Hoge verwachtingen worden ingelost. Bekaert vervijfvoudigt halfjaarwinst" [*Eng.: High expectations are met. Bekaert's first-half profits increase fivefold*], *De Financieel Economische Tijd*, September, 15 1992.

[24]   Excluding these capital gains the net result would decrease by 27.3%. See also note 11.

Also the interim dividend of EUR 2.48 is only 0.77% of the closing price of EUR 322.88 on December 21. It is therefore unlikely that the mere announcement to distribute part of the capital gains through an interim dividend would cause a significant price increase.

Based on the above theoretical considerations, it is therefore very unlikely that the distribution of an interim dividend caused a raw return of 4.32% (or an abnormal return of 2.61%) on December 22.[25] The only possible conclusion based on financial economic principles is that the announcement on December, 21 did not contain any value-relevant information and therefore was not privileged.

4.1.2. Empirical analysis

While the previous section analysed the value-relevance of announcing the distribution of the interim dividend on theoretical grounds, this section determines whether the price impact of the announcement is significant or not. To test if the stock price return of Bekaert on the day that the announcement was made differs from what the return would have been without the announcement, event study methodology is used (Schweitzer, 1989). An event study measures whether the difference between the actual return on the event day ($R_{i,t}$) and the expected return $E[R_{i,t}]$, or the abnormal return, occurred by chance or not (MacKinlay, 1997). The existence of a significant non-zero abnormal return indicates the release of value-relevant information (Strong, 1992). If this is the case, the information can be labelled as 'privileged'.

Over a period of twenty trading days before and after the event, resulting in a 41-day event window, abnormal returns are calculated to examine the return behaviour around the announcement of the interim dividend in order to determine if there was any price impact and if there was any anticipatory price behaviour resulting from insider trading. Share price data for Bekaert and data on the *Brussels All Share Price Index* were collected from *Datastream*.

Three models are used to measure the benchmark expected return for the Bekaert share: the market model, the market-adjusted model, and the Dimson model[26]. The market model abnormal returns are calculated as:

---

[25]   See infra table 6.2 for the exact calculation of this abnormal return.
[26]   The following variables are used: $AR_{i,t}$ = abnormal return of stock i on day t of the estimation period; $R_{i,t}$ = the return of stock i in period t; $R_{m,t}$ = the market index return in period t; a_i, b_i = intercept and slope coefficient of the market model; $e_{i,t}$ = random disturbance term of the market model for stock i in period t; $b_{k,i}$ = parameters of the Dimson model. Finally, 'OLS' denotes ordinary least squares.

$$AR_{i,t} = R_{i,t} - \left(\hat{a}_i + \hat{b}_i \cdot R_{m,t} \right) \qquad [6.1]$$

where '∧' denotes the OLS estimates from the market model:

$$R_{i,t} = a_i + b_i \cdot R_{m,t} + e_{i,t} \qquad [6.2]$$

In order to calculate market model abnormal returns information from outside the event window is used. The parameters of the market model are estimated over a 100-day period from –21 to –120 trading days before the event day. To test for the robustness of the result for the choice of the estimation window calculations were made using a 150 days and a 200 days estimation window.

Besides the market model abnormal returns, also the market-adjusted abnormal returns are calculated:

$$AR_{i,t} = R_{i,t} - R_{m,t} , \qquad [6.3]$$

Although one can expect the Bekaert shares to be relatively tickly traded because they are listed on the most liquid segment of the Brussels stock exchange, the abnormal returns using Dimson's (1979) methodology to correct for thin trading are reported for the sake of completeness.

According to the Dimson model abnormal returns are calculated as:

$$AR_{i,t} = R_{i,t} - \hat{\alpha}_i^D - \hat{\beta}_i^D \cdot R_{m,t} \qquad [6.4]$$

with

$$\hat{\beta}_i^D = \sum_{k=-2}^{k=+2} \hat{b}_{k,i} , \text{ and} \qquad [6.5]$$

$$\hat{\alpha}_i^D = \frac{1}{96} \sum_{t=-118}^{t=-23} R_{i,t} - \hat{\beta}_i^D \frac{1}{96} \sum_{t=-118}^{t=-23} R_{m,t}$$

The estimation of the Dimson-beta consists of the aggregation of five estimated beta coefficients using two lead and two lag variables from[27]:

$$R_{i,t} = a_i + b_{-2,i} \cdot R_{m,t-2} + b_{-1,i} \cdot R_{m,t-1} + b_{0,i} \cdot R_{m,t} + b_{+1,i} \cdot R_{m,t+1} + b_{+2,i} \cdot R_{m,t+2} + w_{i,t} \qquad [6.6]$$

Next, one has to determine whether the calculated abnormal returns are due to the random variation of the security price of Bekaert or to the announcement of the interim dividend. Using a statistical test, one can determine the probability that the calculated abnormal return occurred by chance or not. Assuming stock returns to be normally distributed, one can calculate the Z-score in order to determine the significance of the abnormal return.[28]

---

[27] Alternatively, the Dimson beta is calculated using one lead and one lag variable.

[28] Brown and Warner (1985) point out that the non-normality of daily returns has no obvious impact on event study methodology, implying that the normal distribution is a good approximation for event studies estimations.

Table 6.2. Abnormal returns for the Bekaert share on December, 21 and 22, 1992

	MM-AR1	MM-AR2	MM-AR3	Market adj	Dimson	Dimson
	100 days	150 days	200 days		2 leads & lags	4 leads & lags
Estimation window	(-21,-120)	(-21,-170)	(-21,-220)	(-21,-120)	(-22,-119)	(-23,-118)
Beta	1.61	1.35	1.34	1	2.16	2.38
Stdev	0.013	0.013	0.012	0.014	0.013	0.014
Day (-1)	2.13%	2.31%	2.25%	2.63%	1.73%	1.61%
Day (0)	2.61%	2.87%	2.81%	3.29%	2.04%	1.85%
Z-value (day -1)	1.655	1.847	1.911	1.946	1.284	1.159
Z-value (day 0)	2.023*	2.289*	2.382*	2.434*	1.510	1.332

Legend:

MM-AR = market model abnormal return

Stdev = standard deviation of abnormal returns over the estimation window

Z-value: test statistic for normal probability distribution

Day (0) denotes December, 22nd and day (-1) denotes December, 21st

** denotes significant at the 1% level

* denotes significant at the 5% level

Table 6.2 reports the abnormal returns for the Bekaert share on 21 and 22 December 1992. Using a significance level of 0.1% or 1%, table 6.2 shows that no abnormal return is significantly different from zero on the announcement day of the interim dividend, nor on the preceding day on which the alleged insider trading took place.[29] Although empirical studies in financial economics use the 1% and the 5% levels of significance, I advise using only the 1% significance level in criminal cases. Given the high standard of proof demanded by criminal law in criminal cases, it is sound advice to only use the 1% significance level in criminal cases (or even the more stringent 0.1% significance level). Using a 1% level of significance, there is a probability of 99% that the abnormal return occurred by chance.[30] As such the empirical results confirm the theoretical analysis. The announcement of the interim dividend was not privileged information within the meaning of article 181 SFTFM.

To finish this section on the privileged character, one can conclude that an economic analysis, both on theoretical grounds as well as on empirical grounds, shows that the

---

[29] Only using a significance level of 5% an abnormal return on the announcement day is detected. However, no abnormal price return is detected on the preceding day.

[30] See also section 4.2 on the choice of the level of significance. It shows that a trade-off has to be made between type I and type II errors. We choose to minimize the type I error, i.e. the conviction of an innocent person. By choosing a 1% level of significance we reduce the number of miscarriages of justice. By choosing a 5% level of significance more innocent people are convicted wrongfully.

announcement of the distribution of the interim dividend was not privileged information. By not examining the privileged character of the information explicitly using financial economics, the likelihood increases that both courts can err in their decision. If this analysis had been made explicitly, both courts could have stopped their investigation immediately and acquitted the accused because a major element of the constituent parts of the criminal offence is lacking.

4.2. BURDEN OF PROOF

As seen in section three, the First Instance Criminal Court and the Court of Appeal reached complete opposite conclusions (conviction versus acquittal) although both examined the same insider trading case. At first sight, one has to conclude that one of the courts has made an error. If both accused were innocent in reality, then the First Instance Criminal Court has made an error. On the other hand, if both accused were guilty in reality, an error has been made by the Court of Appeal (see table 6.3).

Table 6.3. Possible errors in criminal trials

	Reality	
Decision of the court	Innocent	Guilty
Innocent	ok	error
Guilty	error	ok

However, this section will show that such a conclusion does not have to be reached necessarily and that both decisions can be reconcilable depending on the standard of proof a criminal court is willing to apply. This can be seen if we reformulate this problem in statistical terms, i.e. hypothesis testing. Since the true state of the nature is rarely known, hypothesis testing is used to determine whether the value of a certain parameter of a sample of a population is true or merely obtained by chance (Chou, 1989). Suppose a carpenter purchases a lot of timbers of 69 inches.[31] After the delivery, the lot is tested to determine if the length of the timbers is correct. Therefore, out of the lot, 25 timbers are selected at random. The average length (μ) of this sample is 67 inches. Is the difference of two inches due to chance or is the difference significant? To determine this, a so-called null hypothesis, generally denoted as H_0, has to be formulated and tested against an alternative hypothesis, denoted as H_1. In our example we can formulate the hypotheses as:

H_0: μ = 69 inch
H_1: μ < 69 inch

---

[31]   Example based on Gujarati (1995, appendix A.8).

Figure 6.4. Hypothesis testing with a 95% confidence interval for μ

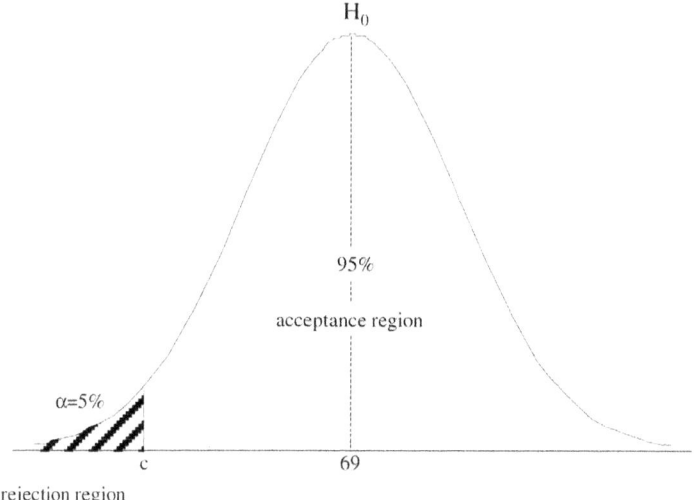

Next, a critical value c has to be established in order to determine whether the difference of two inches is significant or not (see figure 6.4). If the average length of the sample is smaller than c, the carpenter will refuse the lot because of the wrong length. In the opposite case, he will accept the lot. In this case, the difference of two inches was found by chance. The area below c is called the rejection region, while the area outside this region is called the acceptance region. Using a confidence region of 95%, the critical value of c is equal to 64.9.[32]

Similar to the above example, one can formulate a criminal trial in terms of hypotheses. Because the accused is assumed innocent in a criminal trial, the null and alternative hypothesis can be formulated as:

H_0: *innocent*

H_1: *not innocent or guilty*

The criminal trial in terms of hypothesis testing is summarized in figure 6.5. As can be seen in panel b of figure 6.5 different choices of c, which can be interpreted as the standard of proof, lead to different conclusions. Typically the standard of proof in a criminal trial ($c_{crim.}$) is higher than in a civil trial (c_{civil}). However, criminal courts can also reach different conclusions. Suppose the amount of proof is equal to the amount

---

[32]   Assuming a normal distribution and a standard deviation of 2.5 inches, c can be calculated out of: $Z_{5\%} = -1.64 = \dfrac{c - 69}{2.5}$, in which we obtain the value of Z out of the normal distribution table.

X: it is clear from panel b of figure 6.5 that the accused will be convicted by criminal court 1 and acquitted by criminal court 2 ($c_{crim.1} < X < c_{crim.2}$).

Figure 6.5. Hypothesis testing, standard of proof and acceptance region in case of different trials

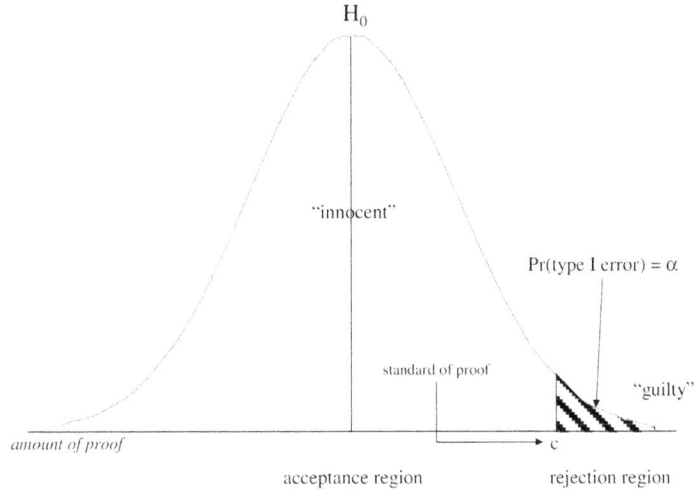

panel a

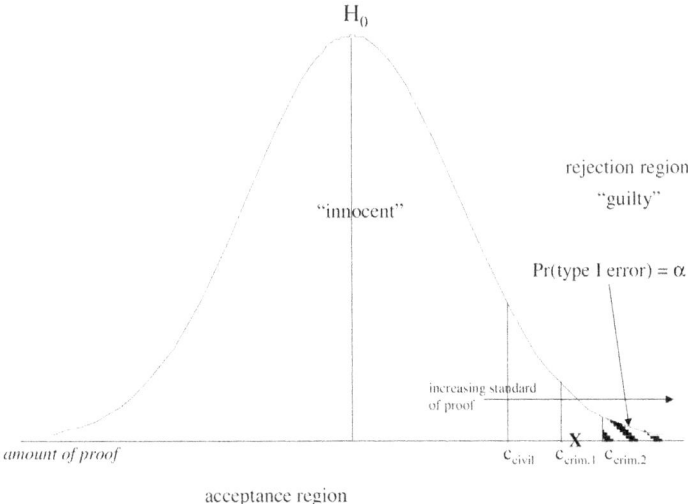

panel b

Before answering the question which court reached the correct conclusion, the level of α has to be determined. With regard to hypothesis testing, two errors can be made: a type I error and a type II error (see table 6.4). A type I error refers to the situation in which the null hypothesis (here: 'the accused is innocent') is rejected when it is true in reality. The probability of type I error amounts to the level of significance α (Chou, 1989). In criminal trial terms, this means that an observation (the accused) is not taken from a certain underlying group (innocent people) when it is really from that group. Consequently, this implies the conviction of an innocent person. A type II error implies that the null hypothesis is not rejected when it is false in reality (probability of type II error is β).[33] Because in this case an observation (the accused) is taken from the underlying group of innocent people while in reality it is from the group of guilty people, a type II error implies the acquittal of a guilty person.

Table 6.4. Possible errors in hypothesis testing

Decision	State of the nature	
	Null hypothesis is true	Alternative hypothesis is true
Accept null hypothesis	ok $Pr(ok) = 1-\alpha$	type II error $Pr(\text{type II error}) = \beta$
Reject null hypothesis	type I error $Pr(\text{type I error}) = \alpha$	ok $Pr(ok) = 1-\beta$

Ideally, one would like to minimize both type I and type II errors. However, this is not possible. Minimizing the probability of type I error (conviction of an innocent person) by making the significance level α small(er), increases at the same time the probability of committing a type II error (acquitting a guilty person) (Kvanli, Guynes and Pavur, 1992). This is illustrated in figure 6.6. By setting the standard of proof (c), the value of α and β is fixed. In turn, by choosing a level of significance α (typically 0.001 or 0.01), the values of c and β are fixed. The court therefore has to make a trade-off between both errors. This choice is not a statistical one but a practical one. In fact, since there is no correct significance level, calibrating this trade-off is ultimately a value judgement based on the costs of incorrectly rejecting the null hypothesis (Larsen and Marx, 1990).

---

[33] The probability of not committing a type II error $(1-\beta)$ is often called the power of the test.

Figure 6.6. Conflict between solving type I and type II errors

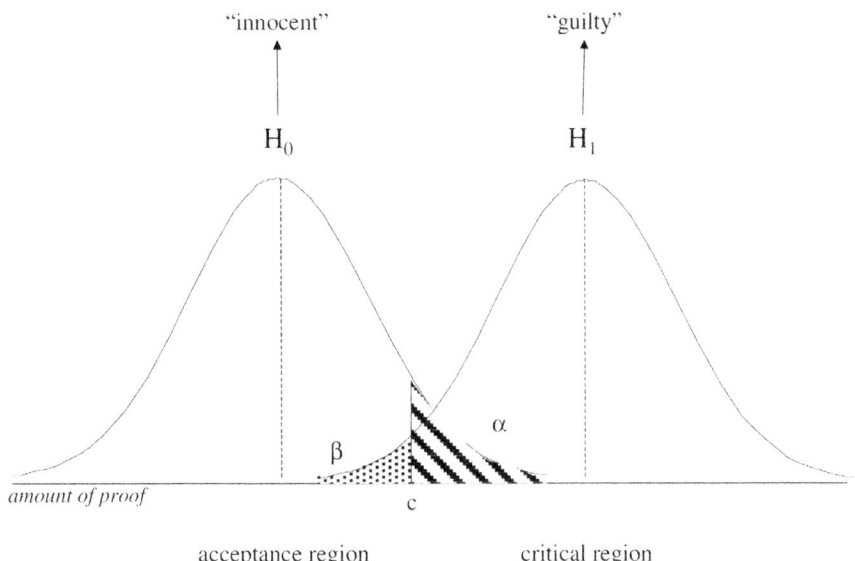

By acquitting both the accused the Court of Appeal implicitly uses a higher level of significance than the First Instance Criminal Court. Figure 6.7 compares both standards of proof. Panel A shows that the First Instance Criminal Court judged that the link between the trader and the information was proven, or as the Court put it: "It is *crystal clear* that the first accused has communicated the privileged information to the second accused."[34] The court based its judgement on the following evidence: the chronology of the facts, the marital status of the two accused, the fact that both accused administrated their assets, including 5,747 Bekaert shares[35], jointly in a public limited company, NV Bekaert Storme Investments (BSI) and the rise of the stock price from EUR 322.88 on December, 21 to EUR 334.67 on December, 31.

---

[34] First Instance Criminal Court of Ghent [27 September 1995], *Bank- en Financiewezen*, 1995, vol.9, 537.

[35] Notification on the basis of article 4 of the Statute of March 2 1989 of 5,747 shares (0.26% of outstanding capital) on June 16 1994. See Bekaert Group, *Annual report*, 1994, 75.

Figure 6.7. Standard of proof applied by the two courts

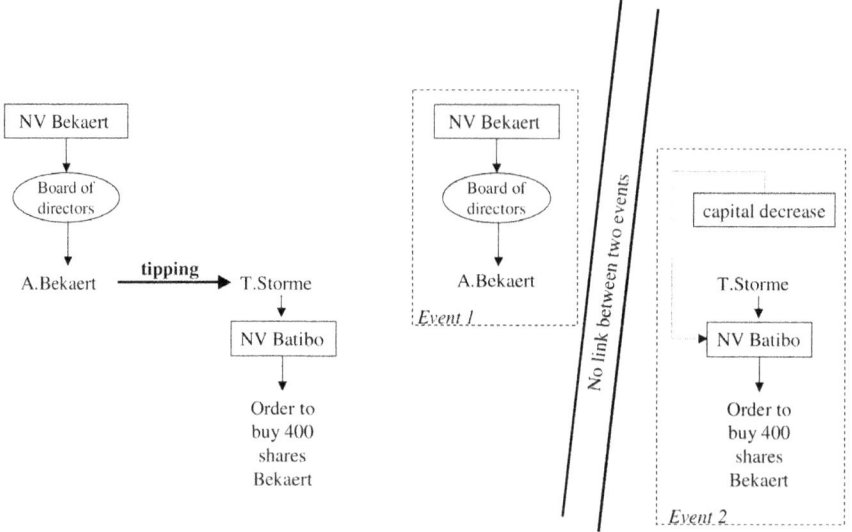

Panel A. First Instance Criminal Court   *Panel B. Court of Appeal*

The Court of Appeal reversed this decision using a higher standard of proof (compare $c_{crim.1}$ and $c_{crim.2}$ in figure 6.5). Although the chronology of the facts and the marital status produce a serious presumption, this presumption in itself is, according to the Court, insufficient to satisfy the standard of proof of insider trading, unless this is supported by other facts or presumptions. According to the Court the participation of the first accused in the meeting of the board of directors of Bekaert deciding on the distribution of the interim dividend and the purchase of Bekaert shares by the second accused are two separate, coinciding events without any link between them (see panel B in figure 6.7).

The Court of Appeal reconstructs the purchase by the second accused quite extensively to conclude that the purchase only coincides with the announcement of the interim dividend[36]. The second accused purchased the shares with funds originating from a decrease of NV Batibo capital. The decision to decrease its capital from EUR 1.74 to 0.99 million was taken at the extraordinary meeting of shareholders on September 24, 1992. This is some considerable time before the meeting of the board of directors of Bekaert of November 20, 1992, during which the idea of distributing an interim

---

[36]   Court of Appeal of Ghent [30 April 1997], *Bank- en Financiewezen*, 1997, 414.

dividend was discussed for the first time and before the meeting of December 18, 1992, during which the formal decision was taken. Therefore, it would be impossible to time Batibo's capital operation in order to obtain funds to trade based on the alleged inside information. Furthermore, it is unlikely that the second accused has timed the actual payment of the funds in order to buy Bekaert shares based on the privileged information, because article 72bis Company Law provides a period of two months after the notice in the Belgian Gazette during which the funds cannot be paid back to the shareholders. Moreover, the Court stipulates that the second accused only invested one third of these funds in Bekaert shares, while he invested the rest in riskless bonds. If he were planning to trade on inside information, he would have bought more stocks and certainly not the day before the announcement of the interim dividend, according to the Court.

Moreover, the Court concluded that neither the number of shares traded on December 21, nor the stock price movement was out of line with previous price and volume patterns on the Brussels stock exchange with regard to Bekaert shares during 1992.

Figure 6.8. Hypothesis testing and standard of proof in determining abnormal returns

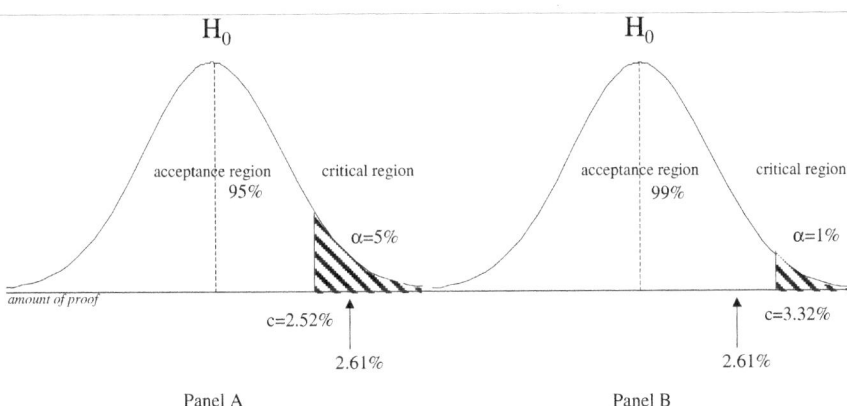

Panel A   Panel B

Again, as seen in the previous section, an economic analysis would reveal that the abnormal returns, using the market model, on 21 and 22 December were 2.13% and 2.61% respectively. In order to determine whether this abnormal return occurs merely by chance or due to announcement of the interim dividend, statistical hypothesis testing is used. Using a high standard of proof, as is the case in a criminal trial and therefore using a 0.1% or a 1% level of significance, on neither day an abnormal return was realized (panel B of figure 6.8). Only using a less stringent standard of proof (e.g. in a civil case) and therefore using a 5% level of significance, an abnormal return on 22 December is detected (panel A of figure 6.8).

5. CONCLUSIONS

This chapter contained a clinical study of the biggest insider trading case in Belgium. Up to now, no economic analysis of this case has ever been conducted. Using a law and economics framework, the Bekaert case study clarifies several aspects compared to a traditional legal analysis. This chapter showed that Belgian courts currently seem to lack knowledge about the functioning of financial markets for assessing an insider trading case. Their decisions therefore provide little guidance to future litigants. The above analysis focused on two aspects of an insider trading case. First, the price-sensitive character of the information must be examined. Current legal literature offers no guidance for determining whether the information is price-sensitive or not. The danger exits that some information may appear to be important when in reality it is not. Only a clinical economic analysis of the case can show whether the information was price-sensitive or not. Using both theoretical models as well as empirical models it was demonstrated that announcement of the distribution of the interim dividend in the Bekaert-case was not privileged information. By not examining the privileged character explicitly, there is a danger that courts may err in their decision, as our analysis showed. Second, the standard of proof was examined. It was shown that the standard of proof has to be linked with statistical hypothesis testing. In such a way, once again, a reliable criterion for determining the standard of proof is established which gives clear guidance for future litigants.

CHAPTER 7
PROSECUTING INSIDER TRADING

0. INTRODUCTION

Chapters five and six analysed insider trading as a strong level of intervention in the trading process. The purpose of insider trading regulations is to prevent trading based on non-public information about a certain firm-specific event that can influence the price of a security. While chapter five analysed the pros and cons of such regulation, chapter six focused on the *Bekaert* case to identify some specific problems. Once the legislator chooses to ban insider trading, the question of the optimal deterrence of insider trading regulations arises.

While Engelen (1997a) analysed the enforcement of insider trading regulation within the classic Becker (1968) model, this chapter elaborates this analysis by including a state-dependent and a rank-dependent expected utility framework. Furthermore, while Engelen (1997a) implicitly assumed that insider traders are risk neutral criminals, the emphasis is now placed on the risk attitudes of insiders and its implications for the optimal choice between the certainty and the severity of punishment in order to prevent insider trading. The analysis is illustrated by the Belgian insider trading regulation, but the conclusions can be extended to other European countries as well.

In the next section we start with the classic expected utility framework of Becker (1968) and extend the analysis with state-dependent and rank-dependent expected utility models. It analyses the impact of criminal risk attitudes on the choice between a change in the certainty of punishment or in the severity of punishment. Next, section two provides an overview of the enforcement of the Belgian insider trading regulation by focusing on these two parameters. Section three applies the different models to a more optimal deterrence of insider trading regulation. Finally, conclusions are drawn in section four.

1. MODELLING CRIMINAL BEHAVIOUR

Different models are presented in literature to analyse criminal behaviour by means of economic models. After analysing the classic expected utility model, the analysis is elaborated by presenting a state-dependent and a rank-dependent expected utility framework.[1]

1.1. TRADITIONAL EXPECTED UTILITY MODELS (EU)

According to the classic economic theory of crime and punishment, criminal behaviour is analysed within an expected utility framework (Cooter and Ulen, 2003 or Posner, 1998). Within this framework, the total number of offences (O) in a society can be represented by the relation (Becker, 1968):

$$O = O(p, f, u) \qquad\qquad [7.1]$$

with

$$\frac{\partial O}{\partial p} < 0 \quad and \quad \frac{\partial O}{\partial f} < 0 \qquad\qquad [7.2]$$

The variable p represents the probability of punishment for the offence and the variable f represents the severity of punishment for the offence. As p or f increases, i.e. the probability of punishment increases or the severity of punishment augments, the total number of offences in society will be reduced (first order conditions smaller than zero). The variable u includes all other factors that have an influence on the number of offences. These are for instance alternatives for a person to increase his prosperity.[2] As the enforcement policy has no direct impact on this variable, it will not be considered in the remainder of the article.

A person will only commit an offence if the expected profits exceed the expected costs. The expected profits are the gains (Y) that result from the offence. In case of insider trading this is the realized capital gains on a share. The expected costs are the result of the probability of conviction p and the level of punishment f. More formally, a criminal will maximize the following expected utility function (Becker, 1968):

---

[1]   See for other approaches Engelen (2003a) and Engelen (2004).
[2]   See on the link between crime rates and economic conditions, for instance, Orsagh and Witte (1981) and Cook and Zarkin (1985). The variable u can also refer to other factors such ethnical backgrounds (DiIulio, 1994 and 1996) or it can refer to aspects covered by other disciplines such as sociology, geography or psychology. For examples on sociological studies, see e.g. Shaw, McKay and Short (1969) and Case and Katz (1991); for examples on geographical studies, see e.g. Evans and Herbert (1989) and Glaeser and Sacerdote (1996); and for an example on psychological studies see e.g. Carroll (1978).

$$EU = pU(Y - f) + (1 - p)U(Y) \qquad [7.3]$$

Some empirical studies such as Wolpin (1978), Willis (1983) and Grogger (1991) show that criminals are more sensitive to changes in the certainty than in the severity of punishment. Combining this finding with the assumption of criminals being risk averse, makes the expected utility model to behave problematic. Becker (1968, p.178) shows that if criminals are more sensitive to a change in p than to a change in f, this implies criminals are risk preferring. This can be illustrated by calculating the elasticity of expected utility of equation [7.3] with respect to the certainty of punishment p:

$$\frac{-\partial EU}{\partial p} \cdot \frac{p}{EU} = [U(Y) - U(Y - f)]\frac{p}{EU} \qquad [7.4]$$

Analogously, the elasticity of expected utility with respect to the severity of punishment f is:

$$\frac{-\partial EU}{\partial f} \cdot \frac{f}{EU} = pU'(Y - f)\frac{f}{EU} \qquad [7.5]$$

For a criminal to be more sensitive to a change in p than to a change in f, the following condition must hold:

$$\frac{U(Y) - U(Y - f)}{f} > U'(Y - f) \qquad [7.6]$$

Assuming a risk averse criminal implies the second order condition of the expected utility function to be negative: $U'' < 0$ (concave utility function)[3]. However, both conditions (i.e. risk averse and more sensitive to the variable p) cannot be satisfied together. This can be seen in figure 7.1. Panel a of figure 7.1 represents a concave utility function of a risk averse criminal. The figure clearly shows that the slope of the tangent to the utility function at Y-f, as expressed by the right hand side of equation [7.6], is steeper than the slope of the chord connecting the two points of the utility function at Y and Y-f, as expressed by the left hand side of equation [7.6]. Within the Becker model, this implies that a criminal who is more sensitive to a change in the probability of punishment than to a change in the severity of punishment, must be risk preferring.

---

[3]   On the other hand, assuming a risk preferring criminal implies the second order condition of the expected utility function to be positive: $U'' > 0$ (convex utility function).

Figure 7.1. A criminals' risk attitude in the expected utility model

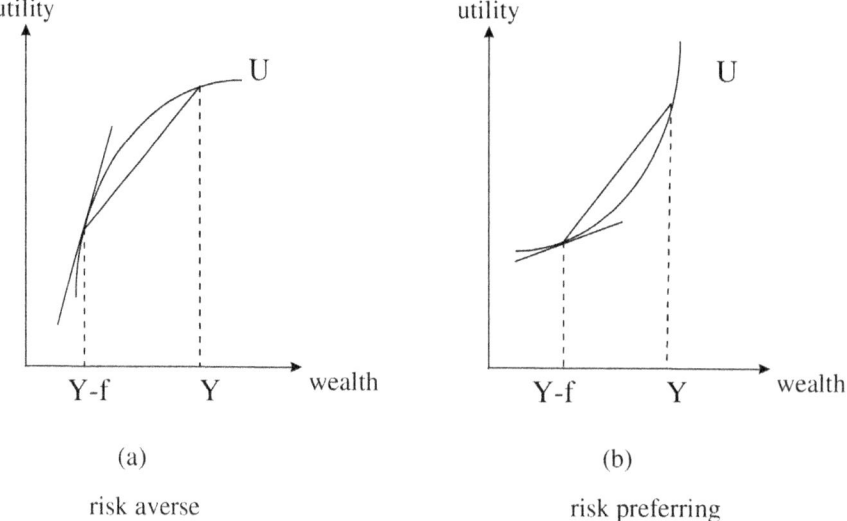

(a)

risk averse

(b)

risk preferring

1.2. STATE-DEPENDENT EXPECTED UTILITY MODELS (SDEU)

A solution to the above problem is offered by Neilson and Winter (1997) who present the following state-dependent expected utility function:

$$SDEU = pU_c(Y - f) + (1 - p)U_n(Y)$$ [7.7]

where U_c is the criminal's utility function if he is punished and U_n is his utility function if he is not caught.

There are very good reasons to assume that criminals take into account a different expected utility function whether they are caught or not. Conviction may lead to more uncertainty about income and to increased job instability (Freeman, 1992; Grogger, 1992, 1995; Nagin and Waldfogel, 1995 and Waldfogel, 1994a) or to a large income reduction for high-income offenders (Lott, 1990 and 1992). This reduction in personal income once they return to the labour force may be caused by a loss of reputation of honesty and integrity (Lott, 1998). Moreover, their human capital decreases while they are in prison. Waldfogel (1994b) shows that these income and employment effects may be persistent.

If the criminals' utility function is state-dependent, Neilson and Winter (1997) show that it is possible for criminals to be risk averse and, at the same time, to be more sensitive to changes in p than to changes in f.

Again, calculating the elasticity of expected utility of equation [7.7] with respect to the certainty of punishment:

$$\frac{-\partial SDEU}{\partial p} \cdot \frac{p}{SDEU} = \left[U_n(Y) - U_c(Y-f) \right] \frac{p}{SDEU} \qquad [7.8]$$

and calculating the elasticity of expected utility with respect to the severity of punishment

$$\frac{-\partial SDEU}{\partial f} \cdot \frac{f}{SDEU} = p\, U_c'(Y-f) \frac{f}{SDEU} \qquad [7.9]$$

yields the following condition for a criminal to be more sensitive to changes in p than to changes in f in a state-dependent expected utility framework:

$$\frac{U_n(Y) - U_c(Y-f)}{f} > U_c'(Y-f) \qquad [7.10]$$

Again, figure 7.2 represents a risk averse criminal implying a concave utility function: $U_c'' < 0$ and $U_n'' < 0$. Within a state dependent expected utility framework, it is possible that the slope of the tangent to the utility function U_c at Y-f, as expressed by the right hand side of equation [10], is flatter than the slope of the chord connecting the point of the utility function U_c at Y-f and the point of the utility function U_n at Y, as expressed by the left hand side of equation [7.10]. Therefore, in a state-dependent expected utility model, criminals can be both risk averse and more sensitive to changes in p than to changes in f.

Figure 7.2. A risk averse criminal in the state-dependent expected utility model

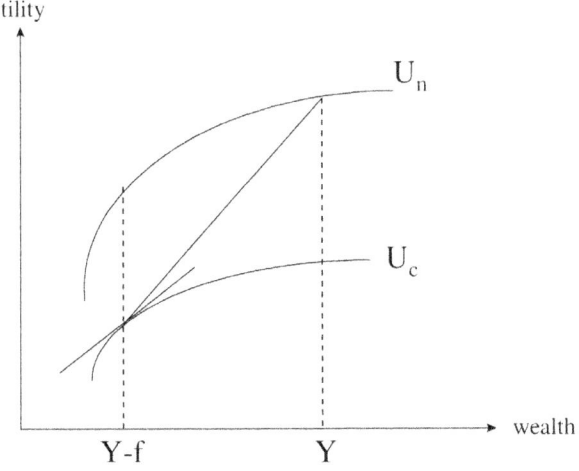

1.3. RANK-DEPENDENT EXPECTED UTILITY MODELS (RDEU)

The same conclusion can be obtained by another refinement of the expected utility hypothesis. If criminals' preferences follow a rank-dependent expected utility function, criminals can be both risk averse and more sensitive to changes in p (Neilson and Winter, 1997). A rank-dependent expected utility model can be expressed as:

$$RDEU = g(p)U(Y - f) + (1 - g(p))U(Y) \tag{7.11}$$

Compared to an expected utility model, the probability of punishment p is transformed by the *function g* in a rank-dependent expected utility model, with g representing the weight on the worse outcome and 1-g representing the weight on the better outcome.[4] There is no consensus concerning the shape of the transformation function g. As such, several shapes can be found in the literature. Quiggin (1982 and 1987) uses an S-shaped function that overweighs extreme low probability outcomes (see panel a in figure 7.3). Although a convex transformation function is sometimes proposed (Quiggin, 1993; see panel c of figure 7.3), most of the time the transformation function is assumed to be concave (Chew, Karni and Safra, 1987 and Segal, 1987). This function is represented in panel b of figure 7.3 and indicates that the worst outcome receives a higher weight than the better outcome. Such a shape is more suited for analysing criminal behaviour. In the RDEU-model a criminal will overweight the event that he is punished and underweight the event that he is not. Technically, a worse payoff gets a higher probability weight by setting *g(p)* higher than p, compared to the classic expected utility model (Neilson and Winter, 1997).

Figure 7.3. Different shapes of the transformation functions in the RDEU

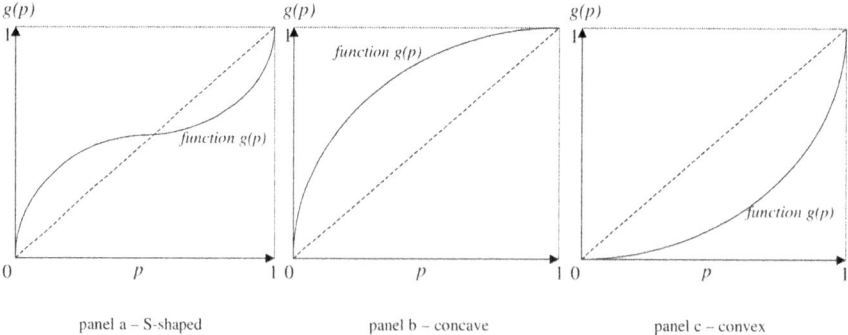

panel a – S-shaped   panel b – concave   panel c – convex

---

[4]   With g(0) = 0, g(1) = 1 and g'(p) > 0. The transformation function is said to be symmetric when g(p) = 1-g(p).

Expressed mathematically, several functional forms for the transformation function g are thus proposed in literature. Quiggin (1993) considers the functional form $g(p) = p^\gamma$. Depending on the value of γ the function will be concave ($0 < \gamma < 1$) or convex ($\gamma > 1$).[5] Several functional forms yielding an S-shape function are proposed.

Karmarkar (1978, 1979) suggests using $g(p) = \dfrac{p^\gamma}{p^\gamma + (1-p)^\gamma}$, yielding a symmetric S-shape function for $0 < \gamma < 1$, while Tversky and Kahneman (1990) suggest using $g(p) = \dfrac{p^\gamma}{\sqrt[\gamma]{p^\gamma + (1-p)^\gamma}}$, yielding an asymmetric S-shape curve for $0 < \gamma < 1$. In our criminal model we propose the use of the functional form $g(p) = p^\gamma$, with $0 < \gamma < 1$, being consistent with a concave utility function of a risk-averse criminal. The functioning of the RDEU-model compared to the ordinary EU-model can be illustrated by means of an example. Suppose the probability of conviction amounts to 55% or 0.55 and the probability of walking away from conviction amounts to 45% or 0.45. Using the transformation function $g(p) = p^\gamma$ with e.g. γ being equal to 0.4812, the probability p is transformed in g(p). This implies that g(0.55) is equal to 75% or 0.75 and 1-g(p) is equal to 25% or 0.25. Compared to the ordinary EU-model the criminal will overweight the event that he is punished (0.75 > 0.55) and underweight the event that he is not (0.25 < 0.45).

Calculating the elasticity of expected utility of equation [7.11] with respect to the certainty of punishment:

$$\frac{-\partial RDEU}{\partial p} \cdot \frac{p}{RDEU} = g'(p)[U(Y) - U(Y-f)]\frac{p}{RDEU} \qquad [7.12]$$

and calculating the elasticity of expected utility with respect to the severity of punishment

$$\frac{-\partial RDEU}{\partial f} \cdot \frac{f}{RDEU} = g(p)U'(Y-f)\frac{f}{RDEU} \qquad [7.13]$$

it can be shown that the following condition must hold for a criminal to be more sensitive to changes in p than to changes in f in a rank-dependent expected utility framework:

$$g'(p)\frac{p}{g(p)} > U'(Y-f)\frac{f}{U(Y) - U(Y-f)} \qquad [7.14]$$

It can be proven that it is possible to choose a function g for which equation [7.14] holds.[6] Again, a rank-dependent expected utility model allows criminals to be both risk averse and more sensitive to changes in p than to changes in f.

---

[5] Notice that the RDEU-model is reduced to the ordinary EU-model when γ is equal to one.
[6] See Neilson and Winter (1997, p.102) for the proof.

2. THE CURRENT ENFORCEMENT OF INSIDER TRADING REGULATIONS IN BELGIUM

In this section the current enforcement of insider trading regulations in Belgium is examined. Insider trading has been prohibited in Belgium since 1989.[7] But it was not until 1995, however, that the first convictions were pronounced.[8] Before analysing the optimal choice between the certainty (p) and the severity (f) of punishment in section three for the insider trading regulation to be deterrent, the value of these two parameters will be examined.

2.1. PARAMETER ONE – THE SEVERITY OF PUNISHMENT (f)

The variable f (severity of punishment) has a very high value. The Belgian criminal law enumerates a very large number of sanctions.[9] Any infringement of prohibition on insider trading is punished with imprisonment ranging from three months to one year *and* a fine of EUR 250 to EUR 50,000. Additionally, the judge can impose a disgorgement up to three times the direct or indirect profit derived or the loss avoided. Moreover, imprisonment automatically imposes professional restrictions on management and board functions in companies.[10] With regard to the prior regulation the sanctions were seriously aggravated.[11] As of 1 September 1998 professional

---

[7] Incorporation of Article 509-4 into the Belgian Criminal Code by Article 27 of the Statute of 9 March 1989 modifying the Commercial Code and Royal Decree No.185 of 9 July 1935 on Bank Control and on the Issuance of Transferable Securities, *Belgian Gazette*, 9 June 1989, erratum, *Belgian Gazette*, 27 June 1989. As a consequence of the European Directive (89/592/EEC) of 13 November 1989 for the Coordination of the Regulations of Insider Trading, *OJ* L 334/30, 18 November 1989, the regulation of insider trading was rewritten in Part V (Art.181-193) of the Statute of 4 December 1990 on Financial Transactions and Financial Markets, *Belgian Gazette*, 22 December 1990, erratum, *Belgian Gazette*, 1 February 1991. At the same time Article 509-4 of the Criminal Code was abolished. The Statute came into force on 1 January 1991. Again, as a consequence of a European Directive (Directive 2003/6/EC of the European Parliament and of the Council of 28 January 2003 on Insider Dealing and Market Manipulation (Market Abuse), *OJ* L 96/16, 12 April 2003 – in short: the *Market Abuse Directive* or *MAD*), this regulation was recently rewritten in Article 40 of the Statute of 2 August 2002 on the Supervision of the Financial Sector and Financial Services, *Belgian Gazette*, 4 September 2002 (edition 2). The Statute came into force on 1 June 2003. See Article 1 of the Royal Decree of 3 April 2003, *Belgian Gazette*, 29 April 2003.

[8] First Instance Criminal Court of Ghent [27 September 1995], *Bank- en Financiewezen*, 9/1995, 535-538 and First Instance Criminal Court of Charleroi [27 September 1995], *Bank- en Financiewezen*, 9/1995, 539.

[9] Article 40 of the Statute of 2 August 2002 and the old Article 189 of the Statute of 4 December 1990.

[10] Old Article 192 of the Statute of 4 December 1990.

[11] Article 509-4 of the Belgian Criminal Code imposed imprisonment ranging from one month to one year and a fine of 250 to 50,000 EUR, *or one of these sanctions alone.* Disgorgement was limited to the profit derived or the loss avoided. As professional restrictions were automatically imposed with

---

restrictions are no longer imposed automatically, but have to be imposed by the criminal court.[12] These sanctions are also being imposed in reality. In the *Bekaert*-case the First Instance Criminal Court imposed the following sanctions: an imprisonment of three months with delay, professional restrictions, a fine of EUR 12,395 and a triple disgorgement of EUR 44,620 (see in detail chapter six).

2.2. PARAMETER TWO – THE CERTAINTY OF PUNISHMENT (p)

Engelen (1997) clearly shows that the variable p (certainty of punishment) has a very low value. The first reason for the low value of the certainty of punishment results from the scope of the prohibition of the Statute. Article 40 paragraph 1 prohibits buying or selling, or giving orders for buying or selling on the basis of inside information. Simply doing nothing is not included within the scope of the Statute. Nevertheless, such a decision is, from an economic point of view, at least as important as a buy or sell decision. Take for instance, a portfolio manager who is planning to rebalance his portfolio by selling a security. On the basis of inside information he decides to keep the security in his portfolio because a sharp increase of the security price is expected. Although the portfolio manager deals on the basis of inside information, he is not affected by the prohibition of Article 40 paragraph 1. Nor is a portfolio manager who renounces a planned purchase. Analogously, Article 40 paragraph 2 does not include the simple dissuasion of a purchase or sale, without the communication of the inside information itself (Engelen, 1999). A considerable number of transactions are thereby excluded from the criminal sanctions.

The second reason why the certainty of punishment p is very small, is the fact that insider trading is difficult to detect. Even if supervisory bodies try to detect abnormal price and volume-patterns with special software, a crafty insider will create such a construction that his transactions will not attract attention. He can obtain this by spreading his transactions over various orders or by using foreign intermediaries, preferably a financial institution in a financial centre where the identity of the principal is covered by banking secrecy. The supervising Market Authority of the Brussels Stock Exchange reported such a case in its 1998 report.[13] In this case a suspicious buying order occurred on the day before a press release under embargo was distributed concerning a participation in a foreign company. Because the buying order originated

---

an imprisonment of three months, these restrictions could be avoided in case of a conviction less than three months.

[12]   Law of 2 June 1998, *Belgian Gazette*, 22 August 1998.

[13]   The Brussels Stock Exchange is now called Euronext Brussels.

from abroad, the Market Authority tried in vain to gather information on the buyer's identity.[14]

A third factor in the effectiveness of the variable p is the judicial inquiry and prosecution. Between 1991 and 1995 first line supervision was assigned to the Belgian Banking and Finance Commission (BFC), while the judicial inquiry and the actual prosecution are carried out by the judicial authorities (courts, investigating magistrate and public prosecutor).[15] This construction shows a double possibility for dismissal: by the BFC on the one hand and by the public prosecutor on the other. Between 1991 and 1995 the BFC opened 108 investigations of insider trading: 89 cases were dismissed, while 19 or 17.5% of the investigations have been passed on the Public Prosecutor's Offices. Only two cases have been prosecuted (see figure 7.4). This means that less than 2% of the possible cases of insider trading have ultimately been prosecuted and that only 10% of the cases handed on by the BFC to the Public Prosecutor's Offices have been effectively prosecuted in court.

Figure 7.4. Inquiry and prosecution of insider trading in Belgium between 1 January 1991 and 31 December 1995

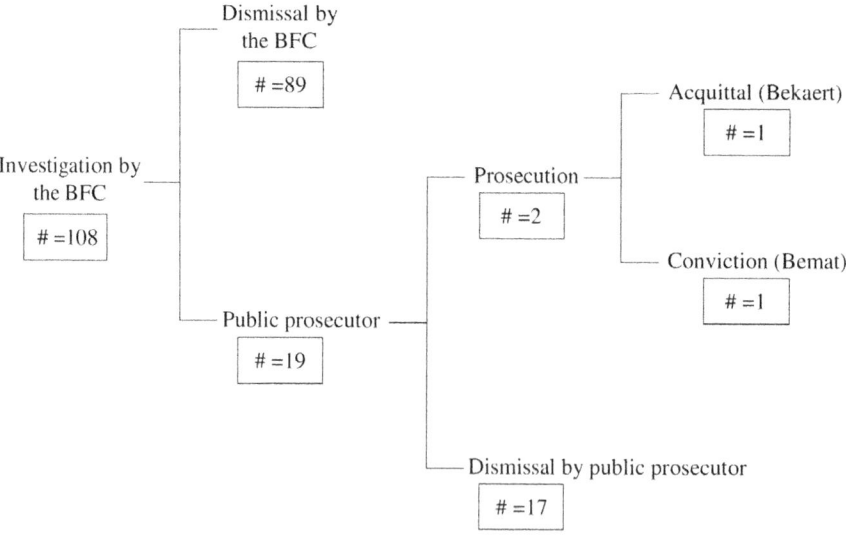

Source: Banking and Finance Commission (2001)

As of 1996 the first line supervision of insider trading was assigned directly to the Market Authority of the Stock Exchange itself. The number of insider trading investigations by the Market Authority is reported in table 7.1.[16] As can be seen from this table, the number has increased steadily over the last years. The Market Authority sees three possible factors contributing to this increased number.[17] First, the detection of insider trading is said to be improved during recent years. Second, the number of transactions (trading volume) increased over the same period, leading to more insider trading cases in absolute numbers (while the relative number did not change). Third, more volatile market prices cause more apparent suspicious price movements.

Table 7.1. The number of insider trading investigations by the Market Authority between 1 January 1996 and 31 December 2000

Year	1996	1997	1998	1999	2000
Number of cases	13	24	31	42	50

Source: Market Authority (2001)

Figure 7.5 shows that of the 160 insider trading investigations in the period 1996-2000, only 31 or 19% of the investigations have been handed on to the Public Prosecutor's Offices. Of the latter, only one case has been prosecuted in court (the *Ter Beke*-case), leading to an acquittal in first instance.[18] This means that less than 1% of the possible cases of insider trading have been prosecuted and that only 3% of the cases handed on by the Market Authority to the public prosecutor has been effectively prosecuted in court. Compared to the period 1991-95, this implies that the Market Authority refers a higher percentage of insider trading cases to the Public Prosecutor's Offices, but in turn, the latter dismiss more cases. The high degree of dismissal by the Public Prosecutor's Offices is likely to be due to the heavy workload, the complicated character of this offence, the limited amounts involved, the high burden of proof in criminal cases and the fact that no victims present themselves.[19] To solve the high degree of dismissal the Market Authority proposed using administrative sanctions as well as increasing the visibility of the prosecution by making the imposed administrative sanctions visible.[20]

---

[16] As of 2003 supervision is again assigned to the Banking and Finance Commission. No recent data on the prosecution of insider trading is available at this moment.
[17] Interview with Mr V. Van Dessel, Head of the Market Authority of Euronext Brussels, November 2001.
[18] First Instance Criminal Court of Ghent, 18 December 2002, *Bank- en Financieel Recht*, 2003, no. 1, 58-61.
[19] Interview with Mr V. Van Dessel, Head of the Market Authority of Euronext Brussels, November 2001.
[20] *Ibidem.*

Figure 7.5. Inquiry and prosecution of insider trading in Belgium between 1 January 1996 and 31 December 2000

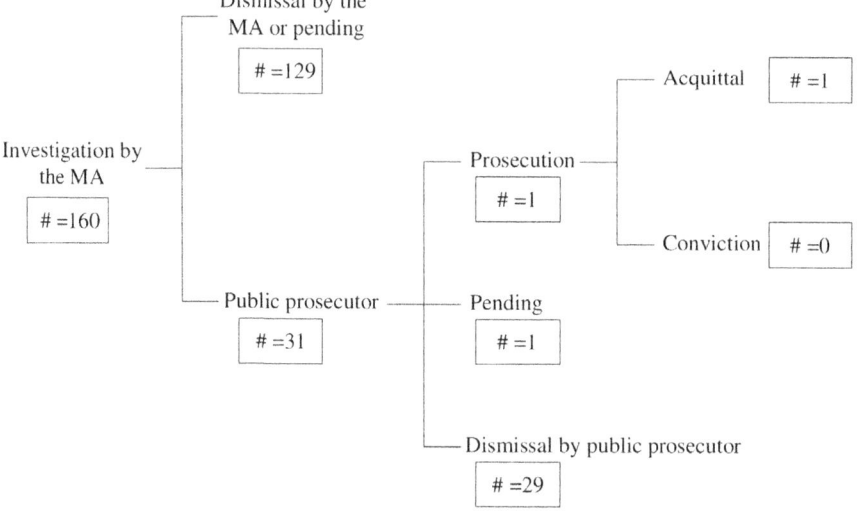

Source: Market Authority (2001)

A fourth reason for the present insider trading regulation to be effective is the very fact of using *criminal* sanctions. The problem is in fact the difficulty in meeting the burden of proof for a criminal case. It is not sufficient to identify the persons involved in insider trading; the link between the trader and the information has to be demonstrated as well. This was why the Court of Appeal acquitted the defendants in the Bekaert case.[21] In this case, the Court of Appeal applied a very high burden of proof. It was demonstrated that a member of the Board of Directors of Bekaert possessed material non-public information and it was demonstrated that her husband bought stocks of this company. While the First Instance Criminal Court judged that the link between the trader and the information was proven, the Court of Appeal reversed this decision. According to the Court of Appeal, "this was a serious presumption, but this presumption in itself is insufficient to satisfy the burden of proof of insider trading, unless this was supported by other facts or presumptions." If other courts follow this view, it will be very unlikely for a person to be convicted for insider trading in the future. A similar problem in the UK was set forward by Naylor (1990, p.58). According to this study, in 75% of the cases the British Stock Exchange believed it had enough proof to meet the civil standard but not the criminal standards. Therefore, Naylor (1990, p.90) suggested that enforcement of insider trading should

---

[21]   Court of Appeal of Ghent [30 April 1997], *Bank- en Financiewezen*, 1997, 413.

concentrate more on civil penalties, which would eliminate the problem presented by the criminal burden of proof.

Figure 7.6 summarizes these problems and offers an overview of the possibility of conviction in case of acting on the basis of material non-public information.

Figure 7.6. The possibility of a conviction of acting on the basis of material non-public information

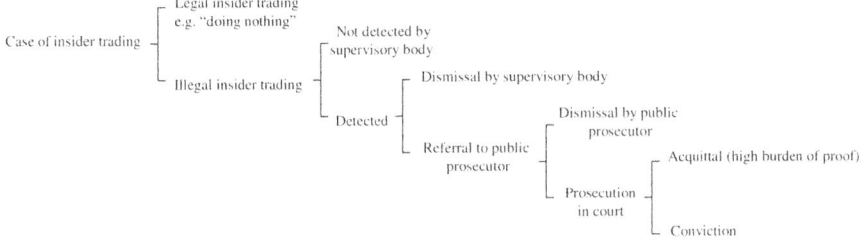

3. THE OPTIMAL DETERRENCE OF THE BELGIAN INSIDER TRADING REGULATION

This section examines the optimal means of deterrence of insider trading regulations. In particular, we apply the above models to the Belgian insider trading law. We examine the choice between increasing the severity (f) or the certainty (p) of punishment.[22] As the previous section showed, it appears that the variable f (severity of punishment) has a very high value. In order to restrict insider trading the certainty of punishment has to be sufficiently high as well. If the probability of conviction is close to nil, the severity of the sanction will not have the appropriate deterrent effect. Or as Naylor (1990, p.89) puts it: "If in many cases criminal sanctions are unenforceable then the potential insider trader will have little reason to refrain from committing the crime no matter how harsh the penalty." The previous section demonstrated that the variable p has a very low value. It appears that the expected costs of the offence are too small compared to the expected payoff of insider trading. For the insider trading regulation to be deterrent, the expected costs component has to be increased. The relevant question is thus: *Should the Belgian legislator focus on the severity of punishment or on the certainty of punishment for insider trading regulation to be more effective?*

---

[22]   In the analysis we ignore the costs of apprehension, prosecution and execution.

The answer to the question of increasing either the certainty or the severity of punishment depends on both the criminals' risk attitude and the model used to describe criminal behaviour. Table 7.2 summarizes the conclusions of the section one, which described how criminal behaviour can be modelled.

Table 7.2. Sensitiveness to p and f according to the criminals' risk attitude and the model being used

| | More sensitive to a change in p than to a change in f? | |
Model	risk averse criminal	risk preferring criminal
Expected utility	no	yes
State-dependent utility	yes	yes
Rank-dependent utility	yes	yes

If insider traders are risk preferring, the classic expected utility model, as well as the state-dependent and the rank-dependent expected utility models indicate that such a criminal will be more sensitive to an increase in p than to an increase in f. Therefore, for a deterrence policy to be optimal, a substantial increase of the certainty of punishment has to be pursued. This is the most effective way to increase the expected costs of the crime of insider trading and to make the insider trading regulation more deterrent.

This conclusion also holds if an insider trader is risk averse in the state-dependent and the rank-dependent expected utility models. In this case as well, a substantial increase of the certainty of punishment has to be pursued. As already explained in section one, this is not the case in the classic expected utility model. According to this model, the legislator should increase the severity of punishment rather than the certainty of punishment (first best solution), for a risk averse criminal is more sensitive to a change in f than to a change in p. If the legislator feels that the severity of punishment is already high enough, this would imply that an increase of p would only be a second best solution. Section three showed that the severity of punishment is already very high in Belgium. Moreover, increasing it even further may cause another problem. As Posner (1998, p.245) points out, the tendency to punish all crimes by a uniformly severe fine, may eliminate *marginal* deterrence, i.e. the incentive to substitute less for more serious crimes. Therefore, as a second best solution, we propose to focus on an increase of the probability of punishment in case of a risk averse insider trader and an expected utility model.

Table 7.3 summarizes the appropriate choice between the certainty and the severity of punishment according to the insider trader's risk attitude and the model being used to describe criminal behaviour.

Table 7.3. Appropriate action for the Belgian insider trading regulation to be more effective according to the criminal's risk attitude and the expected utility model

Model	risk averse criminal	risk preferring criminal
Expected utility	increase of f (first best) increase of p (second best)	increase of p
State-dependent utility	increase of p	increase of p
Rank-dependent utility	increase of p	increase of p

3.1. CAN THE CERTAINTY OF PUNISHMENT BE INCREASED?

The above analysis suggests increasing the value of the variable p in order to make enforcement more effective. However, an increase of the certainty of punishment within the current criminal framework may be difficult for a number of reasons. First, extending the scope of the Statute to include actions such as "doing nothing" besides buying and selling securities on the basis of inside information is useless, for this kind of insider trading can never be traced. It is also extremely difficult to improve the detection of insider trading as the insider covers up his transactions (see supra). The only factor that may increase the certainty of punishment is a more efficient judicial inquiry and prosecution.

Although it may be possible to improve co-operation between the supervising authority on the stock exchange and the judicial authorities, there will still be a structural problem that cannot be solved in the short or medium-term. The Public Prosecutor's Offices do not possess the specialized financial knowledge required for prosecuting such offences. Given the fact that the Public Prosecutor's Offices are also heavily overloaded, priority may be given to the enforcement of other crimes. Even more problematic is the burden of proof in criminal cases. Although it was considered that the public prosecutor disposed of strong evidence in the *Bekaert*-case, it ultimately led to an acquittal by the Court of Appeal. Therefore, it is very unlikely that the Public Prosecutor's Offices will concentrate on insider trading offences in the near future. The problem of the high burden of proof is not unique to Belgium. Similar findings are reported by Naylor (1990) with respect to the U.K. and by Pfeil (1996) with respect to Germany. It is clear that the use of criminal prosecutions for insider trading has serious limitations.

Consequently, a more radical change to the organization of the prosecution of insider trading is necessary. Until recently, the Belgian legislator only adopted a criminal framework in order to restrict insider trading on the Brussels Stock Exchange. It has to be pointed out that the European legislator did not necessarily require criminal sanctions for the implementation of Directive 89/592 (Engelen, 1997a).[23] It only required member states to determine penalties that were 'sufficient to promote compliance' with the measures taken pursuant to the Directive (Art.13 Old Directive). At the same time Article 8 of the Directive required adequate supervision by the assignment of a supervisory body, that must be given all supervisory and investigative powers that are necessary for the exercise of their functions, where appropriate in collaboration with other authorities. The Directive therefore left the organization of enforcement and the extent of penalties largely to the discretion of the member states (Pingel, 1992).

As Pfeil (1996) points out, a wider variety of judicial measures for banning insider trading will reduce the number of insider traders that are able to avoid detection and punishment. The use of administrative sanctions was clearly within the scope of the Old Directive. An administrative sanction is imposed directly by an administrative body on the violator. When the violator does not oppose this sanction within a certain term, the administrative sanction becomes final. If the violator opposes the sanction, the case is brought before the court (Van den Wyngaert, 1999). Such administrative sanctions were already applied in Belgium, for instance, in competition law and financial law (money laundering).[24] However, with respect to insider trading, the Belgian legislator did not enable administrative sanctions to be taken. This was a clear shortcoming. Administrative sanctions will improve the probability of conviction because such a system can react more quickly after the alleged insider trading and lead to less dismissals compared to criminal prosecutions. Figures 7.3 and 7.4 showed that courts have a clear tendency to neglect these violations (Wymeersch, 1991). However, the system should meet some conditions, such as adversary proceedings, a possibility of appeal before a court and the establishment of specialized investigating agents within the BFC.

Recently, the European Commission adopted a new directive to improve the European legal framework against insider trading and market manipulation, the so-called Market Abuse Directive (MAD).[25]

---

[23] European Directive (89/592/EEC) of 13 November 1989 for the Coordination of the Regulations of Insider Trading, *OJ* L 334/30, 18 November 1989 [*In short: Old Directive*].

[24] Law of 5 August 1991 concerning the Protection of Economic Competition, *Belgian Gazette*, 11 October 1991, respectively, Law of 11 January 1993 concerning the Prevention of the Use of the Financial System for Money Laundering, *Belgian Gazette*, 9 February 1993.

[25] Directive 2003/6/EC of the European Parliament and of the Council of 28 January 2003 on Insider Dealing and market Manipulation (Market Abuse), *OJ* L 96/16, 12 April 2003 [in short: the *Market Abuse Directive*].

First, the MAD sets out a minimum list of requirements for supervisory and investigating powers to be given to competent authorities for the detection and investigation of insider trading.[26] According to Article 12 MAD, these powers shall include *at least* the right to: (a) have access to any document and to receive a copy of it, (b) demand information from any person, and if needed, to require the testimony of a person, (c) carry out on-site inspections, (d) require existing telephone and data traffic records, (e) require the cessation of any practice that is contrary to the provisions adopted in the implementation of the MAD, (f) suspend trading of the financial instruments concerned, (g) request the freezing and/or the sequestration of assets and (h) request temporary prohibition of professional activity.

Secondly, the MAD makes administrative sanctions mandatory, parallel to the current criminal sanctions. The Explanatory Memorandum of the proposal of the MAD stresses the speed of administrative sanctions compared to criminal proceedings (Article 14 paragraph 1).[27] Moreover, the MAD stresses the disclosure of sanctions as a very powerful deterrent (Article 14 paragraph 3). Article 15 ensures that any person subject to an administrative decision will have the right to apply to the courts for a full judicial review. Finally, the co-operation between competent authorities is improved by Article 16 MAD.

It should be noted that administrative sanctions and full supervisory and investigative powers were already possible within the framework of the Old Directive. The MAD therefore does not add new instruments, it only makes them *mandatory*. As such, it forces the Belgian legislator to improve the enforcement of its current insider trading regulation by including administrative sanctions next to the existing criminal sanctions.

The new Belgian regulation as enacted in the Statute of 2 August 2002 maintains the criminal sanctions of the former regulation (Article 40 paragraph 6), but adds administrative sanctions and investigative powers by the BFC to the existing regulation.[28] Article 34 and 35 provide the BFC with investigative powers, such as access to documents, the right to demand information from any person, require data traffic records and the right to carry out on-site inspections, with the exception of

---

[26] Every member state has to designate a *single administrative* authority competent to ensure the application of the provisions in the directive (Article 11). As such, the explanatory memorandum stresses the administrative nature of the single competent authority to ensure independence from the markets and to avoid possible conflicts of interest (MAD, consideration nr.36 and 43).

[27] European Commission, *Explanatory Memorandum*, Proposal for a Directive of the European Parliament and of the Council on Insider Dealing and Market Manipulation (Market Abuse), COM(2001) 281 final, 30 May 2001, p.12.

[28] Compare with the Old Article 189 of the Statute of 4 December 1990.

private houses. Moreover Article 36 paragraph 2 provides the BFC with the authority to impose administrative fines for insider trading violations. The BFC can impose a fine between 2,500 and 2,500,000 EUR and a double disgorgement of the benefits.[29] The level of the fine should be proportional to the seriousness of the offence.[30] To meet the standards of the European Treaty for Human Rights and the jurisdiction of the European Court for Human Rights, Article 70 contains detailed procedure to preserve the rights of the suspect[31]. Furthermore, Article 73 avoids the cumulation of administrative and criminal penalties. The amount of the administrative fine imposed by the BFC, which becomes final before the criminal court has reached a decision on the same facts relating to the same person, may be substracted from the criminal fine imposed by the criminal court (*non bis in idem*).

By introducing more extensive investigating powers and authority to impose administrative sanctions to the BFC, it is expected that administrative sanctions will improve the probability of conviction. Future research has to examine whether the introduction of administrative sanctions indeed leads to a higher conviction rate of insider trading violations.

3.2. EFFECTIVENESS

Although the existence of legal rules is an important element for the development of financial markets, the law and finance literature showed that the enforcement of these rules is of equal importance[32]. However, the above analysis revealed that the current criminal framework in Belgium is insufficient to deter insider trading. Some suggestions were made in the above sections to improve the enforceability of insider trading regulation to increase the certainty of punishment. But, the final question remains. Is the enforcement of insider trading laws enforceable in reality?

Examining the effectiveness of the insider trading sanctions in the US, Seyhun (1992) finds that both the increased level of sanctions and its enforcement during the 1980s was ineffective. Neither increased enforcement by the SEC since 1980[33], nor the increased sanctions since the enactment of the Insider Trading Sanctions Act of 1984 and the Insider Trading and Securities Fraud Enforcement Act of 1988 prevented insider trading. On the contrary, both the profitability and the volume of insider trading increased. Even around the time of the increase of the sanctions, no temporary

---

[29] Up to three times in case of recidivism.
[30] *Preparatory works*, Belgian Chamber of Deputies, Doc. 50-1843, no. 1, p.75.
[31] *Preparatory works*, Belgian Chamber of Deputies, Doc. 50-1843, no. 1, p.74 ff.
[32] See chapter one.
[33] After Chiarella v. United States, 588 F. 2d 1358 (2d Cir. 1978), revised 100 S.Ct. 1108 (1980).

effect of these sanctions was found. Or as Seyhun (1992, p.171) puts it: "Data suggest that insiders appeared not to be concerned with changes in statutes even on a temporary basis." Insiders only became more reluctant to trade with regard to earnings announcements and takeover announcements because of the extensive case law.

If the insider trading regulation cannot be enforced in reality, it has some serious consequences. If the insider trading regulation cannot be enforced, then this law will redistribute wealth from honest people, obeying the law, to dishonest people, breaking the law. This is the perverse consequence of an unenforceable law. One can therefore question the social desirability of such a law.

Moreover, the question whether insider trading regulation can be enforced or not, may be irrelevant. The effectiveness of a ban on insider trading was questioned by Hillier and Marshall (2002). This empirical study, with respect to the U.K., examines the impact of a restriction on trading by corporate insiders in periods when they are expected to be advantaged with regard to the information flow. In the U.K. corporate insiders cannot trade prior to the announcement of price-sensitive information. Moreover, a voluntary Model Code specifies a closed period prior to periodic announcements, such as final and interim earnings announcements. Hillier and Marshall (1998) already showed that trading by corporate insiders dropped to zero in the two months prior to an earnings announcement. Given the fact that a listed company typically distributed both an interim earnings report, covering the six-month period since the last annual report and a final earnings report after the annual accounting year-end, this means that corporate insiders are banned from trading during two periods each lasting two months. This is quite drastic: during four months out of twelve or during 33% of the year corporate insiders are prohibited from trading in their company's equity.

However, the empirical results of Hillier and Marshall (2002) show that, although the timing of insider trading has been affected by this rule, the profits realized by corporate insiders are unaffected. Corporate insiders earn statistically significant abnormal profits in every period. Regulating trading by corporate insiders does not appear to curtail their performance because they continue to realize abnormal returns *in tempore non suspectu*. They conclude by questioning the effectiveness or even the need for regulation constraining the activities of corporate insiders. Because the current regulation only affects the timing of the trades, but not the performance of insider trading, "insiders' use of private information may be subtle and consequently very difficult to regulate (p.23)."

4. CONCLUSION

This chapter analyses the optimal deterrence of insider trading regulations. After extending the classic expected utility framework with state-dependent and rank-dependent expected utility models, the impact of criminals risk attitudes on the choice between a change in the certainty of punishment or in the severity of punishment is examined.

The analysis is illustrated by the Belgian insider trading regulation. Focusing on the parameters certainty of punishment and severity of punishment, the article provides an overview of the enforcement of the Belgian insider trading law. It has been shown that the current criminal framework is insufficient to deter insider trading. While the severity of punishment is quite high, the probability of conviction is currently very low. This is due to a number of deficiencies in Belgian insider trading laws, the difficulty of detecting insider trading, the high amount of dismissal by the Public Prosecutor's Offices and the high burden of proof.

Consequently, despite the extensive arsenal of criminal sanctions, the cost of the offence will be too low to restrict insider trading. In order to increase the efficacy of the enforcement of insider trading regulation in Belgium, a choice has to be made between the severity and the certainty of punishment. The answer to this question depends on the criminals' risk attitude and the model used to describe criminal behaviour. The analysis showed that the Belgian legislator should increase the certainty of punishment. To increase the probability of conviction broad investigative powers and the authority to impose administrative sanctions have to be assigned to the supervisory body. In line with the new European Market Abuse Directive, the Belgian legislator recently enabled this framework.

EPILOGUE – DID SOMETHING
CHANGE AFTER ENRON?

In 2002 financial markets were troubled by some major accounting scandals such as Enron, Global Crossing, Halliburton, Tyco and WorldCom to name a few.[1] Especially Enron caused a real shock wave through the financial markets and received at lot of attention in the media. In the US this even led to the enactment of the so-called Sarbanes-Oxley Act.[2] The rise and fall of Enron was remarkable. Through aggressive expansion and acquisitions Enron became the largest energy company in the US and the sixth largest in the world. It was named several times 'The Most Innovative Company in America" by Fortune Magazine. Yet, it lost USD 63 billion of its market capitalisation between January 2001 and January 2002. After announcing in November 2002 it overstated its earnings by USD 600 million, share prices collapsed and Enron even filed for Chapter 11 in December 2002.[3]

It is puzzling that such corporate scandals, which harm investors and the economy as a whole, could ever happen in the US. Especially since the US was considered to have the best corporate governance system, the best disclosure system and the most efficient capital markets (Macey, 2004). Miller (2004) compares the recent accounting scandals of Enron and WorldCom with other classic cases of corporate fraud such as HIH Insurance Group in Australia, EIEI International in Japan, Bank of Credit and Commerce International in Luxembourg and Lincoln Savings & Loan in the US. Examining those six case studies, some striking similarities can be found. The existence of a substantial number of these factors could in the future maybe be used as indicators of possible fraud.

All the fraud cases were characterised by radical growth in a short period of time, often by aggressive expansion through acquisitions and a drastic change in the nature of the business. The problem was often exaggerated by complex corporate structures.[4] In many cases the underlying operating performance of the company was poorly which

---

[1]   See "The Corporate Scandal Sheet", *Forbes*, 28 August 2002 for more examples, online available at
       http://www.forbes.com/2002/07/25/accountingtracker.html.
[2]   H.R. 3763.
[3]   A full analysis of the Enron-case is beyond the confines of this epilogue. More details on the Enron-
       case can be found in Branson (2003), Brickey (2003), Macey (2004), Palepu and Healy (2003) and
       Schwarcz (2002).
[4]   At its time of collapse, Enron had more than 3,000 off-balance sheet subsidiaries and partnerships.

put more pressure to use fraudulent techniques. It starts with creative accounting to end in pure and simple fraud until the point where it can no longer be disguised. Furthermore, a small group or even a single, often charismatic, individual dominated those companies. Often those managers were disproportionately compensated. Every case was characterised by severe conflicts of interest on the part of senior managers. In many of the cases they also had high-level political connections. Corporate image is always an important goal, like in the case of Enron that "spent hundreds of thousands of dollars catering to equity analysts whose opinions were important to sustaining stock prices (Miller, 2004, p.444)."

This epilogue has no ambition to offer a full analysis of all aspects of those recent corporate scandals, or to offer the ultimate solution to all of the problems. The danger exists that regulators overestimate the impact of the Enron case and alike and overreact with all kind of regulations. Changes in corporate governance such as the Sarbanes-Oxley Act and alike are often implemented in a hurry, without analysing the long-term effects and the costs and benefits of those reforms (Miller, 2004). It is thus unclear whether this new regulation would stand a cost-benefit analysis of social desirability. As it was discussed earlier, this furthermore increases the likelihood of adverse effects.

The most important fact the corporate scandals demonstrate is the failing of the U.S. monitoring system. The U.S. system relies on objective monitors such as audit firms, credit rating agencies and financial analysts, who critically hold all management decisions, accounting practices and business transactions to the light. Enron and other cases demonstrated that this was no longer the case in the U.S. system. On the contrary the monitors seemed to be captured by the companies they were supposed to control (Macey, 2004).

Boot and Macey (2004) develop the idea of a trade-off between objectivity and proximity in monitoring companies. It is argued that both goals cannot be reached simultaneously. Objectivity refers to monitoring companies from a distant without any influence from management. Typical examples include credit rating agencies, financial analysts or accounting firms. Proximity refers to a monitoring system in which the monitors have close contact with management and have a better access to information. A typical example is the board of directors. The U.S. system relies heavily on an objective monitoring system. However, if the distant, objective monitors lose their independence from management it is supposed to supervise, the system doesn't function properly anymore, as the recent corporate scandals demonstrated. Several key actors seem to have lost their objectivity in the U.S. monitoring system. Financial analysts cannot produce independent stock recommendations because their employers (i.e. the investment banks) put strong pressure on them to give 'buy' or 'strong buy' recommendations.[5] Michaely and Womack (1999) show that financial analysts' recommendations from investment banks that acted as underwriters for an initial public offering were significantly biased towards a more positive stock advise then other analysts.[6] Macey (2004) also points out that credit rating agencies are reluctant to downgrade a company's credit rating and do not perform the corporate governance role on which investors rely. Audit firms also seem to be captured by their clients, because individual partners in an accounting firm depend completely on auditing one big firm. In such an environment the danger exists that this partner is captured by the firm he is supposed to control because his income and career depends on it.

Some commentators on the recent corporate scandals furthermore questioned the efficient market hypothesis and demanded an even more elaborate system of mandatory disclosure. If anything, the Enron-case and alike demonstrated and supported the semi-strong form efficiency of the stock market. Based on public information the stock price of those companies was correct. Only with knowledge of private information, one could know that the stock price did not reflect the true value of the company. Earlier in this book, ways to improve the strong form efficiency of stock markets were discussed.

One way to achieve this goal is a system of mandatory disclosure. However, as Macey (2004) points out, it is unclear whether the existence of externalities supports or weakens the case for mandatory disclosure. He questions "the assumption that firms generally will disclose negative information about themselves [...] and the assumption that investors will not invest in companies that fail to disclose sufficient information about their financial condition (p.413)" However, as chapter three showed managers must have the incentive to always tell the truth, even in case of bad news. This requires that the incentives for telling the truth and the penalty for telling lies must be high enough. For instance, with respect to Enron (Grinstein, 2004, p. 507, table 2) questions whether the level of equity-linked compensation of management was high enough to be an adequate monetary incentive to maximize the company value. Only if the long-term equity stake of managers is high enough, they will act more in the interest of shareholders. Moreover, more severe punishment for false reporting will eliminate management incentive to cheat (Macey, 2004).

Furthermore, if disclosure of information is easily manipulated, then it puts further questions to the whole system of disclosure. If disclosure is not an effective instrument

---

[5]   It is astonishing to see that two-thirds of all recommendations are 'buy' or 'strong buy', and only less than two percent 'sell' or 'strong sell'.

[6]   For other studies on analyst recommendations, see e.g. Ber, Yafeh and Yosha (2001), Dechow, Hutton and Sloan (2000), Jegadeesh, Kim, Krische and Lee (2004) and Ljungqvist, Marston and Wilhelm (2004).

to distinguish good from bad companies, then it is better abandoned (Grinstein, 2004). As already explained earlier in this book, there exist more efficient ways of companies to incorporate information in security prices and to make stock prices strong form efficient. Several signalling mechanisms exist for companies to signal their true fundamental value to the stock markets, such as capital structure policy, dividend policy, insider trading, share repurchases, etc. Also the amount of short sales on a stock can provide indications on its true value. A focus on signalling mechanisms instead of disclosure rules might therefore be a more fruitful way to avoid corporate scandals in the future.[7]

To conclude how companies should communicate with financial markets and to what extent regulation is necessary, the Enron-case shows that three important actions should be undertaken. First, it is of the utmost importance to increase the level of independence of analyst recommendations, since the monitoring system depends heavily on it. Among others, this requires rules on conflicts on interests between analyst and investment banking activities. Second, the stock market needs independent auditors by improving internal monitoring and control in audit firms. Finally, stimulating signalling devices that can incorporate private information in security prices and make stock markets more strong form efficient is a very powerful way to prevent corporate scandals.

---

[7] See in detail chapter three.

REFERENCES

Aharony, J. and I. Swary (1980), "Quarterly dividend and earnings announcements and stockholders' returns: an empirical analysis", *Journal of Finance*, 1-12.

Akerlof, G. (1970), "The market for lemons: quality uncertainty and the market mechanism", *Quarterly Journal of Economics*, vol. 84, 488-500.

Alford, A., J. Jones, R. Leftwich and M. Zmijewski (1993), "The relative informativeness of accounting disclosures in different countries", *Journal of Accounting Research*, vol. 31, 183-223.

Allen, F. and R. Michaely (1995), "Dividend policy", in R. Jarrow et al. (eds.), *Handbook of operations research and management science: finance*, Amsterdam, North-Holland.

Arcuri, A. (2000), "Product safety regulation", in B. Bouckaert en G. De Geest (eds.), *Encyclopedia of Law and Economics, Volume III, The regulation of contracts*, Edward Elgar, p.329-346.

Arrow, K. (1985), "The potentials and limits of the market in resource allocation", in G.R. Feiwel (ed.), *Issues in contemporary microeconomics and welfare*, London, MacMillan Press, 107-124.

Asquith, P. and D. Mullins (1986), "Signalling with dividends, stock repurchases and equity issues", *Financial Management*, vol. 15, 27-44.

Ayres, I. (1991), "Back to *Basics*: regulating how corporations speak to the market", *Virginia Law Review*, vol. 77, 945-999.

Baesel, J. and G. Stein (1979), "The value of information: inferences from the probability of insider trading", *Journal of Financial and Quantitative Analysis*, 533-571.

Bagehot, W. (1971), "The only game in town", *Financial Analyst Journal*, 12-14.

Bagwell, K. (ed.) (2001), *The economics of advertising*, Edward Elgar, 669 p.

Bagwell, L.S. (1992), "Dutch auction repurchases: an analysis of shareholder heterogeneity", *Journal of Finance*, vol. 47, 71-105.

Bainbridge, S. (2000), "Insider trading", in B. Bouckaert en G. De Geest (eds.), *Encyclopedia of Law and Economics, Volume III, The regulation of contracts*, Edward Elgar, p.772-812.

Baker, G.P., M.C. Jensen and K.J. Murphy (1988), "Compensation and incentives: practice versus theory", *Journal of Finance*, vol. 43, 593-616.

Ball, R. and P. Brown (1968), "An empirical evaluation of accounting income numbers", *Journal of Accounting Research*, 159-178.

Barron, D. (1996), *Business and its environment*, Prentice Hall, 720 p.

Bartel, A.P. and L.G. Thomas (1987), "Predation through regulation: the wage and profit effects of the occupational safety and health administration and the environmental protection agency", *Journal of Law and Economics*, vol. 30, 239-264.

Beales, H., R. Craswell and S. Salop (1981), "The efficient regulation of consumer information", *Journal of Law and Economics*, vol. 24, 491-539.

Beaver, W. (1968), "The information content of annual earnings announcements", *Journal of Accounting Research*, supplement, 67-92.

Beaver, W., R. Lambert and D. Morse (1980), "The information content of security prices", *Journal of Accounting and Economics*, 3-28.

Bebchuk, L.A. and C. Fershtman (1994), "Insider trading and the managerial choice among risky projects", *Journal of Financial and Quantitative Analysis*, vol. 29, no.1, 1-14.

Beccaria, C. (1764), *Dei delitti e delle pene (On crimes and punishment)*, Edited by Franco Venturi, Einaudi Tascabili, Torino, 1994, 680 p.

Beck, T., A. Demirgüç-Kunt and V. Maksimovic (2002), "Financial and legal constraints to firm growth: does size matter?", The World Bank, working paper, nr.2784.

Beck, T., R. Levine and N. Loayza (2000), "Finance and the sources of growth", *Journal of Financial Economics*, vol. 58, 261-300.

Becker, G. (1968), "Crime and Punishment: An Economic Approach", *Journal of Political Economy*, 76(2), 169-217.

Becker, G. (1976), *The economic approach to human behavior*, Chicago, The University of Chicago Press.

Becker, G. (1981), *A treatise on the family*, Cambridge, MA, Harvard University Press.

Becker, G. (1983), "A theory of competition among pressure groups for political influence", *Quarterly Journal of Economics*, 371-400.

Becker, G. (1985), "Public policies, pressure groups, and dead weight costs", *Journal of Public Economics*, 329-347.

Benston, G. (1969), "The value of the SEC's accounting disclosure requirements", *The Accounting Review*, 515-532.

Benston, G. (1973), "Required disclosure and the stock market: an evaluation of the Securities Exchange Act of 1934", *American Economic Review*, vol. 63, 133-155.

Benston, G. (1975), "Required disclosure and the stock market: rejoinder", *American Economic Review*, vol. 65, 473-477.

Benston, G. (1976), "Public (U.S.) compared to private (U.K.) regulation of corporate financial disclosure", *The Accounting Review*, 483-498.

Benston, G. and Hagerman, R. (1974), "Determinants of bid-ask spreads in the OTC-market", *Journal of Financial Economics*, 353 ff.

Bentham, J. (1776), *A fragment on Government*, Edited by J. Burns and H. Hart, Cambridge, Cambridge University Press, 1988.

Bentham, J. (1789), *An introduction to the principles of morals and legislation*, Edited by J. Burns and H. Hart, London, Athlone Press, 1970.

Ber, H., Y. Yafeh and O. Yosha (2001), "Conflict of interest in universal banking: Bank lending, stock underwriting, and fund management", *Journal of Monetary Economics*, vol.47, no.1, 189-218.

Bettis, J., J. Coles and M. Lemmon (2000), "Corporate policies restricting trading by insiders", *Journal of Financial Economics*, vol. 57, 191-220.

Bhattacharya, U. and H. Daouk (1999), "The world price of insider trading", Kelley School of Business, Indiana University.

Bittlingmayer, G. (2000), "The market for corporate control (including takeovers)", in B. Bouckaert en G. De Geest (eds.), *Encyclopedia of Law and Economics, Volume III, The regulation of contracts*, Edward Elgar, p.725-771.

Black, B. and R. Gilson (1998), "Venture capital and the structure of capital markets: bank versus stock markets", *Journal of Financial Economics*, vol. 47, nr.3, 243-277.

Black, F. (1986), "Noise", *Journal of Finance*, vol. 41, 529-543.

Black, F. and M. Scholes (1974), "The effects of dividend yield and dividend policy on common stock prices and returns", *Journal of Financial Economics*, vol. 1, 1-22.

Boot, A. and J. Macey (2004), "Monitoring Corporate Performance: The Role of Objectivity, Proximity, and Adaptability in Corporate Governance", *Cornell Law Review*, vol.89, 356-393.

Bordeaux-Groult, R. (1987), "Problems of enforcement and cooperation in the multinational securities market: a French perspective", *University of Pennsylvania Journal of International Business Law*, vol. 9, nr.3, 453-465.

Bouckaert, B. and G. De Geest (2000b), "Introduction", in B. Bouckaert and G. De Geest (eds.), *Encyclopedia of Law and Economics, Volume I, The history and methodology of law and economics*, Edward Elgar, p.xiv-xv.

Bouckaert, B. and G. De Geest (2000a), *Encyclopedia of Law and Economics*, Edward Elgar, 5 volumes.

Branson, D. (2003), "Enron – When All Systems Fail: Creative Destruction or Roadmap to Corporate Governance Reform?", *Villanova Law Review*, vol.48, no.4, 989.

Brealey, R. and S. Myers (1996), *Principles of Corporate Finance*, McGraw-Hill, 998 p.

Brealey, R. and S. Myers (2000), *Principles of Corporate Finance*, McGraw Hill, 1093 p.

Brennan, M. (1970), "Taxes, market valuation and corporate financial policy", *National Tax Journal*, December, 417-427.

Brickey, K.F. (2003), "From Enron to WorldCom and Beyond: Life and Crime After Sarbanes-Oxley", *Washington University Law Quarterly*, Vol. 81.

Brickley, J., S. Bhagat and R. Lease (1985), "The Impact of Long Range Managerial Compensation Plans on Shareholders' Wealth", *Journal of Accounting and Economics*, April, 115-129.

Brindisi, L. (1985), "Creating Shareholder Value: a New Mission for Executive Compensation", *Midland Corporate Finance Journal*, winter.

Brudney, V. (1979), "Insiders, outsiders and the informational advantages under the federal securities laws", *Harvard Law Review*, vol. 93, 322-376.

Calabresi, G. (1961), "Some thoughts on risk distribution and the law of torts", *Yale Law Journal*, vol. 70, 499 ff.

Carlin, W. and C. Mayer (1999), "Finance, investment and growth", Working paper, University of Oxford.

Carlton, D. and D. Fischel (1983), "The regulation of insider trading", *Stanford Law Review*, vol. 35, 857-895.

Carlton, D.W. and J.M. Perloff (1994), *Modern Industrial Organization*, Harper Collins College Publishers, 973 p.

Carroll, J.S. (1978), "A psychological approach to deterrence: the evaluation of crime opportunities", *Journal of Personality and Social Psychology*, vol. 36, nr.12, 1512-1520.

Case, A. and L. Katz (1991), "The company you keep: the effect of family and neighborhood on disadvantaged youth", *NBER working paper*, nr.3705.

Cassimon, D. and P.J. Engelen (2005), "The impact of the legal and institutional framework on the financial architecture of new economy firms in developing countries", *Information Economics, and Policy*, vol. 17, no.2, 247-269.

Cerfontaine, J. (1997), "Beursdelicten", in *Een strafrecht voor bank- en beursverrichtingen*, TBH-dossier no. 4, Kluwer rechtswetenschappen, 117-172.

Chakravarty, S. and J. McConnell (1997), "An analysis of prices, bid/ask spreads, and bid and ask depths surrounding Ivan Boesky's illegal trading in Carnation stock", *Financial Management*, vol. 26, summer, 18-34.

Chakravarty, S. and J. McConnell (1999), "Does insider trading really move stock prices?", *Journal of Financial and Quantitative Analysis*, vol. 34, 191-209.

Cheek, J.H. (1996), "Approaches to market regulation", in Fidelis Oditah (ed.), *The future for the global securities market*, Clarendon Press, Oxford, 243-255.

Chew, S., E. Karni and Z. Safra (1987), "Risk aversion in the theory of expected utility with rank-dependent preferences", *Journal of Economic Theory*, vol. 42, nr.2, 370-381.

Chou, Y. (1989), *Statistical analysis for business and economics*, Elsevier, 1157 p.

Claessens, S. and L. Laeven (2001), 'Law, property rights and growth', Paper presented at the Third Annual Conference on *Financial Market Development in Emerging and Transition Economies*, Hong Kong, June 28-30.

Coase, R. (1960), "The problem of social cost", *Journal of Law and Economics*, vol. 3, 1-44.

Coffee, J.C. (1986), "Shareholders versus Managers: The Strain in the Corporate Web", *Michigan Law Review*, vol. 85, 37.

Coffee, J.C. (1999), "The future as history: the prospects for global convergence in corporate governance and its implications", *Northwestern University Law Review*, vol. 93, no.3, 641-707.

Cohen, A.K. (1971), *Delinquent boys, the culture of the gang*, Freepress, 198 p.

Cole, D. and B. Slade (1991), "Reform of financial systems", in D. Perkins and M. Roemer (eds.), *Reforming economic systems in developing countries*, Harvard Institute for International Development, Harvard University Press, 313-340.

Comment, R. and G.A. Jarrell (1991), "The relative signalling power of Dutch-auction and fixed-price self-tender offers and open-market share repurchases", *Journal of Finance*, vol. 46, 1243-1271.

Cone, K. and J. Laurence (1994), "How accurate are estimates of aggregate damages in securities fraud cases?", *Business Lawyer*, vol. 49, 505-526.

Cook, P. and G. Zarkin (1985), "Crime and the business cycle", *J.Legal Stud.*, vol. 14, 115 ff.

Cooter, R. and T. Ulen (1997), *Law and Economics*, Addison-Wesley, Reading, 481 p.

Cooter, R. and T. Ulen (2000), *Law and Economics*, Addison-Wesley, Reading, 445 p.

Copeland, T. and D. Galai (1983), "Information Effects on the bid-ask spread", *Journal of Finance*, 1457 ff.

Copeland, T. and J. Weston (1988), *Financial Theory and Corporate Policy*, Addison-Wesley, Massachusetts, 946 p.

Core, J., W. Guay and D. Larcker (2003), "Executive equity compensation and incentives: a survey", *Economic Policy Review*, vol. 9, nr.1, 27-50.

Cornell, B. and E. Sirri (1992), "The reaction of investors and stock prices to insider trading", *Journal of Finance*, vol. 47, 1031-1059.

Cornell, B. and R.G. Morgan (1990), "Using finance theory to measure damages in fraud on the market cases", *UCLA Law Review*, vol. 37, 883-924.

Coughlan, A.T. and R.M. Schmidt (1985), "Executive Compensation, Managerial Turnover, and Firm Performance: An Empirical Investigation", *Journal of Accounting and Economics*, 43-66.

Cowen, T. (1988), *The theory of market failure*, Fairfax, George Mason University Press.

Cox, J.D. (1986), "Insider Trading and Contracting: A Critical Response to the Chicago School", *Duke Law Journal*, 628-659.

Dann, L. (1981), "Common Stock Repurchases: An Analysis of Returns to Bondholders and Stockholders", *Journal of Financial Economics*, vol. 9, 113-138.

Dau-Schmidt, K.G. (1992), "A bargaining analysis of American labor law and the search for bargaining equity and industrial peace", *Michigan Law Review*, vol. 91, 419 ff.

De Geest, G. (1994), *Economische analyse van het contracten- en quasi-contractenrecht*, Maklu Uitgevers, 568 p.

De Geest, G. (2000), "Law and economics in Belgium", in B. Bouckaert and G. De Geest (eds.), *Encyclopedia of Law and Economics, Volume I, The history and methodology of law and economics*, Edward Elgar, p.128-138.

De Vauplane, H. and O. Simart (1997), "The concept of securities manipulation and its foundations in France and the USA", *Brook.J.Intl.L.*, vol. 23, nr.1, 203-240.

DeAngelo, H. and L. DeAngelo (1989), "Proxy contests and the governance of publicly held corporations", *Journal of Financial Economics*, 29-59.

Dechow, P., A. Hutton and R. Sloan (2000), "The Relation between Analysts' Forecasts of Long-Term Earnings Growth and Stock Price Performance Following Equity Offerings", *Contemporary Accounting Research*, vol.17, 1-32.

DeFusco, R., R. Johnson and T. Zorn (1990), "The Effect of Executive Stock Option Plans on Stockholders and Bondholders", *Journal of Finance*, June, 617-628.

Degryse, H. (1995), *Essays on financial intermediation, product differentiation, and market structure*, K.U.Leuven, Doctoral dissertation.

Demirgüç-Kunt, A. and V. Maksimovic (1998), "Law, finance and firm growth", *Journal of Finance*, vol. 53, 2107-2137.

Demirgüç-Kunt, A. and V. Maksimovic (1999), "Institutions, Financial Markets and Firm Debt Maturity", *Journal of Financial Economics*, 295-336.

Demsetz, H. (1986), "Corporate Control, Insider Trading, and Rates of Return", *American Economic Review*, 76, 313-316.

Demsetz, H. (1998), "Property rights", in P. Newman (ed.), *The New Palgrave Dictionary of Economics and the Law*, London, Macmillan, 144-155.

Den Hartog, J. (2000), "General theories of regulation", in B. Bouckaert en G. De Geest (eds.), *Encyclopedia of Law and Economics, Volume III, The regulation of contracts*, Edward Elgar, p.223-270.

Dennis, R.J. (1987), "Mandatory disclosure theory and management projections: a law and economics perspective", *Maryland Law Review*, vol. 46.

Devos, D. (1991), "Les opérations d'initiés en droit positif belge", *Bank- en Financiewezen*, nr.8, 455-470.

Diamond (1985), "Optimal release of information by firms", *Journal of Finance*, vol. 40.

DiIulio, J.Jr. (1994), "The question of black crime", *The Public Interest*, Fall.

DiIulio, J.Jr. (1996), "My black crime problem, and ours", *City Journal*, vol. 6, nr.2, 14-28.

Dimson, E. (1979), "Risk measurement when shares are subject to infrequent trading", *Journal of Financial Economics*, vol. 7, 197-226.

Dnes, A. (1996), *The economics of law*, International Thomson Business Press, 200 p.

Dodd, P. and J. Warner (1983), "On corporate governance: a study of proxy contests", *Journal of Financial Economics*, 401-438.

Dooley, M.P. (1980), "Enforcement of Insider Trading Restrictions", *Virginia Law Review*, vol. 66, 1-89.

Duffhues, P., R. Kabir, G. Mertens and P. Roosenboom (2001), "Employee stock option grants and firm performance in the Netherlands", in J. McCahery et al. (ed.), *Convergence and diversity in corporate governance regimes and capital markets*, forthcoming.

Dye, R. (1984), "Insider Trading and Incentives", *Journal of Business*, vol. 57, 295-313.

Eades, K., P. Hess and E. Kim (1985), "Market rationality and dividend announcements", *Journal of Financial Economics*, vol. 14, 581-604.

Easterbrook, F. (1981), "Insider Trading, Secret Agents, Evidentiary Privileges, and the Production of Information", *Sup.Ct.Rev.*, 309.

Easterbrook, F. (1984), "Two agency cost explanations of dividends", *American Economic Review*, vol. 74, 650-659.

Easterbrook, F. and D. Fischel (1982), "Corporate control transactions", *Yale Law Journal*, vol. 91, 698-737.

Easterbrook, F. and D. Fischel (1984), "Mandatory disclosure and the protection of investors", *Virginia Law Review*, 669-715.

Eide, E. (2000), "Law and economics in Norway", in B. Bouckaert and G. De Geest (eds.), *Encyclopedia of Law and Economics, Volume I, The history and methodology of law and economics*, Edward Elgar, p.309-312.

Eide, E. and R. Van den Bergh (1996), *Law and economics of the environment*, Oslo, Juridisk Forlag.

Elton, E. and M. Gruber (1995), *Modern portfolio theory and investment analysis*, John Wiley, 715 p.

Engelen, P.J. (1997a), "Is the Enforcement of Insider Trading Regulation Enforceable?", *European Journal of Crime, Criminal Law and Criminal Justice*, vol. 5(2), 105-111.

Engelen, P.J. (1997b), *Corporate governance in België: een tour d'horizon* [*Eng.: Corporate governance in Belgium: a first exploration*], Working paper, Departement Bedrijfseconomie, UFSIA, nr.97-259, December, 49 p.

Engelen, P.J. (1997c), "In defense of insider trading. An economic analysis of the Belgian insider trading regulation", *Cahiers Economiques de Bruxelles*, nr.156, 349-372.

Engelen, P.J. (1998a), "De schorsing van de notering op de Brusselse Beurs: 'trading halts'. Kan de Brusselse Beurs leren van buitenlandse ervaringen?" [*Eng.: The interruption of trading on the Brussels Stock Exchange: Trading Halts. Can the Brussels Stock Exchange learn from foreign experiences?*], *V&F*, nr.1, 83-88.

Engelen, P.J. (1998b), "Journalisten, koersgevoelige informatie en handel met voorkennis" [*Eng.: Journalists, price-sensitive information and insider trading*], *V&F*, nr.3, 305-315.

Engelen, P.J. (1999), *Informatieverstrekking door beursgenoteerde vennootschappen* [*Eng.: Information Disclosure by Stock Exchange Listed Companies*], Intersentia Rechtswetenschappen, 331 p.

Engelen, P.J. (2000a), "Hoe communiceren beursgenoteerde vennootschappen met de financiële markten? Naar een nieuwe beleidsdoelstelling voor beursregulering" [*Eng.: How do listed companies communicate with financial markets? Towards a new policy goal for securities regulation*], *V&F*, nr.2, 101-112.

Engelen, P.J. (2000b), Book review of B. Bouckaert and G. De Geest, *Encyclopedia of Law and Economics*, Edward Elgar, 5 volumes, 2000, in *Economisch en Sociaal Tijdschrift*, 2000, nr.4, blz.276-277.

Engelen, P.J. (2003a), "Can reputational damage restrict illegal insider trading?", *European Journal of Crime, Criminal Law and Criminal Justice*, vol. 11, nr 3, 253-263.

Engelen, P.J. (2003b), "Handel met voorkennis: Belgische regelgeving onverenigbaar met Europese Richtlijn" [*Eng.: Insider Trading: Belgian regulation violates European Directive*], *Bank- en Financieel Recht*, 58-61.

Engelen, P.J. (2004), "Criminal behavior: a real option approach. With an application to restricting illegal insider trading", *European Journal of Law and Economics*, vol. 17, nr. 3, 329-352.

Evans, D. and D. Herbert (1989), *The geography of crime*, Routledge London, 360 p.

Fabozzi, F.J. and C.K. Ma (1988), "The over-the-counter market and New York Stock Exchange Trading Halts", *The Financial Review*, vol. 23, nr.4, 427-437.

Fama, E. (1970), "Efficient capital markets: a review of theory and empirical work", *Journal of Finance*, 383-417.

Fama, E. (1980) "Agency Problems and the Theory of the Firm", *Journal of Political Economy*, 288-307.

Fama, E. (1991), "Efficient capital markets II", *Journal of Finance*, 1575-1617.

Farrar, D. and L. Selwyn (1967), "Taxes, corporate financial policy and return to investors", *National Tax Journal*, December, 444-454.

Faure, M.G. (2000), "Environmental regulation", in B. Bouckaert en G. De Geest (eds.), *Encyclopedia of Law and Economics, Volume II, Civil law and economics*, Edward Elgar, 443-520.

Ferguson, A. (1767), *An essay on the history of civil society*, Edited by L. Schneider, New Brunswick, NJ, Transaction Publishers, 1980.

Finnerty, J.E. (1976), "Insiders and Market Efficiency", *Journal of Finance*, 31, 1141-1148.

Firth, M. (1976), "The impact of earnings announcements on the share price behavior of similar type firms", *The Economic Journal*, vol. 86, 296-306.

Firth, M. (1981), "The relative information content of the release of financial results data by firms", *Journal of Accounting Research*, vol. 19, 521-529.

Fischel, D. (1982a), "Use of modern finance theory in securities fraud cases involving actively traded securities", *Business Lawyer*, vol. 38, 1-20.

Fischel, D. (1982b), "The corporate governance movement", *Vanderbilt Law Review*, vol. 35, 1259-1292.

Fischel, D. (1984), "Insider trading and investment analysts: an economic analysis of *Dirks v. Securities and Exchange Commission*", *Hofstra Law Review*, vol. 13, 127-146.

Fischel, D. (1989), "Efficient capital markets, the crash, and the fraud on the market theory", *Cornell Law Review*, vol. 74, 907-922.

Fischel, D. (1996), *Payback. The conspiracy to destroy Michael Milken and his financial revolution*, Harper Business, 332 p.

Flechter, C.E. (1991), *Materials on the law of insider trading*, Carolina Academic Press, 629 p.

Forsgardh, L. and K. Hertzen (1975), "The adjustment of stock prices to new earnings information: a study of the Swedish stock market", in E. Elton and M. Gruber, *International capital markets*, North-Holland Publishing Company.

Foster, G. (1977), "Quarterly accounting data: time series properties and predictive ability results", *Accounting Review*, 1-21.

Foster, G. (1986), *Financial Statement Analysis*, Prentice Hall, New York.

Franks, J., C. Mayer and L. Renneboog (1996), *The role of large stakes in poorly performing companies in the UK*, KUL, Departement TEW, onderzoeksrapport no. 9636, 27 p.

Freeman, R. (1986), "Who escapes? The relation between churchgoing and other background factors to socioeconomic performances of black male youth from inner-city tracts", in R.B. Freeman and H.J. Holzer (eds.), *The black youth employment crisis*, University of Chicago Press.

Freeman, R. (1992), "Crime and the employment of disadvantaged youths", in G. Peterson and W. Vroman (eds.), *Urban Labour Markets and Job Opportunity*, Washington, DC, Urban Institute Press, 201-237.

Freund, J. and R. Walpole (1987), *Mathematical statistics*, Prentice-Hall, 608 p.

Friend, I. and E. Herman (1964), "The SEC through a glass darkly", *Journal of Business*, vol. 37, 382-405.

Friend, I. and E. Herman (1965), "Professor Stigler on securities regulation. A further comment", *Journal of Business*, 106-110.

Friend, I. and R. Westerfield (1975), "Required disclosure and the stock market: Comment", *American Economic Review*, vol. 65, 467-472.

Furbush, D. and J.W. Smith (1994), "Estimating the number of damaged shares in securities fraud litigation: an introduction to stock trading models", *Business Lawyer*, vol. 49, 527-543.

Gaillard, E. (1992), "France", in E. Gaillard (ed.), *Insider trading. The laws of Europe, the United States and Japan*, Kluwer Law and Taxation Publishers, 59-78.

Geens, K. (1991a), "Voorkennis: strafbaar zonder gebruik?", in *De nieuwe beurswetgeving. Commentaar bij de Wet van 4 december 1990 betreffende de financiële markten en de financiële verrichtingen*, Biblo, Kalmthout, 409-471.

Geens, K. (1991b), "Hoe duidelijk moet informatie zijn om bevoorrecht te zijn?", *TRV*, 221-225.

Gilson, R.J. and R.H. Kraakman (1984), "The mechanisms of market efficiency", *Virginia Law Review*, 549-644.

Givoly, D. and D. Palmon (1985), "Insider Trading and the Exploitation of Inside Information: Some Empirical Evidence", *Journal of Business*, 69-87.

Glaeser, E.L. and B. Sacerdote (1996), "Why is there more crime in cities?", *NBER working paper*, nr.5430.

Glendon, M.A., M. Gordon and C. Osakwe (1992), *Comparative Legal Traditions in a Nutshell*, St. Paul, West Publishing Company.

Gordon, J.N. and L.A. Kornhauser (1985), "Efficient markets, costly information, and securities research", *New York University Law Review*, vol. 60, 761-849.

Green, E., D. Braverman and J. Schneck (1996), "Concepts of regulation – the US model", in Fidelis Oditah (ed.), *The future for the global securities market*, Clarendon Press, Oxford, 157-178.

Griffin, P. (1977), "The time-series behavior of quarterly earnings: preliminary evidence", *Journal of Accounting Research*, 71-83.

Grinstein, Y. (2004), "Complementary Perspectives on Efficient Capital Markets, Corporate Disclosure and Enron", *Cornell Law Review*, vol. 89, 503-510.

Grogger, J. (1991), "Certainty vs. Severity of Punishment", *Economic Inquiry*, 29(2), 297-309.

Grogger, J. (1992), "Arrest, persistent youth joblessness, and black/white employment differentials", *Review of Economics and Statistics*, vol. 74, 100-106.

Grogger, J. (1995), "The effect of arrests on the employment and earnings of young men", *Quarterly Journal of Economics*, vol. 110, 51-71.

Grossman, S. (1981), "The informational role of warranties and private disclosure about product quality", *Journal of Law and Economics*, vol. 24, 461-483.

Grossman, S. (1986), "An analysis of the role of insider trading on futures markets", *Journal of Business*, vol. 59, 129-146.

Grossman, S. and J. Stiglitz (1980), "On the impossibility of informationally efficient markets", *American Economic Review*, vol. 70, nr.3, 393-408.

Grundfest, J. (1998), "Securities regulation", in P. Newman (ed.), *The New Palgrave Dictionary of Economics and the Law*, London, Macmillan, 410-419.

Haddock, D. and J. Macey (1986a), "A Coasian Model of Insider Trading", *Northwestern University Law Review*, 1449-1472.

Haddock, D. and J. Macey (1986b), "Controlling insider trading in Europe and America: the economics of the politics", in J.M. Graf von der Schulenberg and F. Skogh (eds.), *Law & economics and the economics of legal regulation*, Dordrecht, 149-167.

Haddock, D.D. and J.R. Macey (1987), "Regulation on Demand: A Private Interest Model, with an Application to Insider Trading Regulation", *Journal of Law and Economics*, 30, 311-352.

Haft, R. (1982), "The effect of insider trading rules on the internal efficiency of the large corporation", *Michigan Law Review*, vol. 80, 1051-1071.

Hart, O.D. (1983), "The Market Mechanism as an Incentive Scheme", *Bell Journal of Economics*, vol. 14, 366-382.

Hatzis, A. (2000), "Law and economics in Greece", in B. Bouckaert and G. De Geest (eds.), *Encyclopedia of Law and Economics, Volume I, The history and methodology of law and economics*, Edward Elgar, p.228-239.

Haugen, R. (1997), *Modern Investment Theory*, Prentice Hall, 748 p.

Haugen, R. (2001), *Modern Investment Theory*, Prentice Hall, 656 p.

Hawawini, G. and P. Michel (1987), *Mandatory Financial Information and Capital Market Equilibrium in Belgium*, Garland Publishing.

Hay, J., A. Shleifer and R. Vishny (1996), "Towards a theory of legal reform", *European Economic Review*, 559-567.

Healy, P. and K. Palepu (1988), "Earnings information conveyed by dividend initiations and omissions", *Journal of Financial Economics*, vol. 21, 149-175.

Healy, P.M. and K.G. Palepu (1995), "The Challenges of Investor Communication. The Case of CUC International, Inc.", *Journal of Financial Economics*, vol. 38, 111-140.

Heinkel, R. and A. Kraus (1987), "The effect of insider trading on average rates of return", *Canadian Journal of Economics*, 588-611.

Heremans, D. (2000), "Regulation of banking and financial markets", in B. Bouckaert and G. De Geest (eds.), *Encyclopedia of Law and Economics, Volume III, The regulation of contracts*, Edward Elgar, 813-836.

Herzel, L. and A. Braendel (1998), "Law-and-economics in action", in P. Newman (ed.), *The New Palgrave Dictionary of Economics and the Law*, London, Macmillan, 492-497.

Hillier, D. and A. Marshall (1998), "The timing of directors' trades", *Journal of Business Law*, September, 454-467.

Hillier, D. and A. Marshall (2002), "Are trading bans effective? Exchange regulation and corporate insider trading transactions around earnings announcements", *Journal of Corporate Finance*, vol. 8, 393-410.

Holden, C. and A. Subrahmanyam (1992), "Long-lived private information and imperfect competition", *Journal of Finance*, vol. 47, 247-270.

Holzhauer, R. and R. Teijl (1995), *Inleiding rechtseconomie*, Gouda Quint, Arnhem, 335 p.

Holzhauer, R. and R. Teijl (2000), "Law and economics in the Netherlands", in B. Bouckaert and G. De Geest (eds.), *Encyclopedia of Law and Economics, Volume I, The history and methodology of law and economics*, Edward Elgar, 274-308.

Hu, J. and T. Noe (2001), "Insider trading and managerial incentives", *Journal of Banking and Finance*, vol. 25, 681-716.

Hume, D. (1739), *A treatise of human nature*, Edited by P. Nidditch, Oxford, Oxford University Press, 1978.

Ikenberry, D. and J. Lakonishok (1993), "Corporate governance through the proxy contest: evidence and implications", *Journal of Business*, 405-435.

Ikenberry, D., J. Lakonishok and T. Vermaelen (1995), "Market Underreaction to open market share repurchases", *Journal of Financial Economics*, vol. 39, 181-208.

Jaffe, J. (1974), "Special Information and Insider Trading", *Journal of Business*, 10-28.

Jaffe, J. (1974a), "The effect of regulation changes on insider trading", *Bell Journal of Economics and Management Science*, 93-121.

Jaffe, J. (1974b), "Special Information and Insider Trading", *Journal of Business*, 10-28.

Jarrell, G. (1981), "The economic effects of federal regulation of the market for new security issues", *Journal of Law and Economics*, vol. 24, 613-675.

Jegadeesh, N., J. Kim, S.D. Krische and C.M.C. Lee (2004), "Analyzing the Analysts: When Do Recommendations Add Value?", *Journal of Finance*, vol. 59, no. 3, 1083-1124.

Jeng, L., A. Metrick and R. Zeckhauser (1999), "The profits to insider trading: a performance-evaluation perspective", working paper, Harvard University.

Jensen, M. (1986), "Agency costs of free cash flow, corporate finance, and takeovers", *American Economic Review*, vol. 76, 323-329.

Jensen, M. and W. Meckling (1976), "Theory of the firm: managerial behavior, agency costs, and capital structure", *Journal of Financial Economics*, vol. 3, 305-360.

Johnson, S., R. La Porta, F. Lopez-de-Silanes and A. Shleifer (2000), "Tunneling", *American Economic Review Papers and Proceedings*, 90, 22-27.

Joskow, P. and N. Rose (1989), "The effects of economic regulation", in R. Schmalensee and R. Willig (eds.), *Handbook of Industrial Organization II*, Amsterdam, North Holland, 1450-1506.

Joskow, P. and R. Noll (1981), "Regulation in theory and practice: an overview", in G. Fromm (ed.), *Studies in Public Regulation*, Cambridge, MA, The MIT Press, 1-66.

Joy, M., R. Litzenberger and R. McEnally (1977), "The adjustment of stock prices to announcements of unanticipated changes in quarterly earnings", *Journal of Accounting Research*, 207-225.

Kabir, R. (1991a), "Het opschorten van de handel op de Amsterdamse Effectenbeurs", *Bedrijfskunde*, 65-71.

Kabir, R. (1991b), *An Empirical Investigation of Trading Suspension and Insider Trading Restriction*, doctoral dissertation, University of Limburg, 155 p.

Kabir, R. (1994), "Share Price Behaviour around Trading Suspensions on the London Stock Exchange", *Applied Financial Economics*, 289-295.

Kabir, R. (1997), "The value relevance of Dutch financial statement numbers for stock market investors", *Center Working Paper*, nr.9758, 23 p.

Kabir, R. and T. Vermaelen (1996), "Insider Trading Restrictions and the Stock market: Evidence from the Amsterdam Stock Exchange", *European Economic Review*, vol. 40, 1594-1603.

Kabir, R., P. Duffhues and G. Mertens (1999), *Personeelsoptieregelingen in Nederland: theorie en praktijk*, Tilburg, Tilburg University Press, 45 pp.

Kahan, M. (1992), "Securities laws and the social costs of 'inaccurate' stock prices", *Duke Law Review*, vol. 41, 977-1044.

Kao, C. and C. Wu (1994), "Tests of dividend signalling using the Marsh-Merton model: a generalized friction approach", *Journal of Business*, 45-68.

Kaplan, S.N. (1994), "Top Executives, turnover and firm performance in Germany", *Journal of Law, Economics and Organisation*, vol. 10, 142-159.

Kaplow, L. and S. Shavell (1994), "Why the legal system is less efficient than the income tax in redistributing income", *Journal of Legal Studies*, vol. 23, 667-681.

Karmarkar, U. (1978), "Subjectively weighted utility: a descriptive extension of the expected utility model", *Organisational Behavior and Human Performance*, vol. 21, nr.1, 61-72.

Karmarkar, U. (1979), "Subjective weighted utility and the Allais paradox", *Organisational Behavior and Human Performance*, vol. 24, nr.1, 67-72.

Karpoff, J.M. and J.R. Lott (1993), "The reputational penalty firms bear from committing criminal fraud", *Journal of Law and Economics*, vol. 36, 757-802.

Kay, M. (1973), "The justice report on insider trading", *The modern law review*, 185-192.

Keeler, T. (1984), "Theories of regulation and the deregulation movement", *Public Choice*, 103-145.

Keown and Pinkerton (1981), "Merger Announcements and Insider Trading Activity: An Empirical Investigation", *Journal of Finance*, 855.

King, M. and A. Roell (1988), "Insider Trading", *Economic Policy*, vol. 6, 165-187.

King, R. and R. Levine (1993), "Finance and growth: Schumpeter might be right", *Quarterly Journal of Economics*, vol. 108, 717-737.

King, R., G. Pownall and G. Waymire (1991), "Corporate Disclosure and Price Discovery Associated with NYSE Temporary Trading Halts", *Contemporary Accounting Research*, 509-531.

Kirstein, R. (2000), "Law and economics in Germany", in B. Bouckaert and G. De Geest (eds.), *Encyclopedia of Law and Economics, Volume I, The history and methodology of law and economics*, Edward Elgar, 160-227.

Kitch, E. (1980), "The law and economics of rights in valuable information", *Journal of Legal Studies*, vol. 9, 683-723.

Kitch, E. (1996), "Competition between securities markets: good or bad?", in Oditah, Fidelis (ed.), *The future for the securities market: legal and regulatory aspects*, Oxford, Clarendon, 233-241.

Kitch, E. (2000), "Regulation of the securities market", in B. Bouckaert en G. De Geest (eds.), *Encyclopedia of Law and Economics, Volume III, The regulation of contracts*, Edward Elgar, 813-836.

Kitch, E., M. Isaacson and D. Kasper (1971), "The regulation of taxicabs in Chicago", *Journal of Law and Economics*, vol. 14, 285-350.

Klapper, L. and I. Love (2002), "Corporate governance, investor protection and performance in emerging markets", *World Bank working paper*, nr. 2818, 32p.

Korhonen, A. (1975), "Accounting income numbers, information and stock prices: a test of market efficiency", *The Finnish Journal of Business Economics*, vol. 24, 306-322.

Krekels, P. (1992), "Misbruik van voorkennis naar Belgisch recht: de repressieve keerzijde van de informatiemedaille?", *Tijdschrift voor Belgisch Handelsrecht*, 3-53.

Kripke (1973), "The myth of the informed layman", *The Business Lawyer*, vol. 28, 631.

Kryzanowski, L. (1978), "Misinformation and regulatory actions in the Canadian capital markets: some empirical evidence", *Bell Journal of Economics*, 355-368.

Kryzanowski, L. (1979), "The Efficacy of Trading Suspensions: A Regulatory Action to Prevent the Exploitation of Monopoly Information", *Journal of Finance*, 1187-1200.

Kvanli, A., C. Guynes and R. Pavur (1992), *Introduction to business statistics. A computer integrated approach*, West Publishing Company, 929 p.

Kyle, A. (1985), "Continuous auctions and insider trading", *Econometrica*, vol. 53, 1315-1336.

La Porta, R., F. Lopez-de-Silanes, A. Shleifer (1999), 'Corporate ownership around the world, *Journal of Finance*, vol. 54, 471-517.

La Porta, R., F. Lopez-de-Silanes, A. Shleifer and R.W. Vishny (1997), 'Legal determinants of external finance', *Journal of Finance*, vol. 52, 1131-1150.

La Porta, R., F. Lopez-de-Silanes, A. Shleifer and R.W. Vishny (1998), 'Law and Finance', *Journal of Political Economy*, vol. 106, 1113-1155.

La Porta, R., F. Lopez-de-Silanes, A. Shleifer and R.W. Vishny (2000), 'Agency problems and dividend policies around the world', *Journal of Finance*, vol. 55, 1-34.

La Porta, R., F. Lopez-de-Silanes, A. Shleifer and R.W. Vishny (1999), 'Investor protection and corporate valuation', *NBER Working Paper*, no. W7403.

La Porta, R., F. Lopez-de-Silanes, A. Shleifer and R.W. Vishny (1999), 'Investor protection: origins, consequences and reform', *NBER Working Paper*, no. W7428.

La Porta, R., F. Lopez-de-Silanes, A. Shleifer and R.W. Vishny (2000), "Investor protection and corporate governance", *Journal of Financial Economics*, vol. 58, 3-27.

Laffont, J.J. and E.S. Maskin (1990), "The efficient market hypothesis and insider trading on the stock market", *Journal of Political Economy*, 70-93.

Lambrecht, P. (1991), "La réforme financière de 1990. Livre V. Du délit d'initié (Loi du 4 décembre 1990)", *J.T.*, 671-675.

Lando, H. (2000), "Law and economics in Denmark", in B. Bouckaert and G. De Geest (eds.), *Encyclopedia of Law and Economics, Volume I, The history and methodology of law and economics*, Edward Elgar, 139-145.

Lang, L. and R. Litzenberger (1989), "Dividend announcements: cash flow signalling vs. free cash flow hypothesis", *Journal of Financial Economics*, vol. 24, 181-191.

Langevoort, D.C. (1982), "Insider Trading and the Fiduciary Principle: A Post-Chiarella Restatement", *California Law Review*, 70, 1-53.

Langevoort, D.C. (1990), "Investment Analysts and the Law of Insider Trading", *Virginia Law Review*, 76, 1023-1054.

Larcker, D. (1983), "The Association Between Performance Plan adoption and Corporate Capital Investment", *Journal of Accounting and Economics*, April, 3-30.

Larsen, R. and M. Marx (1990), *Statistics*, Prentice-Hall, 829 p.

Lee, H.C. (1993), "Market manipulation in the US and UK", *The Company Lawyer*, vol. 14, no.5, 84-89 (part I) and 123-129 (part II).

Lee, R. (1998a), *What is an exchange?*, Oxford, Oxford University Press, 405 p.

Lee, R. (1998b), "Ownership of market information", in P. Newman (ed.), *The New Palgrave Dictionary of Economics and the Law*, London, Macmillan, 730-734.

Lee, R. (1998c), "Regulation of capital markets in the European Union", in P. Newman (ed.), *The New Palgrave Dictionary of Economics and the Law*, London, Macmillan, 228-232.

Lee, R. (2000), "Property rights in price and quote information", in B. Bouckaert en G. De Geest (eds.), *Encyclopedia of Law and Economics, Volume III, The regulation of contracts*, Edward Elgar, 315-331.

Leland, H. (1981), "Comments on Grossman", *Journal of Law and Economics*, vol. 24, 485-489.

Leland, H. (1992), "Insider Trading: Should It be Prohibited?", *Journal of Political Economy*, 859-887.

Leland, H. and D. Pyle (1977), "Informational asymmetries, financial structure and financial intermediation", *Journal of Finance*, vol. 32, 371-377.

Leland, H., (1992) "Insider Trading: Should It be Prohibited?", *Journal of Political Economy*, 859-887.

Lev, B. (1989), "On the usefulness of earnings and earnings research: lessons of two decades of empirical research", *Journal of Accounting Research*, 153-192.

Levine, R. (1997), "Financial development and economic growth: views and agenda", *Journal of Economic Literature*, vol. 35, 688-726.

Levine, R. and S. Zervos (1998), "Stock markets, banks, and economic growth", *American Economic Review*, vol. 88, 537-558.

Levitt, A. (1998), *A question of integrity: promoting investor confidence by fighting insider trading*, SEC Speaks Conference, February 27th.

Levmore, S. (1982), "Securities and secrets: insider trading and the law of contracts", *Virginia Law Review*, vol. 68, 117-160.

Levy, A. (1999), "Access denied", *Bloomberg*, December, 32-38.

Lewisch, P. (1991), "The political economy of barriers to entry: the example of the amendment for taxicab regulation in Austria", in Weigel, W. (ed.), *Economic Analysis of Law – A collection of applications*, Vienna, Österreichischen Wirtschaftsverlag, 222-234.

Lin, J. and J. Howe (1990), "Insider trading in the OTC market", *Journal of Finance*, vol. 45, 1273-1284.

Litzenberger, R. and K. Ramaswamy (1979), "The effect of personal taxes and dividends on capital asset prices: theory and empirical evidence", *Journal of Financial Economics*, vol. 7, 163-195.

Litzenberger, R. and K. Ramaswamy (1982), "The effects of dividends on common stock prices: tax effects or information effects", *Journal of Finance*, vol. 37, 429-443.

Ljungqvist, A., F. Marston and W. Wilhelm (2004), "Competing for Securities Underwriting Mandates: Banking Relationships and Analyst Recommendations", *NYU – Stern School of Business Working Paper*, No. FIN-03-015.

Lorie, J.H. and V. Niederhoffer (1968), "Predictive and Statistical Properties of Insider Trading", *Journal of Law and Economics*, 11, 35-53.

Lott, J.R. (1990), "The effect of conviction on the legitimate income of criminals", *Economic Letters*, vol. 34, 381-385.

Lott, J.R. (1992a), "Do we punish high-income criminals too heavily?", *Economic Inquiry*, vol. 30, 583-608.

Lott, J.R. (1992b), "An attempt at measuring the total monetary penalty from drug convictions: the importance of an individual's reputation", *Journal of Legal Studies*, vol. 21, 159-187.

Lott, J.R. (1996), "The level of optimal fines to prevent fraud when reputations exist and penalty clauses are unenforceable", *Managerial and Decision Economics*, vol. 17, 363-380.

Lott, J.R. (1998), "Criminal conviction and future income", in P. Newman (ed.), *The New Palgrave Dictionary of Economics and the Law*, London, Macmillan, 550-553.

Macey, J. (1991), *Insider trading. Economics, politics, and policy*, AEI Press, 76 p.

Macey, J. (2004), "Efficient Capital Markets, Corporate Disclosure, and Enron", *Cornell Law Review*, vol. 89, 394-422.

Macey, J. and G. Miller (1990), "Good finance, bad economics: an analysis of the fraud-on-the-market theory", *Stanford Law Review*, vol. 42, 1059-1092.

Macey, J., G. Miller, M. Mitchell and J. Netter (1991), "Lessons from financial economics: materiality, reliance, and extending the reach of *Basic v. Levinson*", *Virginia Law Review*, vol. 77, 1017-1049.

Macey, J.R. (1999), "Securities trading: a contractual perspective", *Case Western Reserve Law Review*, vol. 50, 269-290.

MacKinlay, A.C. (1997), "Event studies in economics and finance", *Journal of Economic Literature*, vol. 35, 13-39.

Magat, W.A. (1998), "Information regulation", ", in P. Newman (ed.), *The New Palgrave Dictionary of Economics and the Law*, London, Macmillan, 307-311.

Malkiel, B. (1992), "Efficient Market Hypothesis", in Newman, P., M. Milgate and J. Eatwell (eds.), *New Palgrave Dictionary of Money and Finance*, Macmillan, London.

Manne, H.G. (1965), "Mergers and the Market for Corporate Control", *Journal of Political Economy*, 110-120.

Manne, H.G. (1966), *Insider Trading and the Stock Market*, New York, Free Press, 189 p.

Manne, H.G. (1970), "Insider Trading and the Law Professors", *Vanderbilt Law Review*, 23, 547.

Manne, H.G. (1985), "Insider trading and property rights in new information", *Cato Journal*, vol. 4, 933-943.

Marris (1963), "A model of the managerial enterprise", *Quarterly Journal of Economics*, 185-209.

Masulis, R. (1980), "Stock repurchase by tender offer: an analysis of the causes of common stock price changes", *Journal of Finance*, vol. 35, 315-319.

Maug, E. (2000), "Insider trading legislation and corporate governance", *Discussion papers in business*, Department of Business and Economics, Humboldt-Universität zu Berlin, January, nr.5, 46 p.

Mehran, H. (1995), "Executive Compensation Structure, Ownership, and Firm Performance", *Journal of Financial Economics*, vol. 38, 2 ff.

Mendelson, M. (1969), "Book review: the economics board of insider trading reconsidered", *University of Pennsylvania Law Review*, vol. 117, 470-492.

Mendelson, M. (1972), "From automated quotes to automated trading: restructuring the stock market in the US", *The Bulletin*, Institute of Finance, New York University.

Mercuro, N. and S.G. Medema (1997), *Economics and the law. From Posner to post-modernism*, Princeton University Press, Princeton, New Jersey, 235p.

Merton, R. and Z. Bodie (1995), "A conceptual framework for analyzing the financial environment", in D.B. Crane, R.C. Merton, K.A. Froot et al. (eds.), *The global financial system. A functional perspective*, Harvard Business School Press, 3-32.

Meulbroek, L. (1992), "An empirical analysis of illegal insider trading", *Journal of Finance*, 1661-1699.

Michaely, R., R. Thaler and K. Womack (1995), "Price reactions to dividend initiations and omissions: overreaction or drift?", *Journal of Finance*, vol. 50, 573-608.

Michaely, R. and K. Womack (1999), "Conflict of Interest and the Credibility of Underwriter Analyst Recommendations", *Review of Financial Studies*, vol. 12, 653

Milgrom, P. (1981), "Good news and bad news: representation theorems and applications", *Bell Journal of Economics*, 380-391.

Miller, G. (2004), "Catastrophic Financial Failures: Enron and More", *Cornell Law Review*, vol. 89, 423-455.

Miller, M. (1986), "Behavioral rationality in finance: the case of dividends", *Journal of Business*, vol. 59, 451-468.

Miller, M. and B. Scholes (1978), "Dividends and taxes", *Journal of Financial Economics*, vol. 6, 333-364.

Miller, M. and F. Modigliani (1961), "Dividend policy, growth, and the valuation of shares", *Journal of Business*, vol. 34, 411-433.

Mishra, C., D. McConaughy and D. Gobeli (2000), "Effectiveness of CEO pay-for-performance", *Review of Financial Economics*, vol. 9, 1-13.

Mitnick, B. (1980), *The political economy of regulation*, New York, Columbia University Press.

Moerland, P.W. (1992), "Economische theorievorming omtrent de onderneming (deel 1)", *MAB*, Jan.-Febr., 57-65.

Moerland, P.W. (1995a), "Corporate Ownership and Control Structures: An International Comparison", *Review of Industrial Organisation*, 1995, vol. 10, 446.

Moerland, P.W. (1995b), "Alternative disciplinary mechanisms in different corporate systems", *Journal of Economic Behavior and Organisation*, vol. 26, 17-34.

Montagné, L. (2000), "Law and economics in France", in B. Bouckaert and G. De Geest (eds.), *Encyclopedia of Law and Economics, Volume I, The history and methodology of law and economics*, Edward Elgar, 150-159.

Morck, R., A. Shleifer and R.W. Vishny (1988), "Management Ownership and Market Valuation: An Empirical Analysis", *Journal of Financial Economics*, 293-315.

Murphy, K. (1985), "Corporate Performance and Managerial Remuneration: An Empirical Analysis", *Journal of Accounting and Economics*, 179-203.

Murphy, K. (2004), "Stock-based pay in new economy firms", *Journal of Accounting and Economics*, vol. 34, 129-147.

Myers, S. (1999), "Financial architecture", *European Financial Management*, 133-141.

Nabben, S. (1995), *Circuit breaker. Funktionen und Auswirkungen bedingter Börsenregeln*, Neue bedriebswirtschaftliche Forschung Wiesbaden, Gabler, 287 p.

Nagin, D. and J. Waldfogel (1995), "The Effects of Criminality and Conviction on the Labor Market Status of Young British Offenders", *International Review of Law and Economics*, vol. 15, 109-126.

Naylor, J.M. (1990), "The use of criminal sanctions by UK and US authorities for insider trading: how can the two systems learn from each other?", *The Company Lawyer*, vol. 11, 53-61 (part 1) and 83-91 (part 2).

Needham, D. (1983), *The economics and politics of regulation: a behavioral approach*, Boston, Little Brown, 482 p.

Neilson, W. and H. Winter (1997), "On Criminals' Risk Attitudes", *Economic Letters*, 55, 97-102.

Noe, T.H. (1997), "Insider trading and the problem of corporate agency", *Journal of Law, Economics, and Organization*, vol. 13, 287-318.

Noll, R. (1989), "Economic perspectives on the politics of regulation", in R. Schmalensee and R. Willig (eds.), *Handbook of Industrial Organization II*, Amsterdam, North Holland, 1253-1287.

Nuolimaa, R. and P. Timonen (2000), "Law and economics in Finland", in B. Bouckaert and G. De Geest (eds.), *Encyclopedia of Law and Economics, Volume I, The history and methodology of law and economics*, Edward Elgar, 146-149.

Ogus, A. (1996), *Regulation. Legal form and economic theory*, Clarendon Press, Oxford, 355 p.

Ogus, A. (1998), "Law-and-economics from the perspective of law", in P. Newman (ed.), *The New Palgrave Dictionary of Economics and the Law*, London, Macmillan, 486-492.

Oliver, J.M. (1979), *Law and economics an introduction*, George Allen & Unwin, London, 108 p.

Olson, R.N. (2000), "The regulation of medical professions", in B. Bouckaert en G. De Geest (eds.), *Encyclopedia of Law and Economics, Volume III, The regulation of contracts*, Edward Elgar, 1018-1054.

Orsagh and Witte (1981), "Economic status and crime: implications for offender rehabilitation", *J.Crim.L.&Criminology*, vol. 72, 1055 ff.

Overdahl, J. and H. McMillan (1998), "Another day, another collar: an evaluation of the effects of NYSE Rule 80A on trading costs and intermarket arbitrage", *Journal of Business*, vol. 71, 27-53.

Pagano, M. and A. Roëll (1993), "Auction markets, dealership markets and execution risk", in Conti, V. and R. Hamaui (eds.), *Financial markets' liberalization and the role of banks*, Cambridge University Press, 200-212.

Palepu, K. and P.M. Healy (2003), "The Fall of Enron", *Journal of Economic Perspectives*, Vol. 17, No. 2.

Pardolesi, R. and G. Bellantuona (2000), "Law and economics in Italy", in B. Bouckaert and G. De Geest (eds.), *Encyclopedia of Law and Economics, Volume I, The history and methodology of law and economics*, Edward Elgar, 244-261.

Pashigian, B.P. (1984), "The effect of environmental regulation on optimal plant size and factor shares", *Journal of Law and Economics*, vol. 27, 1-28.

Pastor, S. and J. Pintos (2000), "Law and economics in Spain", in B. Bouckaert and G. De Geest (eds.), *Encyclopedia of Law and Economics, Volume I, The history and methodology of law and economics*, Edward Elgar, 346-369.

Patell, J. and M. Wolfson (1984), "The intraday speed of adjustment of stock prices to earnings and dividend announcements", *Journal of Financial Economics*, 223-252.

Peltzman, S. (1976), "Towards a more general theory of regulation", *Journal of Law and Economics*, 211-240.

Penman, S. (1982), "Insider Trading and the Dissemination of Firm's Forecast Information", *Journal of Business*, 478-503.

Perry, M. (1996), "Approaches to market regulation – the United Kingdom", in Fidelis Oditah (ed.), *The future for the global securities market*, Clarendon Press, Oxford, 179-198.

Pfeil, U. (1996), "Finanzplatz Deutschland: Germany enacts insider trading legislation", *Am. U. J. Int'l L. & Pol'y*, vol. 11, 137-193.

Philippe, D. (1991), "Les opérations d'initiés", *R.P.S.*, 107.

Phillips, R.M. and R.J. Zutz (1984), "The Insider Trading Doctrine: A Need for Legislative Repair", *Hofstra Law Review*, 71.

Phillips, S. and R. Zecher (1981), *The SEC and the public interest*, Cambridge, MA, MIT Press, 175 p.

Pigou, A.C. (1920), *The economics of welfare*, London, Macmillan.

Pingel, I. (1992), "The EC Directive of 1989", in E. Gaillard (ed.), *Insider trading. The laws of Europe, the United States and Japan*, Kluwer Law and Taxation Publishers, 5-22.

Plott, C.R. (1965), "Occupational self-regulation: a case study of the Oklahoma Dry Cleaners", *Journal of Law and Economics*, vol. 8, 195-222.

Polinsky, A.M. (1983), *An introduction to law and economics*, Little Brown and Company, Boston, 138 p.

Posner, R. (1971), "Taxation by regulation", *Bell Journal of Economics*, 22-50.

Posner, R. (1974), "Theories of economic regulation", *Bell Journal of Economics and Management Science*, 335-358.

Posner, R. (1984), "Some economics of labor law", *University of Chicago Law Review*, vol. 51, 988-1011.

Posner, R. (1987), "The law and economics movement", *American Economic Review*, vol. 77, 1-13.

Posner, R. (1990), "Law and economics *is* moral", *Valparaiso University Law Review*, vol. 24, 163-173.

Posner, R. (1998), *Economic analysis of law*, Aspen Law & Business, 5th edition, 802 p.

Posner, R. (2000), "Foreword", in B. Bouckaert and G. De Geest (eds.), *Encyclopedia of Law and Economics, Volume I, The history and methodology of law and economics*, Edward Elgar, xii-xiii.

Posner, R. and K. Scott (1980), *Economics of corporation law and securities regulation*, Little Brown and Company, Boston, 381 p.

Pound, J. (1988), "Proxy contests and the efficiency of shareholder oversight", *Journal of Financial Economics*, 237-285.

Pound, J. (1991), "Proxy voting and the SEC. Investor protection versus market efficiency", *Journal of Financial Economics*, 241-285.

Pratt, S. and Ch. DeVere (1970), Relationships between insider trading and rates of return for NYSE common stocks, 1960-1966, in *Modern Developments in Investment Management*, eds. J. Lorie and R. Brealey, New York.

Quiggin, J. (1982), "A theory of anticipated utility", *Journal of Economic Behavior and Organization*, vol. 3, nr.4, 323-343.

Quiggin, J. (1987), "On the nature of probability weighting: response to Segal", *Journal of Economic Behavior and Organization*, vol. 8, nr.4, 641-645.

Quiggin, J. (1993), *Generalized expected utility theory*, Kluwer Academic Publishers, Boston, 208 p.

Rajan, R. and L. Zingales (1998), "Financial dependence and growth", *American Economic Review*, vol. 88, 559-586.

Reiss, A.J. (1984), "Selecting strategies of social control over organizational life", in K. Hawkins and J.M. Thomas (eds.), *Enforcing regulation*, Kluwer-Nijhoff Publishing, 1984, 23-35.

Reiss, A.J. and A.D. Biderman (1980), *Data sources on white-collar law-breaking*, Washington D.C., National Institute of Justice.

Rendleman, R., C. Jones and H. Latane (1982), "Empirical anomalies based on unexpected earnings and the importance of risk adjustments", *Journal of Financial Economics*, 269-287.

Renneboog, L. (1996), *Ownership, Managerial Control and the Governance of Companies Listed on the Brussels Stock exchange*, KUL, Departement TEW, onderzoeksrapport no.635, 37 p.

Reynolds, T. and A. Flores (1989), *Foreign Law: Current Sources of Basic Legislation in Jurisdictions of the World*, Littleton, Rothman and Co.

Robbins, L. (1932), *An essay on the nature and significance of economic science*, Macmillan, London, 141 p.

Robbins, S. and W. Werner (1964), "Professor Stigler revisited", *Journal of Business*, vol. 37, 406-413.

Robert, M.C. and M. Svetchine (1991), "Insider dealing – remedies and enforcement in France", in K. Hopt and E. Wymeersch (eds.), *European Insider Dealing*, London, Butterworths, 331-337.

Ross, S.A. (1977), "The determination of financial structure: the incentive-signalling approach", *Bell Journal of Economics*, 23-40.

Rousseau, P. and P. Wachtel (1998), "Financial intermediation and economic performance: historical evidence from five industrialized countries", *Journal of Money Credit and Banking*, 657-678.

Rowley, C. (1998), "Law-and-economics from the perspective of economics", in P. Newman (ed.), *The New Palgrave Dictionary of Economics and the Law*, London, Macmillan, 474-486.

Rozeff, M. and M. Zaman (1988), "Market efficiency and insider trading", *Journal of Business*, vol. 61, 25-44.

Rubin, P.H. and J.B. Kau (1981), "The impact of labor unions on the passage of economic regulation", *Journal of Labor Economics*, 133-145.

Saari, C.P. (1977), "The Efficient Capital Market Hypothesis, Economic Theory and the Regulation of the Securities Industry", *Stanford Law Review*, vol. 29, 1031-1076.

Santoni, G.J. and T. Liu (1993), "Circuit breakers and stock market volatility", *The Journal of Futures Markets*, vol. 13, 261-277.

Schmidt, H. (1991), "Insider Regulation and Economic Theory", in Hopt and Wymeersch (eds.), *European Insider Dealing*, 21-38.

Schotland, R. (1967), "Unsafe at Any Price: A Reply to Manne, Insider Trading and the Stock Market", *Va.L.Review*, vol. 53, 1425.

Schwab, S. (1987), "Collective bargaining and the coase theorem", *Cornell Law Review*, vol. 72, 245-287.

Schwarcz, S.L. (2002), "Enron, and the Use and Abuse of Special Purpose Entities in Corporate Structures", *University of Cincinnati Law Review*, Symposium Issue, April.

Schwartz and Wilde (1979), "Intervening in markets on the basis of imperfect information: a legal and economic analysis", *Pacific Law Review*, vol. 127, 630.

Schweitzer, R. (1989), "How do stock returns react to special events?", *Business Review*, 17-29.

Scott, K. (1980), "Insider Trading: Rule 10b-5, Disclosure and Corporate Pricing", *J.Legal Stud.*, 801.

Scott, K. (1998), "Insider trading", in P. Newman (ed.), *The New Palgrave Dictionary of Economics and the Law*, London, Macmillan, 410-419.

Segal, U. (1987), "Some remarks on Quiggin's anticipated utility", *Journal of Economic Behavior and Organization*, vol. 8, nr.1, 145-154.

Serafino, P. (1999), "Disclosure. Big investors get the first word on big news", *Bloomberg*, February, 50-54.

Seyhun, H.N. (1986), "Insiders' profits, costs of trading, and market efficiency", *Journal of Financial Economics*, 189-212.

Seyhun, H.N. (1992), "The effectiveness of the insider-trading sanctions", *Journal of Law and Economics*, 149-182.

Seyhun, H.N. (2000), *Investment intelligence from insider trading*, The MIT Press, Cambridge, Massachusetts, 402 p.

Shapiro, C. (1982), "Consumer information, product quality and seller reputation", *Bell Journal of Economics*, vol. 13, 20-35.

Shapiro, S. (1980), *Detecting illegalities: a perspective on the control of securities violations*, Ann Arbor, Michigan.

Sharpe, W.F., G.J. Alexander and J.V. Bailey (1999), *Investments*, Prentice Hall, New Jersey, 962 p.

Shavell, S. (1985), "Criminal law and the optimal use of nonmonetary sanctions as a deterrent", *Columbia Law Review*, vol. 85, 1232-1262.

Shaw, C., H. McKay and J. Short (1969), *Juvenile delinquency and urban areas*, University of Chicago Press, 394 p.

Shleifer, A. and D. Wolfensohn (2002), "Investor protection and equity markets", *Journal of Financial Economics*.

Sirri, E. and P. Tufano (1995), "The economics of pooling", in Crane, D.B. et al. (eds.), *The global financial system: a functional perspective*, Boston, MA, Harvard Business School Press, 81-128.

Skogh, G. (2000), "Law and economics in Sweden", in B. Bouckaert and G. De Geest (eds.), *Encyclopedia of Law and Economics, Volume I, The history and methodology of law and economics*, Edward Elgar, 370-379.

Smith and Watts (1982), "Incentive and tax effects of executive compensation plans", *Austl.J.Mgt.*, vol. 7, 139 ff.

Smith, A. (1776), *The wealth of nations*, Volume 2, Edited by E. Cannan, London, Methuen & Co, 1904.

Soderquist, L.D. (1994), *Securities regulation*, The Foundation Press, 786 p.

Stephen, F.H. and J.H. Love (2000), "Regulation of the legal profession", in B. Bouckaert en G. De Geest (eds.), *Encyclopedia of Law and Economics, Volume III, The regulation of contracts*, Edward Elgar, 987-1017.

Stigler, G. (1964a), "Public regulation of the securities markets", *Journal of Business*, vol. 37, nr.2, 117-142.

Stigler, G. (1964b), "Comment", *Journal of Business*, vol. 37, 414-422.

Stigler, G. (1970), "The optimum enforcement of laws", *Journal of Political Economy*, vol. 78, 526-536.

Stigler, G. (1971), "The theory of economic regulation", *Bell Journal of Economics and Management Science*, vol. 2, 3-21.

Stiglitz, J. (1997), *Economics*, W.W. Norton & Company, 997 p.

Stoll, H. (1992), "Principles of Trading Market Structure", *Journal of Financial Services Research*, 84-103.

Strong, N. (1992), "Modelling abnormal returns: a review article", *Journal of Business Finance & Accounting*, vol. 19, 533-553.

Subrahmanyan, A. (1994), "Circuit breakers and market volatility: a theoretical perspective", *Journal of Finance*, 237-254.

Subrahmanyan, A. (1995), "On rules versus discretion in procedures to halt trade", *Journal of Economics and Business*, vol. 47, 1-16.

Svorny, S. (2000), "Licensing, market entry regulation", in B. Bouckaert en G. De Geest (eds.), *Encyclopedia of Law and Economics, Volume III, The regulation of contracts*, Edward Elgar, 296-328.

Taggart, R.A. (1996), *Quantitative Analysis for Investment Management*, Prentice Hall, 306 p.

Tian, Y. (2004), "Too much of a good incentive? The case of executive stock options", *Journal of Banking and Finance*, vol. 28, 1225-1245.

Tighe, C. and R. Michener (1994), "The political economy of insider trading", *Journal of Finance*, vol. 47, 5, 1661-1699.

Tversky, A. and D. Kahneman (1990), "Cumulative prospective theory: an analysis of attitudes towards uncertainty and value", working paper, Duke University.

Ulen, T.S. (1993), "The Coasean firm in law and economics", *Journal of Corporation Law*, Winter, 301-331.

Van Calbergh, G. and S. Odeurs (1998), "Wie, wat, waar, wanneer? Voorkennis en bekendmakingsverplichtingen", *Vennootschapsrecht- en Fiscaliteit*.

Van den Bergh, R. (1986), "Belgian public policy towards the retailing trade", in J.-M. Graf Von Der Schulenberg and G. Skogh (eds.), *Law and Economics and the Economics of Legal Regulation*, Dordrecht, Kluwer, 185-205.

Van den Bergh, R. (1991), "Wat is rechtseconomie?", in E.H. Hondius, J.J. Schippers and J.J. Siegers (eds.), *Rechtseconomie en recht. Kennismaking met een vakgebied in opkomst*, Tjeenk Willink, Zwolle, 8-49.

Van den Bergh, R. (1992), "Law and economics in Europe: present state and future prospects", in B.Bouckaert and G. De Geest (eds.), *Bibliography of law and economics*, Dordrecht, Kluwer, 5-19.

Van den Bergh, R. (1996), "The growth of law and economics in Europe", *European Economic Review*, vol. 40, 969-977.

Van den Bergh, R. (2000), *Averechts recht*, Intersentia, 62 p.

Van den Bergh, R. and D. Heremans (1987), "Recht en economie", *Tijdschrift voor Economie en Management*, vol. 32, nr.2, 139-164.

Van den Bergh, R. and M. Faure (1991), "Self regulation of the professions in Belgium", *International Review of Law and Economics*, vol. 11, 165-182.

Van den Wyngaert, C. (1999), *Strafrecht en strafprocesrecht in hoofdlijnen*, Maklu, Antwerpen, 1010 p.

Van Horne, J.C. (1998), *Financial management and policy*, Prentice-Hall.

Van Nieuwerburgh, S. and F. Buelens (2000), "Stock market development and economic growth in Belgium: 1300-2000", paper presented at the doctoral seminar of the University of Antwerp, December, 35 p.

Van Velthoven, B. and P. Van Wijck (1997), *Recht en efficiëntie. Een inleiding in de economische analyse van het recht*, Kluwer, Deventer, 424 p.

Veljanovski, C. (1984), "The economics of regulatory enforcement", in K. Hawkins and J.M. Thomas (eds.), *Enforcing regulation*, Kluwer-Nijhoff Publishing, 1984, 171-188.

Vermaelen, T. (1986), "Encouraging information disclosure", *Tijdschrift voor Economie en Management*, 435-449.

Vermaelen, T., "Common Stock Repurchases and Market Signalling", *Journal of Financial Economics*, 1981, vol. 9, 139-183.

Viscusi, W.K. (1978), "A note on lemons markets with quality certification", *Bell Journal of Economics*, vol. 9, 277-279.

Waldfogel, J. (1994a), "The effect of criminal conviction on income and the trust reposed in the workmen", *Journal of Human Resources*, vol. 29, 62-81.

Waldfogel, J. (1994b), "Does Conviction Have a Persistent Effect on Income and Employment?", *International Review of Law and Economics*, vol. 14, 103-119.

Wang (1986), "Some arguments that the stock market is not efficient", *U.C. Davis L. Rev.*, vol. 19, 341 ff.

Warner, J.B., R.L. Watts and K.H. Wruck (1988), "Stock Prices and Top Management Changes", *Journal of Financial Economics*, 461-492.

Watts, R. (1978), "Systematic abnormal returns after quarterly earnings announcements", *Journal of Financial Economics*, 127-150.

Weigel, W. (2000), "Law and economics in Austria", in B. Bouckaert and G. De Geest (eds.), *Encyclopedia of Law and Economics, Volume I, The history and methodology of law and economics*, Edward Elgar, 118-127.

Weisbach, M. (1988), "Outside Directors and CEO Turnover", *Journal of Financial Economics*, vol. 20, 431-460.

Weston, J.F. and T.E. Copeland (1989), *Managerial Finance*, The Dryden Press, 1035 p.

White, R. (1974), "Towards a policy basis for the regulation of insider dealing", *The Law Quarterly Review*, 494-511.

Willis, K. (1983), "Spatial variations in crime in England and Wales", *Regional Studies*, vol. 17, 261-272.

Wilson, J. (1974), "The politics of regulation", in J. McKie (ed.), *Social responsibility and the business predicament*, The Brookings Institution, Washington, D.C., 135-168.

Wilson, J. (1980), "The politics of regulation", in J. Wilson (ed.), *The politics of regulation*, New York, Basic Books, 357-394.

Wolpin, K. (1978), "An Economic Analysis of Crime and Punishment in England and Wales 1894-1967", *Journal of Political Economy*, vol. 86, 815-840.

Wonnacott, T. and R. Wonnacott (1984), *Introductory statistics for business and economics*, John Wiley, 743 p.

Wu, H.K. (1968), "An economist looks at section 16 of the Securities Exchange Act of 1934", *Columbia Law Review*, 260-269.

Wymeersch, E. (1991), "The insider trading prohibition in the EC Member States: a comparative overview", in K. Hopt and E. Wymeersch (eds.), *European Insider Dealing*, London, Butterworths, 65-128.

X. (2000a), "Labor law and employment regulation: general", in B. Bouckaert en G. De Geest (eds.), *Encyclopedia of Law and Economics, Volume III, The regulation of contracts*, Edward Elgar, 533-540.

X. (2000b), "Collective bargaining and worker participation", in B. Bouckaert en G. De Geest (eds.), *Encyclopedia of Law and Economics, Volume III, The regulation of contracts*, Edward Elgar, 626-630.

Young, S.D. (1985), "Insider trading: why the concern?", *Journal of Accounting, Auditing and Finance*.

Zerbe, R.O. Jr. (2001), *Economic efficiency in law and economics*, Edward Elgar, 328 p.

Zhang, G. (2001), "Regulated managerial insider trading as a mechanism to facilitate shareholder control", *Journal of Business Finance and Accounting*, vol. 28, 35-62.

Zweigert, K. and H. Kotz (1987), *Introduction to Comparative Law*, Oxford, Clarendon Press.

INDEX